Planet Earth at its Limits:
Human Trafficking, Overpopulation, Climate Change, and Religious Wars (Book 3)

A Novel-Trilogy
Women, the New Architects of Society

Ambrose Goikoetxea, Ph.D.   *(Laguardia, 1952)*

Planet Earth at its limits is the third Volume of the novel-trilogy, *Women the New Architects of Society.* On his Web site, www.euskalherriasiglo21.org, the author shares information on the making of this novel and other books of his published in the *USA, Basque Country, and Spain*. As a *Basque-American*, he shares his experiences having lived in the USA all his life, and then returning to the "old Country", Basque Country, in 2004. He finds a people still fighting to gain independence from a central government in Madrid, and since matters appeared blurry and unclear from the very beginning, he spent the next four years learning about its society, its political leaders who say one thing and do another, its church leaders with loyalty to the *Vatican*, first, to the Madrid government, second, and to the people, last. In the middle of it there are the women, as main characters in this novel-trilogy, the ones that are emerging as doers, the ones fighting for EQUALITY among men and women, the new leaders of society. It is through their eyes mainly, that the author explores similarities and differences in those three societies: American, Basque, and Spanish. The result is a revealing American perspective on a number of social, religious, cultural, and political issues, exacerbated by a global economic crisis. A *politically and religiously incorrect novel-trilogy* in the interest of the readers in those three societies, revealing, and entertaining, he hopes.

A Novel-Trilogy
Politically and Religiously Incorrect

Planet Earth at its Limits:
Human Trafficking, Overpopulation, Climate
Change, and Religious Wars
(Book 3)

Novel-Trilogy:
Women, the New Architects in Society

16 June 2016

Ambrose Goikoetxea, Ph.D.

Euskal Herria 21st. Century Publishers
Boston, Massachusetts, USA
Arrasate, Gipuzkoa, Basque Country, and
Laguardia-Biasteri, Alava, Basque Country
www.euskalherriasiglo21.org

Published by:
Euskal Herria 21st. Century Publishers
La Rioja 15, Laguardia 01300, Alava, Basque Country
Tel: 011 34 628 70 36 16
www.euskalherriasiglo21.org

Novel-Trilogy: Women, the New Architects of Society

Book 3: Planet Earth at its Limits

A Novel-Trilogy
Copyright © Ambrose Goikoetxea 2016
16 June 2016

ISBN-13: 978-1534747784
Printed in the USA

Dedicated to:

*To **Aloña** who shares my dreams, with my love and passion.*

To all women, *who have suffered over the centuries and millennia, persecuted, tortured, exiled, and executed by the Church's Inquisition, through the many societies that negated them an education, participation in decision making, public office, that ignored and ridiculed their minds, and that utilized their bodies as machines of procreation, sexual objects, and instruments of production of goods.*

To Esperanza*, Cristina, Nancy, Juliana, Andrea, Marta, Sofía, Jennifer, Ava, Joanne, Jean-Lucia, Maria Angeles, Pino, Veronique, Fatima, Mireille, Fu Li, Carrie, Begoña, Roda, Yolanda, and Asun.*

*My parents, **Teresa** and **Eusebio**, who left the Basque Country and came to America looking for change and a better life for their children, as did so many families in the Basque Diaspora.*

My sons, Charles and Miguel, who know of Euskal Herria, its green mountains, fields of wheat and grapes, and who contribute to the Basque Community in the USA with their work and solidarity.

To Lucien Duckstein, Wayne Wymore, Istvan Bogardi, and Ferenc Szidarovszky*, my teachers and tutors, for sharing their work ethic, knowledge, and sense of justice at the University of Arizona, my alma mater.*

*My people of **Biasteri-Laguardia**, Alava, for their work ethic, music, dignity, and hospitality.*

*Mi people of **Zugarramurdi** and **Bargota** today, in Nafarroa, who remember every day the women and men executed by the Spanish Inquisition's Auto-de-Fe carried out in Logroño City, Spain, in 1610.*

To ALL the victims of violence, everywhere.

*My people of **Arrasate-Mondragon**, and their mountain Udalaitz, their political prisoners (women and men), their struggle for the liberty, independence, and the future of the Basque people.*

Preface

In this third volume, *Planet Earth at its Limits*, of the Novel-Trilogy *Women, the New Architects of Society*, the players interact in situations relevant to societies still dominated by men in the USA, Spain, Basque Country, and other countries in the global community. A main theme is that of a planet Earth approaching its limits in critical areas such as overpopulation, scarce land and sea food resources, the trafficking of women, men, and children for purposes of forced prostitution and forced labor, religious wars, and the imminent climatic change.

Both *narrative (essay)* and *novel* are combined in this book. Generally a chapter presents narrative on a particular topic, followed by a chapter with novel format, followed by another chapter with narrative, and so on. In this manner each narrative chapter addresses a topic in some depth, thus supporting the dialogue developed by the characters in the other chapters, hopefully. Accordingly, "reader A" may choose to read both "narrative chapters" and "novel chapters" and thus arrive at a set of conclusions and a level of entertainment of his/her own. On the other hand, "reader B" may choose to read the novel chapters only, which will also perfectly allow the reader to arrive at a set of conclusions and a level of entertainment of his/her own. The "novel chapters" are: 1, 2, 4, 10, 11, 12, 14, 15, and 17. Yes, each one of these two experiences may be somewhat different, but one is not necessarily better than the other, simply somewhat different. It is up to our reader to decide which entertainment experience to pursue.

For years I contemplated the opportunity of reviewing specific periods in history to take a second look at the reasons and circumstances under which *women* were ostracized, denied the right to participate in decision making in their homes, places of worship, public assemblies, their minds and bodies were relegated to the task of procreation, treated as sexual objects, and otherwise persecuted, accused of being witches, tortured, condemned, and finally burned at the stake or executed in other criminal ways. It made no sense, I thought, to treat women that way, those dear human beings all around us that gave us life in the beginning that worked and harvested our fields that gave us our first milk and means of sustenance that put together our broken bodies destroyed by internal wars, wars made by men. It made no sense to believe that those special and generous human beings later in life would become in evil human beings, despicable creatures that had to be chased like animals, caught, tortured, and then killed for the "good of society." It was in that manner, then, that I set out to research a number of episodes in history and, fortunately, I was able to come across a number of answers and circumstances that created a pattern of behavior on the part of the perpetrators of those crimes against our women: the Church and the State, in symbiotic and criminal conspiracy. It is because of the ample evidence gathered here that points towards the Church and the State as conspiring entities, that this is *a politically and religiously incorrect trilogy*, as many may surmise, and appropriately so.

Accordingly, in the first book, "*When the Parallel Worlds Co-Existed*", I gave myself the task of reviewing some periods of history to try to identify a list of powers and circumstances that would have been responsible for the segregation and subordination of women. At the same time, I proceeded to create a list of leading characters for the novel, women and men that live in those three societies, and that can talk to us about how they interact and how they go about changing their respective societies. Changes in their life styles, their ways of thinking, their participation in situations of decision making at work, at home, their behavior towards people of other religions and races, and in some cases changes towards their appreciation of life.

In this second book, "*The Pope's Red Shoes*", I have asked the same leading characters –and a few new ones—to carry out their inquiry and investigation into some difficult but potentially interesting areas, to arrive at some findings and conclusions, and to ultimately share these with our readers. I have asked them, for example, to take a look at the *major religions that existed before Christianity*, and to observe how those major religions served to give content and shape to Christianity, the new religion. As a second task, I have also asked them to look into the dynamics of a very specific socio-political set of circumstances taking place today in the Basque Country and known as the "*Basque political conflict*". Why is it that this particular group of people, very possibly one of the oldest in Europe, if not the oldest, remains caught politically and institutionally between two larger powers and states, as are Spain and France, while many other peoples in similar circumstances have already gained their independence and freedom? As a third task, I asked the leading characters in that second book to review for us *the recent history of women, feminists and non-feminists, their long struggle for women's rights,* and to bring up the personal stories, the wins and loses, and the statistics on monies and budgets spent by governments in those three societies over the last 50-75 years in order to advance women's rights and EQUALITY. It is not enough for a modern state to keep track and denounce the number of women killed yearly in its society. As a fourth task, I asked the leading characters to take a look at the politicians and banks in the USA and in the European Union, their incompetence, sagacity, and fraudulent ways in many personal cases, and to try to explain to the rest of us mere mortals why and how so many countries and societies in our Western World got into accumulating such a gigantic external debt. Only once we realize how gigantic, obscene, dangerous, and contagious is that external debt, country by country, and year after year, we may be in a position to consider and to work together towards changes in the way we work, ways of saving money, ways or relating to each other and other societies, ways of growing and distributing food, family planning, birth control, and regained appreciation for life in our planet, as individual and collective effort among women and men in our global community.

Why I chose the format of a novel to write about women's issues? Although I have managed to publish several articles on women's issues in scientific journals, I feel these issues are too important and relevant today to be read by just a few people in academic circles and, therefore, I decided I should try to reach a larger audience through the novel formal, readers of all ages and interests.

This trilogy, then, hopes to change for the better the perspective the reader may have on a number of issues, including being able to see *women as the new leaders and architects in society today*, the *secret lives of politicians* with their multiple sources of income and their extravagant life styles, *the true origins of the Christianity as an early pirated version of Buddhism*, the making of Jesus from parts of hundreds of stories until becoming *a "biblical Frankenstein"*, the myth behind the *"Basque political conflict"* created by a renegade Basque group and the Spanish State in order to grab, retain, and try to mold to its liking the Basque people in Europe and, while we are at it, taking a look at the *European Union*, how it began with a number of a sound and noble set of goals, and how it is quickly becoming a debt-fraught international community of nation-states, a socially and politically unbalanced institution. In taking a look at these issues and events I tried to re-create a woman's perspective by listening to women on these and related issues, and next creating a number of women characters that view and interpret those issues and events in different ways, for a change, in their own ways, hopefully.

It is with a sense of amazement that as a man I look at what I believe is *woman's abundant and incredible sexual capacity*, her ability to have *multiple orgasms* in a single coitus session, for example, to create and give birth to new human beings. Abilities and attributes that must have scared some men throughout the ages, and which motivated these men to try to restrain her, to cover her face and body, to limit her space, to denounce her sexual abilities as sinful and diabolical, to prohibit her own expressions of sexual freedom and, instead, to try to prostitute her power and beauty to serve man's own appetites, fantasies, and sense of power and control.

In this trilogy I started with a few, well bounded set of issues to study, I thought, but soon I realized that such a study would reflect my own personal experience as a *Basque American*, with my own set of perspectives, prejudices, realities, and sensitivities. And, as such, this exercise tries to convey what I have seen, heard, and touched with my own senses while living most of my adult life in the USA, having benefited from a wonderful, multi-colored, richly varied culture that has seen women organize themselves in the slums and cloth districts of New York, in the tomato fields of San Jose, California, and in the campuses across dozens and hundreds of schools and universities in the USA. It is that perspective from *my own American experience*, that I can't help but carry with me as I take a look at women in the their societies in the Basque Country,

10

Spain, and Europe, in an effort to encourage them to dream, to think of their own ways of doing things, to beg them to please continue looking at the universe in their own, creative, beautiful, and different ways. Why? 'Cause some of us men are tired of five thousand years of recorded history fraught with wars, wars designed and carried out by men, wars that have created a few new cultures, yes, but at the expense of hundreds of other cultures that could have added more beauty, vitality, color, and purpose to our planet, to our species. Some of us men now hope for a much larger and equal role for women in the advancement of our societies, in the creation of new worlds, where the rule of force is left behind, and a new era of dialogue among women and men begins, where reason is the norm over superstition, prejudice, and power of the few.

Towards that end I opted for creating two main characters and a cast of support characters to venture into this trilogy of self discovery. *Kathy Thompson* is a young American Jewish woman in search of her own identity and purpose in life in a society still dominated by men, mostly, who lives and attends college in Tucson, Arizona, USA; she is intelligent, beautiful, and independent in her thinking. *Xabier Elurmendi* is a young man in an Ertzaintza unit (Basque police) with a main role in breaking up demonstrations led by young people that oppose the construction of a giant, high-speed train (AHT) through the green valleys and mountains of the Basque Country today, until one day when his unit in involved in a nearly fatal bus accident, and afterward Xabier decides to enter a seminary in Arantzazu, Basque Country, to become a priest one day. Shortly thereafter Xabier is sent to the USA to visit two Franciscan seminaries in an effort to learn how to attract young people to life in seminaries when he meets Kathy one day. Together they face a variety of challenges, including the deciphering of Gnostic codes of unknown origins, the riddle of ritualistic murders of people around them, paedophiles intent on murder from the Vatican, romance, and corrupt politicians in an array of towns and cities such as Tucson (USA), Arantzazu (Basque Country), Rome, Madrid, Istanbul (Turkey), New Delhi (India), Lhasa (Tibet), Jerusalem, and Tel-Aviv (Israel) along the old "Silk Road".

The multiple plots unfold against *five backgrounds* in the course of this novel trilogy. *The first background (Book 1)* is made up of elements that attempt to characterize and describe the varied and complex fabric of Basque society today, torn with choices among pro-independence groups (Izquierda Abertzale), socialism, self-autonomy, and pro-Madrid monarchy political parties, all depicted from an Anglo-Saxon perspective, hopefully, the author's own Basque-American perspective. The personal and party interests of the various political parties are exposed, revealing in many cases an inept and selfish cast of politicians that lives off an "Indian Basque Reservation" subject to Madrid's rule, and an European Union that uses its institutional frame in order to achieve economic gains, mainly, at the expense of Europe's social, ethnic, and cultural diversity.

Reflected in *a second background (Book 1)*, is today's Spanish Society with its centuries-old legacy of absolutist monarchies, endless state coup-d'etats led by the military, the clergy, and well-to-do families, wars of conquest in dozens of countries in Latin America and the American South West financed by the Crowns of Spain in a large-scale and futile attempt to subdue and annihilate rich and vibrant cultures, its tragic and well documented religious intolerance towards Jews, Moslems, and Protestants. Thus, two main trends in Spain's society today are contrasted: (1) one conservative society that insists in a social order under the influence and the powers of the Church and the State, and (2) one liberal and progressive society that demands a new model governed by the premise of true separation of Church and State.

A new perspective, or at least an enhanced perspective on the origins of Christianity is depicted in *a third background (Book 2)*, as the leading characters expand on their theory of *Christianity as a pirated version of Buddhism* that originated three hundred years earlier and saw its dogma and principles move towards town and cities in Middle East and later in Central Europe along the old "Silk Road" trail. The violent history of the Catholic Church in Spain, the cruel and bloody legacy of its Spanish Inquisition in Europe and Latin America are revisited in an effort to better understand the radical, global changes occurring in the Catholic Church today. In this exercise, the key elements in the "Concordats" of the Vatican with military dictators in Nazi Germany, Fascist Italy, and Franco's Spain are revealed in order to trace in the last one hundred years the origins of women's status as second-class citizens, but also to establish a connection with women's search and struggle today to fully achieve women's rights in our societies.

*A **fourth background** (Book 2)* attempts to reflect the current global financial crisis, the initial economic successes of the European Union, its dramatic ups and downs in the last twenty years, and the futile attempts of its inept and self-indulging politicians to stabilize their countries' diverse economies in the light of high-cost labor, China's massive economic power and its entrance into European markets, the revolution and overthrowing of dictators in the Arab World led by the young and destitute but ideals-rich masses all across the Middle East. The politicians and people-heavy government bureaucracies of the 27 nation-states that make up the European Union frantically and irresponsibly contribute to the gigantic external debts of their respective countries seeking personal gain and political representation, in tune with a US Government unable or unwilling to restrain military intervention in oil-rich countries, or poor countries whose ideologies differ from ours and are deemed a threat to the current global order, the status quo. Are we seeing the beginning of the end of the European Union (EU) as it is and the reign of the G8 powers, and the beginnings of a new global order?

A *fifth background* (Book 3) gets right into areas where our planet Earth is reaching its limits, such as overpopulation, scarce land and sea food resources, trafficking of human beings for forced prostitution and labor, religious wars, and the overwhelming climatic change. This author sees those three major religions of Judaism, Christianity, and Islam as competing with each other to gain additional power and control of the masses and, in the process, contributing to an uncontrolled use of our Earth resources. The players eventually manage to get into the Vatican Secret Archives for purposes of learning more about leading figures and decisions made in Western culture which have contributed over the centuries to the unstable social, political, military, and physical make up of our planet Earth today. Solutions? Yes, this Book 3 does suggest a number of alternatives to the current trend in order for our human species to be able to continue on our planet beyond the next 500 years.

It is then, against those *five backgrounds* that we are led by Kathy, Xabier, and their multi-cultural support cast, to see how women are finally emerging in our societies today, after centuries of abuse, discrimination, and condemnation as "witches", as the new leaders and architects of society in industry, education, the arts, the world of finances, politics, and the business world. Two thousand years are now about to be left behind, with men-dominated societies, an endless chain of men-orchestrated wars, a thousand civilizations destroyed, and a planet risking an apocalyptic end. Now, women and men demand a deep structural and ideological change in their lives and destiny. This is the dawn of a new global order, many of us believe, women and men, and we say it all in this *novel-trilogy.*

PEOPLE AND PLACES

- *Kathy Thompson*, is a young American woman from Tucson, Arizona, USA, 26 years old, half Anglo, half Jewish, and one-hundred percent intelligent and beautiful. A researcher of *Gnostic codes* at the University of Arizona where she studies to earn a degree and make a living in a society dominated by men, mostly. She's independent, sure of herself, ready to tackle most challenges in life, and not willing to limit herself to men's view of the world, until one day she meets Xabier Elurmendi, her life takes on new meaning, and together they venture into romance, corruption in high places, and a mission to save the Pope's life..

- *Xabier Elurmendi,* is a young man in the town of Bergara, Gipuzkoa, Basque Country, 32 years old, beginning a new career as an *Ertzaina* (Basque policeman). He gets involved in a bus accident on a mountain road carrying a group of young men and women that earlier had participated in a peaceful demonstration to "stop the TAV", a high-speed train that would run across the Basque Country. The bus slides down a mountain, several people get killed including friends of his. Impacted by this experience, Xabier joins the Arantzazu Seminary, a Franciscan seminary, to become a priest one day, to redirect his life. His interest for the history and life of the first Christians takes him on a one-year trip to the USA where he meets the very attractive and intelligent Kathy Thompson. There, his new faith, love, and carnal desires compete for his soul and body.

- *Dr. Eugene Finley,* is a professor, mentor of Kathy Thompson, and chief of a team of investigators at the University of Arizona, Tucson, Arizona. This team is trying to decipher a *Gnostic code* dating back to the 3rd. century, and suspected to have been stolen from the *Vatican Secret Archives* in Rome.

- *Nerea Arana,* a young teacher of Euskera, the ancestral Basque language, in the town of Bergara, 28 years old, a friend of Xabier from childhood, attractive, temperamental, and secretly in love with Xabier.

- *Andoni Arana,* Nerea's brother.

- *Aitor Larrañaga,* a nephew of Andoni Arana, and member of Xabier Elurmendi's team in Oñati, Basque Country.

- *Dorothy Larson,* a business woman, 33 years old, mother of David, 9 years old, on a sabbatical, one-year visit from Brussels, Belgium. She has arrived in the town of Arrasate nearby, next to Bergara, to join a movement of young men and women that would like to stop the construction of TAV, the high-speed train. Dorothy brings her own experience in the preparation of legal suits against large multinational corporations, plus a list of contacts in several European countries, Canada, and the USA.

- *Father Muxika,* Superior and abbot at the Arantzazu Seminary, where Xabier is a young seminarian in search of answers to the meaning of life. A series of events lead Father Muxika to ask Xabier to make a trip to the USA to deliver a closed envelope to Father Altuna, an old Jesuit priest, with instructions to carry out a mission intended to save the Pope's life, but without his knowledge or the Vatican's.

- *Father Altuna,* is an old Jesuit priest with a hidden past, who Works at the Hopi Indian reservation in Four Corners, an area in parts of Arizona and New Mexico. He is suspected of having lived in *El Salvador* and to have participated as a "guerrillero" in that and other nearby countries in Central America. He is also suspected of belonging to a centuries-old secret society that protects the life of the Pope utilizing all means, including murder. This time *Pope Benedict XVI* is in the eyesight.

- *Father Walter Altuna,* nephew of Father Altuna, also works in the Native American community of Hopis and Navajos in the Four Corners area.

- *Iñaki Issasa*, leader of the Anti-TAV/AHT movement, with base in Aramaio, another small town next to Bergara and Arrasate.

- *Helen Odriozola*, a young woman, spokesperson for the Anti-TAV/AHT movement.

- *Olaia Salegi*, a young woman, independent, beautiful, and Iñaki's girlfriend. She is also involved in a secret lesbian relationship with another woman.

- *Sergio Balboa*, is a lieutenant in the **Guardia Civil** headquarters based in Oñati, Gipuzkoa. He is tireless in his pursuit of Xabier whom he suspects is a collaborator of ETA, the Basque Terrorist Organization, even as a seminarian in the Arantzazu Seminary.

- *Galindo Sanz,* a lieutenant in an *Ertzaintza unit*, "Basque police", an anti-riot unit in San Sebastian, with an eye on young demonstrators in the Anti-TAV/AHT movement.

- *Walter Belluci,* an Kosovo, former secret police officer, now working as an agent of **INTERPOL** at its office in Washington, D.C.

- *Txomin Elosetegi,* a first cousin of Xabier Elurmendi in the town of Bergara. Together, Txomin, Xabier, and Nerea decide to join an Ertzaintza police unit in Bergara.

- *Emilio Beistegi*, a 24-year old student from Laguardia-Biasteri, Alava, Basque Country. With a one-year scholarship he attends the University of Arizona where he works towards a Masters degree and, in the process, he makes the acquaintance of Kathy and Xabier.

- *Itziar Beistegi,* a 24-year old student, from Bakersfield, California, a 3rd. generation Basque American, and she's visiting friends in Logroño, La Rioja, Spain.

- *Dr. Emilia Abhayawansa*, an expert in the **Tipitaka**, the Buddist Pali Canon, as well as a member of Dr. Finley's research team at the University of Arizona.

- **Dr. Fuad Fahim,** an expert and translator of Coptic codes, also a member of Dr. Finley's research team at the University of Arizona.

- **Giovanni Bruni**, an Observant Franciscan monk and director of the project "Leonardo" at the Vatican Secret Archives, including the Nag Hammadi codes.

- **Luis Mendes,** a young priest from Rio de Janeiro, and a member of the *Vatican's Eagles*, a clandestine organization.

- **Emily Connely**, a librarian at the University of Arizona, and member of the "**Circle of Wise Women of Jerusalem**", a centuries-old secret organization and keeper of the "Three Commandments of Getsemani."

- **Juan Jose Mudanca,** an architect, chief of the archaeology section in Logroño's City Hall.

- **Vatican Eagles,** a secret organization of members of the Vatican which have has existed for centuries, an advocate of equality among men and women within the hierarchy of the Church.

- **Father David Donovan,** lead person of the Vatican Eagles organization.

- **Father Thomas Paulson,** member of Vatican Eagles organization.

- **Guards of the Secret Oath**, an international secret society of men which has existed for centuries, and which wants only men to safeguard the power and control of the Vatican.

- **Delta International Mafia**, a multi-national criminal organization which kidnaps people in order to obtain information for secret service entities of democratic governments. That is, it does the "dirty work" for democratic entities.

- **Gregory Chong**, director of the China State Farm Agri-Business Corporation (CSFAC).

- **Fu Li,** associate of Gregory Chong, a member of the CSFAC.

- **Eugene Mutombo,** a representative of the Democratic Republic of Congo (DRC).

- **Sister Esperanza Carlson,** member of the **Circle of Wise Women of Jerusalem.**

- **Sister Constanza Altuna,** member or the **Circle of Wise Women of Jerusalem.**

PLACES IN THIS NOVEL

- **Arrasate-Mondragon,** a town of 23,000 inhabitants in Gipuzkoa, Basque Country, home of Mondragon University (MU) and of Mondragon Corporation Cooperative (MCC), the multinational industrial complex.

- **Bergara,** a small city in Gipuzkoa, in the middle of the Alto Deba valley, population 15,000, known for its long history of battles between followers of the Crown of Castille, Kingdom of Navarre, Liberals and Carlists. Home to Xabier Elurmendi, Txomin, and Nerea.

- **San Prudencio, "Sanpru",** a neighbourhood of Bergara, population 255.

- **University of the Basque Country (EHU/UPV),** with location in Bilbao, Basque Country.

- **Atapuerca Museum,** with location in Burgos, Spain.

- **Mondragon Unibertsitatea (MU),** with location in Arrasate-Mondragon city, Basque Country.

- **Tucson City,** a city in Arizona, USA, population 1.1 million, 35% Hispanics, second largest city in the State, home of the University of Arizona (UofA) and Kathy Thompson.

- **Oñati,** a small town in Gipuzkoa, Basque Country, population 10,750, home of the Arantzazu Basilica and Seminary. A town that contributed many mercenary men and women to the Crowns of Castille, several of whom founded numerous towns and cities in the new lands of the American continent. Home (Araoz) of Lope de Aguirre, the ill-fated "conquistador". Today, for a change, its people search for its own freedom and destiny.

- *Laguardia-Biasteri,* a town in Alava, Basque Country, population 2,000, home of Emilio Beistegi and his cousin Itziar Beistegi.

- *Boise City,* a city Idaho, USA, with a large and prosperous Basque American community, home of the Euskal Jaiak every five years. Population 205,345.

- *Los Angeles,* the most densely populated and extended city in California, USA, with a population of 4.1 million distributed over five counties. Home to major cultural, economic, scientific, and entertainment centers in the USA and the world.

- *Vatican Secret Archives,* located within an infrastructure of basements under the Vatican buildings, where thousands of documents are kept, many of which are not accessible to the general public, related to Vatican councils, documents, "concordats" between the Vatican and dictators, and letters among bishops, cardinals, and other members of the Vatican hierarchy.

- *Council for World Peace (CWP),* an intergovernmental organization which conducts a "systematic" search for "red spots" in societies, communities, and countries in the global community, with the intent of assisting those societies in the task of staying above "critical levels" for a number of areas, such as poverty, education, religious tolerance, overpopulation, and others. Similar to the United Nations (UN) organization, but different in that it acts *before* an outbreak of violence occurs in the global community.

- *Kinshasa,* capital city of the Democratic Republic of Congo, population of 11 Million.

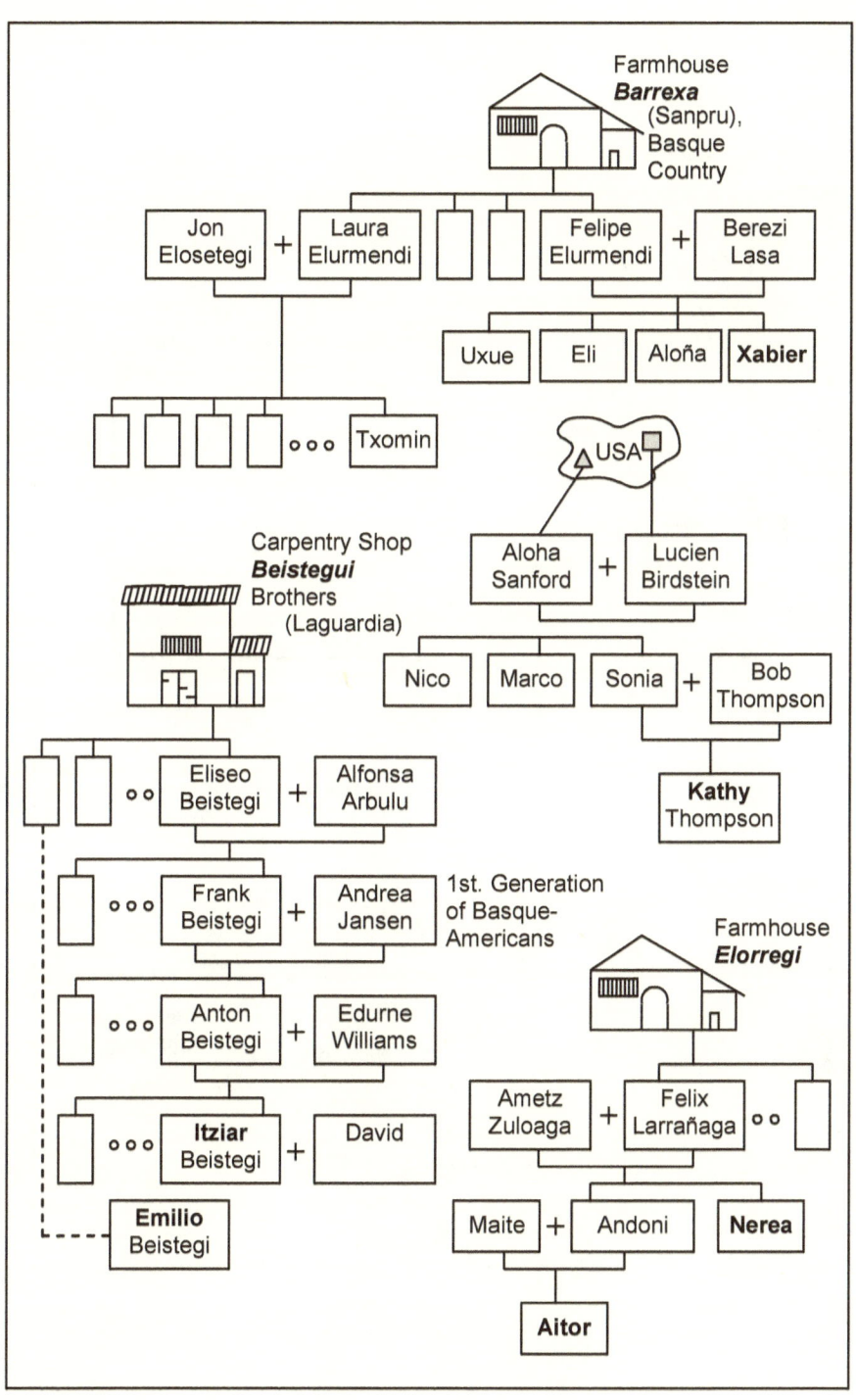

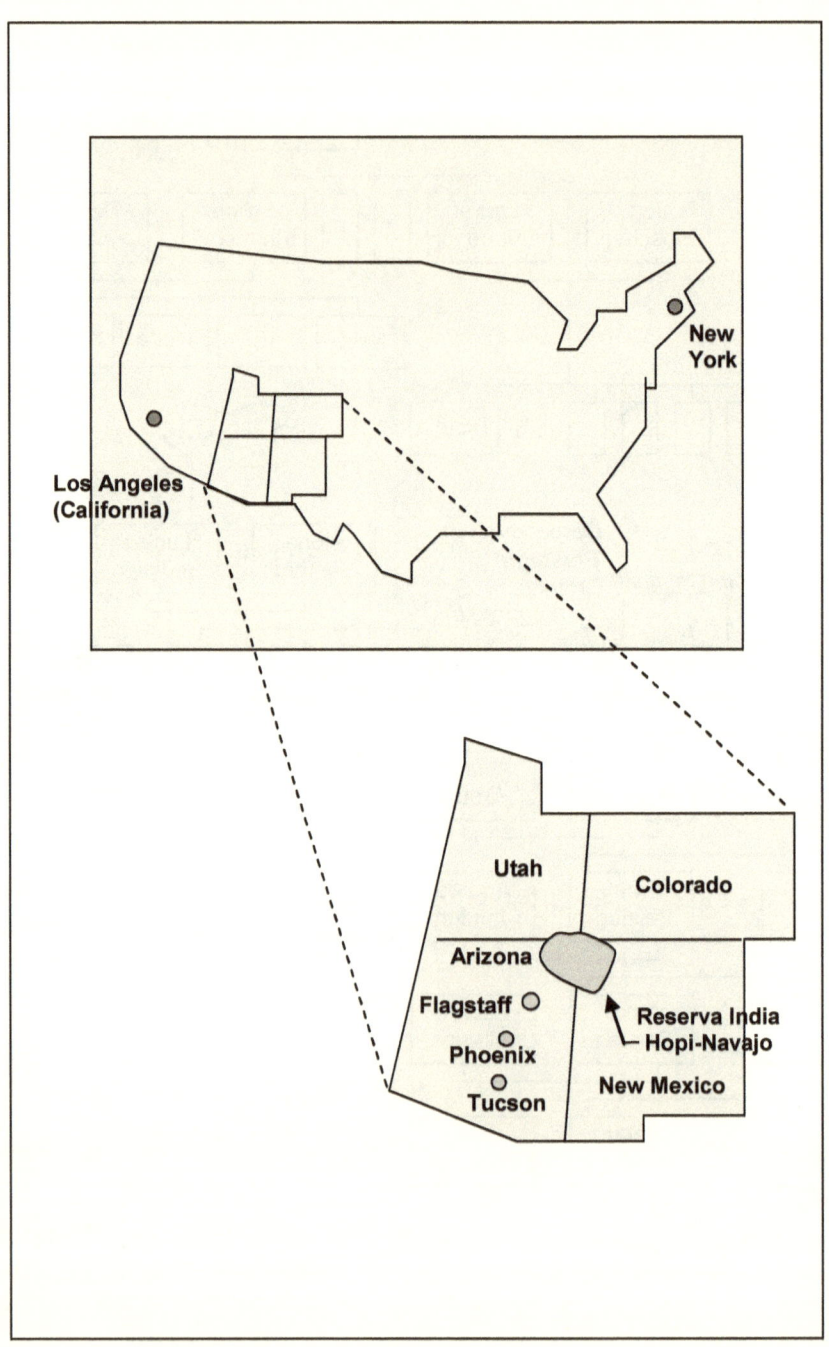

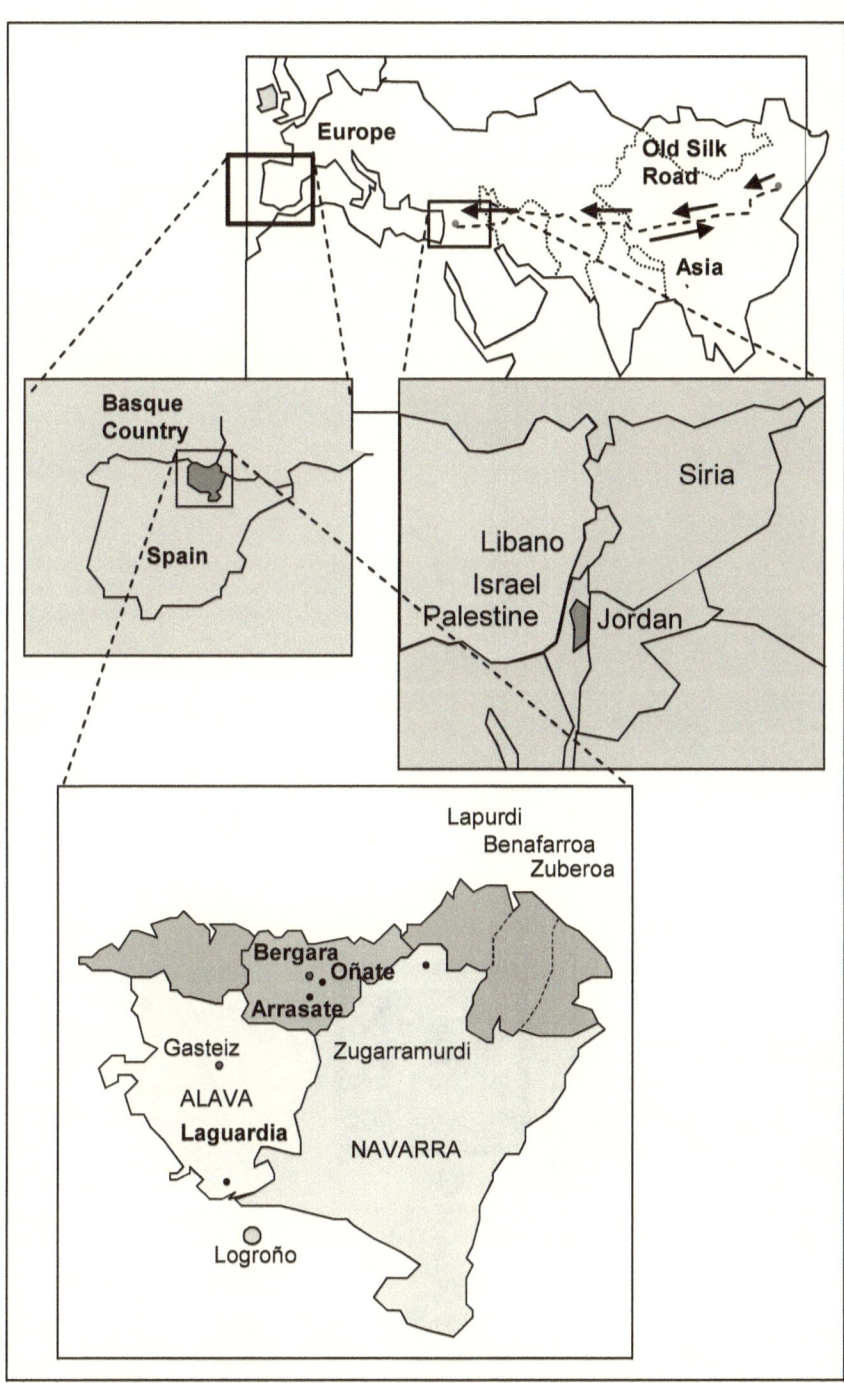

Table of Contents

Part I:
Kathy and Xabier, together again

Chapter

1

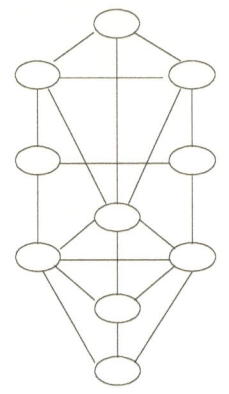

"When one door of happiness closes, another opens; but often we look so long at the closed door that we do not see the one which has been opened for us."

--Helen Keller, Writer[1]

"If you observe a really happy man, or woman, you will find him building a boat, writing a symphony, educating his son, growing double dahlias in his garden. He will not be searching for happiness as if it were a collar button that has rolled under the radiator."

--W. Beran Wolfe, Writer[1]

Kathy and Xabier, Together Again

-Is that you, Xabier? How incredible! I have been waiting for your phone call for weeks now, months, really! Are you OK? –It was **Kathy**, answering **Xabier's phone call**. From her office at the University of Arizona, Tucson, Arizona, USA, she could see the many palm trees on the campus while smiling freely.

-Yes, it's me Kathy…Sorry it took me so long to call you back again…Too many things going on over here in the Basque Country as you can imagine…Please forgive me, but I will explain in detail when…

-It's OK, Xabier, I understand…Too many things happened during your stay here in the USA…It must not have been easy to go back to the Basque Country and communicate those things and events to your people…I understand. –Kathy realized that it was more important at that moment to get reacquainted, the two of them, and that explanations could be said later, once they got together again, for example.

-Well, yes, it has been difficult… Well, more than difficult it has required a long time to go over those events in the USA, too many things happened and my people over here wanted to know the reasons for those things and events, but…

-But what? What has happened Xabier? —Interrupted Kathy, concerned by Xabier's tone in his voice.

-I was just going to say that they approve… They approve and realize that it is important to know what's inside the **Secret Archives of the Vatican**; too many strange events are happening in our world today, happening too fast, and that there may be an answer in those Secret Archives, really.

-Great! It means we can resume our work and do the planning needed to try and see if we can get inside the Secret Archives!

-Exactly! —Added Xabier.

-It so happens that our work here at the University of Arizona has also made progress, despite the unfortunate death of Dr. Fuad Fahim, as you know, and perhaps this time I could travel to the Basque Country to help with that project. Would that be OK with you, Xabier?

-Yes, yes, of course! Right after our conversation I will send you a couple of e-mails with a list of names, people that you would be meeting over here, and places that we may want to visit… Also, the names of a few organizations that we need to keep in mind. —By then Xabier felt more relaxed and gratified to hear that Kathy would be able to assist in that next project and, not only that, she would travel to the Basque Country to join Xabier and other people in the project!

Bilbao Airport

A futuristic design by the architect *Santiago de Calatrava*, the International Airport of Bilbao is located in the town of Loiu, some 6 miles northeast of Bilbao, Basque Country. Its main building looks like a supersonic aircraft about to take off. A large batch of concrete, otherwise, set on a green and gentle countryside, a few hills, and a dozen houses by the name of "baserriak" built on those hills. While the landing is taking place one has the feeling that one is about to land in the middle of a large country farm.

Nervous as he was that day, Xabier stood in the waiting area, just outside the gate for flight BILBO-23 coming in from Frankfurt, Germany. The airplane was scheduled to arrive at 11:30 hours. A cup of coffee and a donut had made it possible for Xabier to relax a bit as he waited to see Kathy again. I had been eight months since the last time they both saw each other at the Marriott Hotel in Los Angeles, California, USA. Well, they did more than seeing each other, as Xabier's visit to the USA lasted 10 months during which time they encountered a long list of events, events which that morning rushed through Xabier's mind. The last two

Figure 1.1: International Airport at Bilbao, a design by Santiago Calatrava, located at Loiu, Bizkaia, Basque Country.

months were particularly recorded in his mind, as their love affair had been particularly torrid as well as uneasy.

-Kathy, over here! –Xabier had just seen Kathy's face in the approaching crowd of passengers in the distance, getting off the airplane, walking through the rectangular metal passage from the airplane to the waiting room.

She could hear his voice, but it took her a few seconds to learn where that voice was coming from in the crowd in the large waiting room. Finally she saw a man frantically waving his arms. It had to be Xabier, she thought. She began to wave her arms too as she kept walking.

-Welcome to the Basque Country, Kathy! –Were Xabier's first words as he warmly embraced Kathy.

-Likewise, Xabier, it feels great to be here!

-You look great, Kathy, as always… With such a long trip I thought you might look tired and sleepy, but no, you look like it was a short trip, like you took a nap and then you woke up.

-Well, in Frankfurt there was a one-hour stop so I had a chance to have some breakfast, comb my hair, and put on another shirt… And here we are!

-Did you bring any luggage?

-No, just this small suitcase that I'm carrying with me… I thought I might buy some things while I visit with you and friends.

The conversation went on as Kathy and Xabier walked to the parking lot of the airport to take Xabier's car, although not before giving each another warm hug and this time a lusty kiss as well. Within a few minutes they were on their way to Bergara.

Staying with Andoni's family

Where would Kathy stay during her visit with Xabier? That was a main question in Xabier's mind, as he thought of several friends and families in the towns of Bergara, Oñati, and Arrasate. Finally, he figured that it might be best to suggest to Kathy to stay with *Maite*, by now a widow of Andoni who had been kidnapped and killed a few months earlier. He had talked with Maite and she was receptive to the idea, having company, someone to talk with besides her own son Aitor.

-This is a beautiful town… What's its name? –Asked Kathy.

-This is the town of *Bergara*… The town I mentioned to you last time we spoke on the phone. I thought it might be a good place for you to know, as well as a good base of operations for us in the months ahead.

-Yes, I remember the name.

-I have asked a good friend of the family, Maite, if she would be able to offer you a room in her house where she lives with her son Aitor. Her husband Andoni was kidnapped a few months ago and killed, as I will explain in greater detail to you in the days ahead. She said she would welcome your company, an opportunity to practice her basic English, and someone to talk with at home. Would staying with Maite be OK with you? –Xabier had other options in mind as well, but he was hoping Kathy would agree staying with Maite.

-Ohh, yes, certainly! I rather stay with someone you know, a town person, rather than in a hotel. –Replied Kathy, trying to show some enthusiasm.

Within a few minutes Xabier and Kathy arrived at Maite's house, a "baserria" on the hills of *Oñati*. A two-story stone house with an ample view of the city of Añati. As Xabier's car approached the house, Maite was already waiting at the house's porch.

-Hi, guys! I figured you both might be arriving right about now, on time for lunch. Welcome to Oñati! –Said Maite with a smile and open arms.

-Hi, Maite, this is Kathy… Kathy, this is Maite, a friend of the family. Hugs and kisses. The few chickens in the backyard were also noisy, as if also welcoming Kathy.

-I am going have to leave the two of you alone, Maite and Kathy… Cannot stay for lunch this time, as I have a meeting at the Seminary, here at Arantzazu, a few kilometres away, but I will be back by 6:00 o'clock this afternoon to help with things, and so we can talk some more, OK?

Where are we, Xabier?

Later that afternoon Xabier comes back to Maite's house, picks up Kathy, and they drive to a tavern in Oñati where they can continue with their plans. Kathy has been somewhat quite in the car, while Xabier has been talking about the very rich history of Oñati and its people. At the tavern Xabier orders two beers and a ration of green olives while they sit at a round table.

-Where are we, Xabier? –Asks Kathy, almost interrupting Xabier in his enthusiastic presentation of the town's history.

-What do you mean? We are in the town of Oñati, of course. –Responds Xabier, a bit surprised.

-No, no, Xabier...I mean where are you and I now? In our relationship, I mean... You asked me to join you in the Basque Country for our next project, that of entering the **Secret Archives of the Vatican**, if you recall, and you ask me to stay at Maite's house while you are going to live somewhere else, it appears. I mean you and I got to know each other quite well back in the USA, in fact we spent many nights together, if you recall, and now...Where are we now, Xabier? –A bit of concern and anguish could be detected in Kathy's face.

- Ohh, I understand now... Sorry Kathy, I was coming to it and, yes, I realize that I have to explain some things to you. It's my fault, it's all my fault, really, as I have been struggling with a number of matters in my mind, certainly our relationship, of course, as well as my position within the Seminary of Arantzazu, really. – Xabier wanted to continue, to go further, but Kathy wanted to say more.

-Xabier, as I see it, you and I got very close to each other in the USA, as you know, and I thought that our getting together now would mean living together while we work with other people to carry out that project... There are many things that we talked about doing together, you and I, really. And what is this struggle that you are talking about? Back in the USA we had many challenges that we had to address together, and we did it all successfully, side by side, so I don't understand yet what is our current situation.

-It's my entire fault, Kathy, I feel caught between two very powerful desires... One such desire is to continue within the Catholic Church, trying to help with internal problems of low count of new seminarians, the wishes of **Father Muxika** before his tragic death, and my concern for an end to the religious wars... On the other hand I feel a lot for you, as a friend and as a woman... One part of me wants to leave all this religion and concern about world peace and go away with you to some remote place in our planet where we could be happy, just you and I... That's what I mean, Kathy.

Xabier and Kathy looked at each other's eyes, while Xabier reached for Kathy's hands, wanting to touch her, wanting to embrace her.

-I hear you, Xabier, it must not have been easy for you either...Certainly, and it has been difficult for me as well. Back in Tucson, Arizona, I thought about you many times, about your earlier commitments to your friends at the Arantzazu Seminary, and whether it was selfish of me to try to have you as part of my life.

-Still, Kathy, I don't want to lose you... I just need some more time to clarify my mind, to make up my mind about what I really want to do with my life... You are very special, someone like you does not appear every day, at least that's how I feel. I also want you to be part of my life, and that is why... -- Kathy was feeling more relaxed, to the point that felt it would be OK to interrupt Xabier to make a suggestion.

-I have a suggestion, Xabier, how about going ahead with our project, which is a lot of work, and is going to require the cooperation of many people, and afterwards decide?

-Thank you, Kathy, I like that, a very good suggestion, another good reason why I feel you are so special in my life.

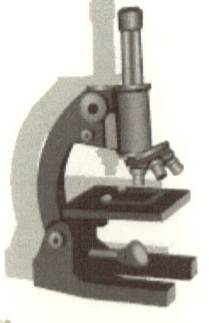

Chapter

2

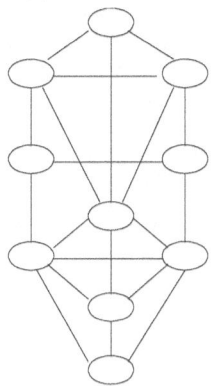

"It is indeed strange that with all the knowledge we have gained in the past hundred years we preserve and practice the methods of an ancient and barbarous world in our dealing with crime. So long as this is observed and exercised there can be no change except to heap more cruelties and more wretchedness upon those who are the victims of our foolish system.

Clarence Darrow, *The Story of My Life,* Writer[1]

A list of Crimes Resolved, Maybe

On the second day of her visit with Xabier in Oñati, Basque Country, Kathy brings up the subject of crimes unresolved, people that both have known and who have met tragic deaths in the past few months. Is there a single killer on the loose, or an international crime organization behind it all? That morning, having a light breakfast at a tavern near the Seminary of Arantzazu, both address the subject.

Father Muxika's tragic end

-What do we know so far about Father Muxika's tragic murder after all, after all these months? He was your boss and friend at the Seminary of Arantzazu, was he not? —Asked Kathy trying to get the conversation going in that direction.

-Yes, you recall correctly, he was my boss and dear friend... Since I got back from the USA there has been a lot of investigation on the subject, I mean the Guardia Civil has been looking into it, specially **lieutenant Balboa** has been leading the investigation, the INTERPOL people have also looked into it, but there has not been an arrest of an individual, or evidence that points to some sort of crime organization, local or international, not yet.

-Did they not cut part of his tongue, if I recall correctly?

-Yes, you are right, and now I remember that a main theory about that murder came out, yes. He was a Franciscan monk, as you know, and there are reasons to believe that he was murdered by members of the Croatian families who were persecuted by the *Ustashi* organization... --Began to remember Xabier.

-The Ustashi organization? –Interrupted Kathy.

-Those Croatian families were Christian Orthodox and many of them died at the hands of the Ustashi police forces in Croatia during World War II, and many officers in the Ustashi police were Franciscan monks, it all being hard to believe. The Vatican and the Ustashi wanted those Christian Orthodox families to convert to Catholicism, and those who refused were sent to concentration camps in Croatia, and many of those who refused to convert got their throats cut, murdered.

-But that was years ago, during the war... --Added Kathy, still hoping to understand where the investigation was going.

-Well, some of the surviving Christian Orthodox families ended up migrating to Latin America after the war, and it is suspected that the sons of those families later murdered many Franciscan monks in retaliation, that's what I meant to say. The investigation is still going on. –Xabiers said, relieved at remembering the details, finally.

Who killed Dr. Fuad Fahim?

It was still early in the morning, so Xabier thought they had time to catch up on other unresolved murders, such as the murder of Dr. Fuad Fahim. An expert in Coptic writings, he worked with Kathy and her chief of research Dr. Finley in the *Department of Anthropology and Social Studies*, at the **University of Arizona**, in Tucson, Arizona, USA.

-And whatever happened to Dr. Fahim, yes, Dr. Fuad Fahim? He was an expert on Coptic writings, I believe. –Asked Xabier, thinking that by then, months later, Kathy would know more about such murder case.

-That murder case is still unresolved, I hate to say…A great loss to our research team at the University of Arizona. There are a number of theories on the subject, and agents of INTERPOL are still working on this case, but nothing clear has emerged yet.

-Yes, I remember your mentioning an inspector Belluci from the office of Interpol. –Said Xabier, and then added more comments. – But if Dr. Fahim was working on the CDs that supposedly came out of the Vatican's Secret Archives, why not investigate that international sect with the name of *Guards of the Secret Oath*, for example. The name of that organization came up several times during the investigation.

-Exactly, and that is the main suspect in this murder case, at this time. Those people, we have reason to believe, are a bunch of fanatical, ultra-conservative Catholics, whose aim is to protect the Vatican, anything that has to do with the Vatican, including its popes, hierarchical power structure, its Secret Archives, etc. The problem is that there are hundreds of Catholic organizations throughout the world, and it takes time to investigate each one of them, really.

-Well, I hope the investigation is looking into figures in the Vatican itself. –Added Xabier – Someone, a person or group of people connected with the contents of the two CDs which got out of the Vatican and later ended in the hands of Dr. Fahim.

-I agree, I agree, Xabier… But we have to remember that the Vatican itself is a State of its own in the international community, with all the institutional and executive powers of any other nation, and there is much paper work to be done to secure an investigation into departments of the Vatican.

-True, true, a major task to carry out, even for agents at INTERPOL…But the investigation is still going on, right?

-Yes, of course, and every few months we receive an update at our Department at the University of Arizona. –Said Kathy, as though wanting to reassure Xabier.

Andoni's murder and the international Mafia

Xabier and Kathy are finishing their coffee, enjoying each other's company once again, when Kathy realizes that she has another question.

-And why am I staying in Maite's house here in Oñati...Is she an old friend of yours, Xabier? –Asked Kathy, somewhat casually, not wanting to reveal her serious interest in the question.

-Oh, no, she is not an old friend of mine, if that's what you meant...But she is a special person, very close to me and other friends of mine, really.

-Special, how... Is she a relative?

-No, she is not a relative. What I mean is that her husband Andoni was kidnapped and later murdered, and many of us have felt very close to her during that tragedy. –Xabier finally came to the point, and he continued.

-As a young man, Andoni had been involved in some activity with *ETA* (*Euskadi eta Askatasuna*), taking young men in his car to meetings and gatherings in Iparralde, the Basque Country on the "French side", nothing else. He was sort of the "taxi driver" to some of those young people. Years later some members of ETA had to flee the country and ended up in Venezuela, as it was reported in some newspapers. As it turned out, a judge in the *Audiencia Nacional* by the name of *Velasco* came out in the newspapers claiming that there was a "cooperation on the part of the Venezuelan government" regarding a collaboration between *ETA* and *FARC* (*Fuerzas Armadas Revolucionarias de Colombia*), and that there was reason to believe that such two organizations contemplated assassinating Columbia's President *Alvaro Uribe* on his tour through Europe.

-What are you saying, Xabier, where is all that going?

-Well, to summarize, the governments of Spain and Columbia eventually got into an exchange of statements and apologies and nothing much else, at least on the newspapers. Getting to the point, Andoni was kidnapped by members of the *Delta international mafia* because those thugs thought that Andoni might have more information of that supposed collaboration between ETA and FARC members, a mafia working in secrecy for either an anti-terrorist cell within the Spanish Government or within the French Government. Months later Andoni was found dead in a parking lot next to Palacio Miramar in **San Sebastian**. He had been drugged during his capture to try to extract information from him but he died in the process, it is suspected. The guy, many of us believe, knew nothing of any supposed collaboration between ETA and FARC, but unfortunately he was caught in the middle of that pull between two governments, we think.

-Has it been determined which government was involved at all?

-Not really. In fact, there is also reason to believe that such international mafia is in the business of procuring unsolicited information and later trying to sell it to interested governments. So, that murder has not been resolved yet, really.

-I hear you. Still, why did you choose Maite's house for my stay in the Basque Country? –Asked Kathy, trying to get an answer to her original question.

-It is only for a couple of days, as we try to get in touch with other contacts that you and I know in order to plan our entry into the Secret Archives of the Vatican. She is a person that I trust, and I know that you will be safe there.

Giovani Bruni knew too much

-Since we are on the topic of murders, do we know of any recent information of the **Giovanni Bruno** case, the administrator of the system of libraries at the Vatican? – This time it was Xabier asking the question.

-No, not really, not yet. –Quickly added Kathy. –As we all know he was found dead floating on the River Tiber near Rome. The case is still open.

-That is a strange case, again, as such murder may have to do with the two CDs which must have been sent out from the Vatican, as many of us suspect. Yes, it was believed that members of the so called *"Guardians of the Sacred Oath"* might have taken revenge on their master librarian for releasing into the open market such CDs, revealing its lethal contents, but others are suspected as well.

-Yes, possibly an individual or international organization interested in getting more information from Mr. Bruno, information with which to blackmail the Vatican and thus obtain large sums of money from such entity.

-Right! –Added Xabier. –The more reason for wanting to know what is inside the walls of the *Secret Archives of the Vatican*, as we have proposed in our next project. We are all doing much conjecturing, when the answers may well be inside those secret archives.

✳✳✳

Chapter
3

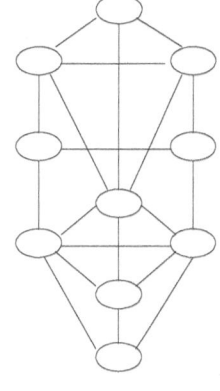

*"On the morning of September 29, 1978, Pope John Paul I was found dead, sitting up in his bed, after only 33 days in office. Although **Vatican** officials claimed the 65-year-old pope died of a heart attack, there was never an autopsy, and at the time, the Vatican definitely had ties to organized crime. Sure enough, in 1982, Vatican Bank president Father Paul Marcinkus resigned from his post after a series of scandals exposed the bank's ties to the Mafia. Eventually, the bank had to repay more than $200 million to its creditors."*

--David Goldenberg, writer[1]

The Vatican Secret Archives

If the **Library of Alexandria** was the crown jewel of the ancient world serving as its repository of thousands of books and documents, then the **Vatican's Secret Archives** would have to be called the most-holy jewel of the Church, underneath the Vatican in catacombs that collect, guard, and maintain the documents that attest to the power and glory of the Roman Catholic Church over the last two-thousand years. The *Archivum Secretum Vaticanum* is spread over several underground sections of Vatican City with the exact distribution and location being unknown, although the section located directly under the **Cortile della Pigna** is generally acknowledged and accessible to the general public. Over 53 miles (84 kms) of shelving space containing over 35,000 volumes and documents of selective, disclosed catalogue. Photographing of documents and copying of content indices are forbidden, the interested reader must request access to specific documents available in the disclosed catalogue. When the request is granted, the document of interest is brought to a study area, and the reader can only bring with her/him paper and pencil. Officially, "transfers and political upheavals nearly caused the total loss of the archival material preceding Innocent III (1198-1216)", so that documents produced by the Christian world during the first ten centuries are basically non-existent, or so the Vatican claims.

A bit of History, Please

The beginnings the Secret Archives are to be found at the end of the 12th Century in response to confrontations among the Popes during councils and conclaves. Those of Viterbo (1269-1271) and Perugia (1292-1294) promoted Celestino V to the papacy. The current archive stores many documents of that period of much conflict between the civil powers and the papacy. Clemente (1305-1314) is crowned at the Cathedral of Lyon, and his personal archive in Avignon was expanded.

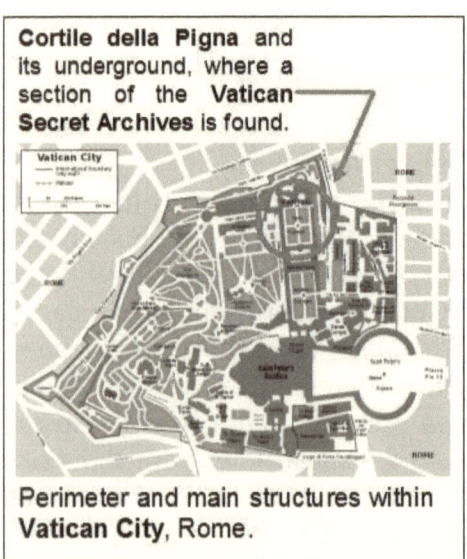

Cortile della Pigna and its underground, where a section of the **Vatican Secret Archives** is found.

Perimeter and main structures within **Vatican City**, Rome.

In 1377, Gregorio XI (1370-1378) returns to Rome taking with him his archive opening a new a dramatic chapter of *schism* in the Western World. After his death Urbano VI (1378-1389) is elected and everything seemed to proceed well until some of the cardinals considered that election invalid; gathered in Fondi they elected al Frances Roberto de Generous with the name of Clemente VII (1378-1394), the "anti-Pope." The papal archive continues to gather materials related to that event, and those later associated with following popes like Benedict XIII (1394-1423). In Rome, at about the same time, the other archive gathers volume with the proceedings of Bonifacio IX (1389-1404), Inocencio VII (1404-1406), and Gregory XII (1406-1415). Yes, the times were difficult and each one of those papacies lasted only a few years, as noted.

Things get complicated with the **Council of Pisa** where another anti-Pope gets elected, Alejandro V (1409-1410), followed by still another anti-Pope Juan XXIII (1410-1415). There existed three centers: Rome, Avignon, and Pisa, each one with its own curia and archive. Finally, with the election of Martin V (1417-1431), of the Colonna family, in the Council of Constanza the schism ends making possible the **unification** of those three archives. It is believed that many of those documents ended up in a complex of buildings which belonged to the Colonna family. The archive was steadily taking shape and location.

As Sixto IV (1471-1484) enters the picture, he founds the **Library of the Vatican**, and within it a part is named the "*secret Library.*" It is there where

An underground bunker of the **Secret Archives of the Vatican**.

some of the oldest papal letters were confined, whereas other documents with information on the privileges of the Roman Church and arrangements with kings were sent to the fortress of *Castel Sant'Angelo*. The need for a single central archive became greater as the years went by, and Pio IV (1559-1565) promoted such concept, and the archives grew in volume and importance with the documents produced by the *Council of Trento* (1545-1563), in Bologna, Italy.

Contents of the Secret Archives

It is with Innocence III (1198-1216) that begins the collection of *Registros Vaticanos*, which contain copies of the official letters among popes, generally called "***bulas***", which were sent to secretaries of the popes. This volume of some 2,047 documents is considered one of the main sources of information about the history of Europe in the period 13th-14th centuries.

This is the *"diplomatic" floor* of the Vatican Secret Archives. It was constructed by Pope Alexander VII in 1660 and contains documents from the 15th century to the Napoleonic period. (Courtesy of Vatican Secret Archives and VdH Books via CNS)

Considered as important are the *Avignon Registros* with a volume of some 353 documents; they begin with a registry of the first year of Clemente V (1305), continues with Juan XXIII (1316-1334), until the anti-papa Benedicto XIII. Another series began in 1389 with the *Lateran Registros*, although it lost many documents as a result of the transfer of those documents from the Vatican Archive in Rome to Paris in 1809 during the Napoleonic period. Some 2,467 documents remain catalogued. Another collection is that which originates in the 15th century with the name of the *Archivo Consitorial* and the annexes of the *College of Cardinals*, with a total of 1,308 documents.

Next, is another very voluminous archive with the name of *Secretary of State*, for the period 16th century to the Napoleonic period. Integral components of this archive, with documents still not accessible to the general public even today. Since then this archive has been augmented to contain a long list of documents, including *Prisoners of War, Office of Information* (related to the first and second world wars), the *Noble Guard, Council Tridentino, Council Vatican I, Council Vatican II*, and *Personal Archive of Pio IX*.

Archives of *Armarios XXXI* began in the 17th century and continued to today. They are distributed along 15 wardrobes and contain documents such as *Liber Diurnus*, and *Liber Censuum* (13th century) with an extract of the **Galileo Galilei** trial.

Despite Vatican efforts in modern times to open up portions of the Vatican Secret Archives and to make them available to the general public for scrutiny and study, the controversy continues.

"I wish they'd spend a higher percentage of their time in efforts to open the archives, and less in spinning what they're selectively presenting,"

A prelate studies Inquisition documents in the **Vatican Archive**. (Photo by Arturo Mari, L'Osservatore Romano, HO via AP)

*said **Abraham Foxman** of the **Anti-Defamation Jewish League (ADL)** to the National Catholic Reporter recently. Foxman and the ADL have consistently opposed beatification for Pius. "They're protesting too much. We are willing to withhold our judgement and the Vatican should withhold its (own) until scholars have been able to openly examine the material and see what's there."* [68]

Management and up keeping of the Secret Archives

The current administrators of the Secret Archives are Cardinal **Sergio Pagano** (since 1997), as Prefect, and **Jean-Louis Bruges** (since 2012), as Cardinal Archivist. The care and maintenance of the documents is carried out by three laboratories of restauration, photography, and copying.

Each year some 1.500 carnets of admission are issued. Very high is also the correspondence from all parts of the world asking for information, photographs, micro-films, and photo-copies of documents.

Research in the Secret Archives is free-of-charge and open to qualified scholars conducting scientific studies. All researches must have a university degree. Yes, it must be mentioned that permission is granted to consult documents in the archives up to the end of the papacy of Pius XI (1939). That is correct, subsequent documents, including those that might involve the late *Pius XII* with activities in Hitler's *Nazi regime* are not available to scholars, not yet.

In order to conduct research, the protocol calls for sending an application to the Prefect providing personal details (name, address, nationality), qualifications, profession, and reasons for research; a letter from a recognized institute of scientific research; must specify the latest academic qualification obtained (e.g., Ph.D., other); attach photocopy of valid identification (e.g., passport); photograph of researcher. Indexes of desired documents may be consulted at the "Leone XIII" Index Room. Photography is not allowed, and researchers can only use pencil and paper. To request access the researcher can use e-mail asv@asv.va, and telephone +39 06 69883211.

✳✳✳

Chapter

4

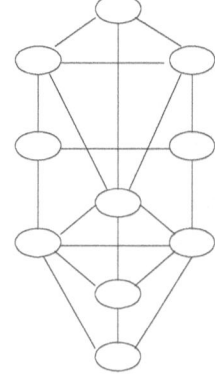

*"**Peace** is the beauty of life. It is sunshine. It is the smile of a child, the love of a mother, the joy of a father, the togetherness of a family. It is the advancement of man, the victory of a just cause, the triumph of truth. Peace is all of these and more and more."*
--**Menachem Begin**, 1978 Nobel Peace Price[1]

*"Today, **peace** means the ascent from simple coexistence to cooperation and common creativity among countries and nations."*
-- **Mikhail Gorbachev** (1931-), Russian Politician, Environmentalist, Social Activist, 1990 Nobel Peace Prize Winner[2]

Creation of the Council for World Peace (CWP)

It is Kathy's third day in *Oñati,* Basque Country, where she is meeting with Xabier and close friends to plan the entry into the Vatican's Secret Archives. Those meeting have addressed a myriad of preparations and needs, including a study of the *Swiss Guard* numbering some 100 guards, their positions at key points in the Vatican, and their relieve hour times by other guards; the participation of members of the *"Circle of Women"*; as well as the cooperation offered by members of the secret society *"Eagles of the Vatican"* headed by Father David Donovan of Trinity College of Maryland, USA.

There is another major piece of information that Kathy wants to share with Xabier, and that she patiently has kept to herself during those two earlier days. Finally the timing is right, Kathy believes, and she is about to share with Xabier. That morning Xabier Arrives to pick up Kathy at Maite's *caserio*, so both can go to a nearby "jatetxea" to have breakfast and continue their conversation.

-Good morning, Kathy!

-*Egun on, Xabier*! –Answers back Kathy, surprising Xabier.

-Hey, someone has already taught you how to say "Good morning" in Euskera. – Replies Xabier with a big smile.

-Yes, I was curious, so I asked Maite how to say a few words, and she told me…it's easy, really. So where are you taking me this morning?

-I thought you would like to see this place called the Etxe Handi, a restaurant in the outskirts of Oñati, a great place to have breakfast. –Suggested Xabier.

Ten minutes later their car arrives at the jatetxea. Not many customers have arrived yet, but the waiters are busy moving tables and chairs, bringing up bottles of wine from the cellar, and unloading food supplies from a van and taking them into the kitchen. Once seated at a table, Xabier senses that Kathy wants to share something with him.

-You started to say something while we were driving the car, but I could not follow you. What was it about? – Asked Xabier.

-Yes, I wanted to bring to your attention a project that my boss, Dr. Finley, at the University of Arizona, has been putting together in the last six months. Actually it is a global organization, an international organization. He and other influential people are still playing with the name but right now they are calling it the **Council for World Peace (CWP)**, although they have also considered the name other names like United Governments for World Peace.

-Hey, that sounds big! And what's the purpose of such organization? – This time Xabier is giving Kathy his full attention.

-Well, it's still a bit early, but Dr. Finley has already managed to contact and invite some 20-30 people that he knows in several governments all over the world, including current political leaders, presidents and vice presidents of corporations, a few university professors, and activists for various causes, and most of them have said yes to his project, they have joined in, in fact. Its purpose is to monitor societies and their well-being all over the world.

-Really? But we already have a United Nations (UN) organization with base in New York City, USA. Doesn't the UN monitor situations of political instability around the world and then it sends a military force in a place where a war conflict has erupted? – Asked Xabier with a smile, at the same time that it gave a two-page breakfast menu to Kathy.

Yes, but the United Nations (UN) does one thing while the Council for World Peace (CWP) would do other things. I'll explain myself. The UN is an intergovernmental organization which seeks to promote international co-operation, so that when a war erupts somewhere in the world the UN reacts and its sends soldiers, equipment, and administrative personnel to that hot spot somewhere in the planet, an *after-the-fact* event. Right? Well, what Dr. Finley has in mind is an intergovernmental organization that goes around identifying areas, societies, and countries where we monitor a number of factors or levels, such as poverty, economic development, food resources, education, political situation, ethnic and religious wars, and other critical situations. The idea is that when a society or country falls below critical factor levels, to be determined, the CWP would alert the world community at-large, and participating countries are invited to send in resources (e.g., people, money, food supplies, teachers, etc.) to remedy such situation. This would be a preventive measure and effort, a *before-the-fact* event. Without such an inter-governmental organization "multiple hot spots" would surface, threatening the quality of life in our planet.

-Yeah, I hear you Kathy, and potentially such organization would render a great service to societies around the globe, but we already have hundreds of Non-Governmental Organizations (NGOs) which are already helping in many societies.

-Yes, those NGOs are already helping in many societies and countries, and I am coming to it, but let me give you some *examples* first to try to describe the function of the CWP. Consider if you will the as example of an automobile. An automobile is only as good on the road its weakest part, so that if its braking system is not monitored and it eventually fails on the road, fatalities can occur. Similarly, the human body is only as good as its weakest organ, so that a person can have all the muscles in the world, but if his/her heart is weak such person may collapse and die). We may also have successful and powerful democracies in the planet, but if one or more societies elsewhere in the planet are below economic and educational thresholds, then those societies are potential targets of opportunistic "religious leaders" and "political leaders" such as the "*Islamic State*" who will recruit its members in order to cause mass destruction and agony in other societies. The main idea, then, is to alert the community of governments, the "system", that a major calamity, a war conflict, is about to occur before it actually happens, and then be there with resources to remedy such drastic situation. It would be like having actualized a map of all the "good" and "hot-spots" in the planet, with a plan and resources to prevent major disasters. A sort of preventive medicine program for planet Earth. – Kathy said, looking at Xabier, and waiting for his next question or comment.

-OK, I hear you, it could work, but there would be many dimensions, many activities, personnel with many areas of expertise, communication systems, multiple databases, trips and missions to carry out, decisions to make, recommendations to offer, follow up activities, etc., which would call for a very large budget, I would think. – Added Xabier, this time raising an eyebrow.

-Exactly! And that is one main reason why such global organization has not been tried before… -- Kathy advanced.

-And where did such idea come from? Probably many world leaders have thought about it before over the years, but nothing that large has been created and put into place yet, I would say.

-Agree. Dr. Finley says that a few years ago a group of professors and students in the *Systems Engineering Department* of the *University of Arizona* (UofA), with the cooperation of professors, students, and business people from other universities and corporations created a research program that they called something like *"multiple criteria decision making"* (MCDM), with the idea of making decisions in the corporate and business world based on several parameters, such as production costs, market demand for products, tax incentives, capital availability, and other parameters. So it occurred to Dr. Finley that a similar list of parameters could be identified to monitor and classify societies and countries around the world as "healthy" and "not healthy" in order to monitor the health of the planet as it reaches it limits in terms of overpopulation, food resources, religious wars, epidemics, and climate change, to mention just a few of the critical conditions that our planet is reaching these days, or about to reach in the near future.

-Really? You really think that we human beings are approaching critical conditions on Earth, our planet Earth?

-Yes, I believe that is the case. – Suggested Kathy – Many scientists, including the astrophysicist **Stephen Hawking**, of the *Royal Society of London* and the *National Academy of Sciences* of the USA, and other renown scientists believe that humans and human societies as we know them today may come to an end in 500 years or so due to reaching limits in those areas of overpopulation, food resources, religious wars, epidemics, and climate change mentioned earlier. The importance, therefore, of making some major changes in our societies if we want to live a few more thousand years as a species in the planet, I would say.

-"500 years or so." Wow! I did not realize that some people thought things were getting so drastic worldwide. – *Xabier* could not help saying, and added: -How advanced is that program? I mean, is this new program something that is going to impact our plans to enter the Secret Archives of the Vatican in the months ahead?

-Such Council and its program is not going to change our plans to enter the Secret Archives, Dr. Finley has assured me of that, but he has suggested that we may want to do some other things as well.

"Other things as well", like what?

-The Council's advisory board has asked Dr. Finley and myself to visit four countries in Africa to investigate and prepare a report on the lands being leased to other countries for agricultural purposes. Yes, for several years now countries like Russia, Germany, China, the USA, and other countries have been getting 50-year leases from those countries in Africa. The Council anticipates that economic conditions in some of those countries are deteriorating fast, that thousands of people are being displaced from their agricultural countries in Africa to nearby cities, and that in some 8-10 years we may be seeing thousands, if not millions, of people trying to migrate and reach political asylum in countries in the European Union (EU).

-This is crazy! I did not know that other countries... I mean rich countries like Germany, China, the USA, and others, were already leasing agricultural lands in Africa. As if that continent did not have enough problems already! – Xabier could not help saying.

-But Dr. Finley feels that going ahead with the plans to enter the Secret Archives, try to find a number of critical documents, and to obtain information which might help resolve that list of murders has top priority. He also has other activities to suggest to you and associates in the Basque Country should you decide to join in the Council.

-Well, I also needed to communicate to you, my dear Kathy, that our plan to enter the Secret Archives may have to delayed a few months, that we may have to wait until next year, due to recruitment activities within the *Vatican Eagles* group... Yes, they are trying to recruit a few more people, this time inside the Vatican, before we all carry out such plan. Sorry about it, but just found out last week, and...

-It's OK, no problem. I will let Dr. Finley about this delay on the part of the Vatican Eagles, and maybe then he decides to re-schedule some of those other activities. –Kathy opened her eyes wide, threw her arms up in the air, and smiling added: -So now you and I can have *a few days* off before going back to the USA while Dr. Finley works with others to reset the timeline for those Council activities!

-Kathy, my dear friend, have you ever visited the beaches in San Sebastian, eaten at some of its fancy restaurants, and danced all night?

-Nope, but I would love to do so with you.

-Great! Have your small luggage ready after lunch!

Part II:

Planet Earth at its Limits

Chapter

5

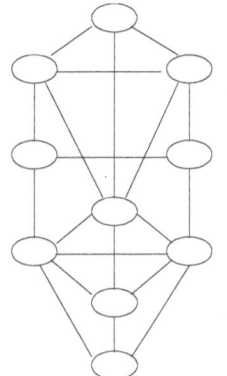

*""Ozone depletion, lack of water, and pollution are not the disease—they are the symptoms. The disease is **overpopulation**. And unless we face world population head-on, we are doing nothing more than sticking a Band-Aid on a fast-growing cancerous tumor."*

— **Dan Brown**, *Inferno*, writer[7]

World Population at its Limits

As we may recall from earlier chapters, our *Homo Sapiens Sapiens* species began with some 200 families who left Africa some 50,000 years ago, migrating into southern Europe, and later dispersing into all five continents. In that period of time we have managed to reproduce ourselves to reach **a population of some 7,000 Million**, in spite of several massive natural disasters due to erupting volcanoes, floods, and plagues as the ones that occurred in Europe during the Middle Ages, a population that would otherwise be much larger today, at the beginning of the 21st century. How is a population of this size a threat to our species and the health of our planet? Good question. I have traveled all along the USA, several countries in Europe and Latin America, and I have seen many cities, yes, but also many vast areas of land with little population, being used mostly for agricultural purposes. Only a few years ago I travelled by car from the Basque Country south all the way to Madrid and, not taking the Burgos route, and I saw mostly empty spaces and agricultural lands, with very few small towns. In fact, much of the population in Spain and many other countries is to be found along its rivers and along its coastlines. So what is all this concern about overpopulation? Let us begin to look at the facts.

Pakistan, with 180 million people, 2.6% of the world's population, is the **sixth most populous country in the world**. Its total fertility rate (TFR) is 3 children per woman, and its economic growth rate is only 3%, compared with China's 9.2% and Bangladesh's 6.1%. Bangladesh has a TFR of 2.2. If Pakistan's TFR does not change, its population will reach nearly 380 million by 2050 and the country will face a devastating scarcity of resources, according to the UN. The Malthusian Theory of Population is still workable to understand the relation of population growth in *geometric means* and food growth in *arithmetic means* while technology remains constant. Unfortunately, the Government of Pakistan and political parties still do not have a clear vision to address this issue, imposing birth control panic with slogans like "bachay do hi achay" (Two Children are enough), which created further fear and confusion among masses.

Little or no progress has been made in *Balochistan*, with a TFR of 4.1, Sindh and Khyber-Pakhtunkhwa 4.3, Punjab 3.9. Major political parties chant slogans for the empowerment of women but when it comes to women's health, they hesitate to include the population issue in their manifestos. The MQM is the only political party whose manifesto reflects the need for family welfare.[3]

We are still looking at Asia. So what is the overpopulation situation in the Philippines?

The *Philippines*, a country the size of Arizona, has about 1/3 the U.S. population of 313 million and is expected to double in size by 2080. To feed its people, the Philippines imports more rice than any other country on the planet and its oceans show severe signs of overfishing. The Philippines has *one of the highest birth rates in the world* and the highest teen pregnancy rate in the Asian Pacific.

Two thirds of native plant and animal species are endemic to the islands and nearly half of them are threatened. Less than 10% of the islands' original vegetation remains and 70% of the 27,000 square kilometers of coral reefs are in poor condition." Late last year Philippine President Benigno Aquino signed the *Responsible Parenthood and Reproductive Health Act of 2012*. This means that government health centers will have to make reproductive health education, maternal health care and contraceptives available to everyone. The *Catholic Church* is vehemently opposed to it and has threatened excommunication for the president and any politicians who support it. One 44-year-old woman, *a devout Catholic with 16 children*, said, "We don't pay attention to (the Church's opposition). They are not the ones who are giving birth again and again. We are the ones who have to find a way to care for the children." In the slums of its capital, Manila, a woman who had 22 pregnancies and has 17 surviving children, reported, "Many times, we sleep without eating." One of the reasons for enacting the reproductive health law is to help break the cycle of poverty. Pilot studies from USAID and UNFPA have shown that integrated population, health and environment (PHE) programs have made inroads in saving the environment. [5]

In some countries the fertility rate may be falling, but overall, the world population is *exploding.*

There more than 3 billion people worldwide under the age of 25. About 1.2 billion of them are adolescents just entering their reproductive years and there are political and cultural forces against contraception So even though birthrates are falling globally, the population explosion is far from over. In many parts of the world children are married at an early age, even at 10 or 11. Often they have babies as soon as they reach adolescence. If they choose, collectively, not to bend to parental and community pressure, and have smaller families than their elders did, the world's population -- now 7 billion -- will continue to grow, but more slowly.

According to UN projections, the number *will rise to 9.3 billion by 2050* -- the equivalent of adding another India and China to the world. This assumes that the worldwide average birthrate will decline from the current 2.5 children per woman to 2.1. If birthrates fail to fall, *population could reach 11 billion by midcentury* - the equivalent to adding three Chinas. Whether 9.3 billion or 11 billion, water, food and arable land will be more scarce, cities more crowded and hunger more widespread, but it will be worse with 11 billion.

John Bongaarts, a demographer at *Population Council in New York* told the Times, "*We're still adding more than 70 million people to the planet every year - which we have been doing since the 1970s.*"

By 2030, India, now with 1.2 billion people, will probably see its birthrate drop from 2.5 children to 2.1. But even then, India's population will continue to grow because of momentum, and is not expected to peak until 2060, at 1.7 billion people. In some of the poorest parts of the world, fertility rates remain high, driven by tradition, religion, the inferior status of women and limited access to contraception. These are the same parts of the world where hunger, political instability and environmental degradation are already pervasive.

Africa is *expected to double in population by the middle of this century*, adding 1 billion people.

With 7 billion people in the world today, about 1 in 8 people lives in a slum and 1 billion are chronically hungry, according to FAO. At least 8 million die every year of hunger-related illnesses. When the population reaches 9 billion - around 2050 - 1 in 3 will be living in a slum, assuming poverty and migration to cities continue at their current rates. And there will be at least 2 billion more mouths to feed, but no one can say where the food will come from. *David Tilman*, a University of Minnesota expert on global agriculture, says *crop production will have to be doubled. William G. Lesher*, a former USDA chief economist, said "*We're going to have to produce more food in the next 40 years than we have in the last 10,000*," he said. "Some people say we'll just add more land or more water. But we're not going to do much of either."

Most of Earth's best farmland has already been utilized, and cities and desserts are replacing it. Soil erosion, chemical contamination and salt buildup from irrigation are despoiling prime acreage. With climate change, higher temperatures and violent weather will stunt or destroy crops. Increased flooding will imperil millions living in low-lying regions.

But instead of worrying about this, in *Europe*, Japan and North America, leaders are worried about having too few young people to care for aging populations and to fund benefits for the elderly. And in developing countries, leaders often consider large youthful populations a source of economic vitality and political strength. In the U.S., political battles are being fought over contraception and abortion, causing some environmental and humanitarian groups to retreat from family planning initiatives.

Nearly 20 years after 179 nations signed a pledge to provide universal access to *family planning*, supplies of contraceptives remain erratic in much of the developing world.

Although *India's* population growth has slowed among the urban middle class, birthrates remain high among the rural poor. *Uttar Pradesh*, a state in India 166 million people 10 years ago. Today it has 200 million and *may double by 2050*. If it were a country, it would be the fifth-most populous in the world. Women in the state still have 3.5 children each on average.

An extensive push is needed to make *contraceptives* widely available in scattered villages and rural areas, many of which lack paved roads or clinics. Government efforts have been haphazard and limited, reflecting ambivalence about family planning. A national law restricts women under 18 from marrying, but the tradition to marry early is still going strong. India's leaders view their country's youth bulge as a competitive advantage over China, whose workforce is older because of long-standing restrictions on family size. *Hania Zlotnik*, former director of the *U.N. Population Division* says: "But most of their growth is in the poor. Is it a good thing to have a larger number of poor people in your population?"

Advances in agriculture, followed by the Industrial Revolution, pushed humanity to the 1-billion mark around 1810. From there, the numbers began a steep ascent. *It took only 12 years to go from 6 to 7 billion.*

Although use of contraceptives worldwide has climbed steadily in the last 40 years, led by the industrialized West and China, it remains extraordinarily low in the least developed parts of Africa and South Asia.

In *Nigeria* only about 8% of reproductive-age women who are married or in relationships use contraception, compared with 72% in the US. Nigeria may surpass the U.S. as the third-most- populous country by 2050. *Kenya*'s family planning program was once held up as a model on the continent. In the late 1970s, the government joined with international donors in a high-profile effort that reduced the birthrate from more than eight per woman to fewer than five by the late 1990s.

Then *Kenya* was shaken by political turbulence, and a Republican-controlled U.S. Congress slashed family planning budgets. Supplies of contraceptives were interrupted across the East African nation and the decline in the birthrate stalled. The projection for Kenyans population in 2050 has been bumped up from 44 million to nearly a 100 million."[6]

There we have the *effects of overpopulation*: (1) an increase in poverty and disease among families worldwide, (2) abuse of women's rights, (3) depletion of natural resources, (4) degradation of the environment, and (5) conflicts and wars. Along this same issue, some of the *solutions to overpopulation* can be: (1) better education, (2) family planning, and (3) knowledge of sex education.

Chapter
6

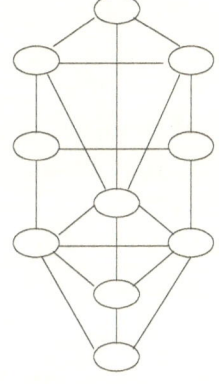

*"Agriculture is not crop production as popular belief holds - it's the production of food and fiber from the world's **land and waters**. Without agriculture it is not possible to have a city, stock market, banks, university, church or army. Agriculture is the foundation of civilization and any stable economy."*

--**Allan Savory**, writer, scientist.[1]

*"Everybody wants to support his own region and economy and farming. If we can **preserve the land** and if we can preserve the ocean, we all know, deep inside that we're doing the right thing.*

--**Eric Ripert**, chef, writer.[2]

Land and Sea Food resources

Vast amounts of foods are needed to maintain the world population today. In this section we take a look at the *changes* that the various types of foods, agricultural areas, and their statistics are undergoing due to a variety of reasons, including overpopulation and climate change.

The world needs to produce *at least 50% more food* to feed 9 billion people by 2050. But climate change could cut crop yields by more than 25%. The land, biodiversity, oceans, forests, and other forms of natural capital are being depleted at unprecedented rates. Unless we change how we grow our food and manage our natural capital, food security --especially for the world's poorest --will be at risk. Already, *high food prices* are the new normal. When faced with high food prices, many poor families cope by pulling their children out of school and eating cheaper, less nutritious food, which can have severe life-long effects on the social, physical, and mental well-being of millions of young people. Malnutrition contributes to infant, child, and maternal illness; decreased learning capacity; lower productivity, and higher mortality. One-third of all child deaths globally are attributed to under-nutrition. *Investment in agriculture and rural development* to boost food production and nutrition is a priority for the *World Bank Group*, which works through several partnerships to improve food security; from encouraging climate-smart farming techniques and restoring degraded farmland to breeding more resilient and nutritious crops to improving storage and supply chains for reducing food losses.[7]

In *Bangladesh* unplanned growth of population is complicating the process of meeting the *demand for food*, basic health requirements and educational facilities, which, in turn, is expected to lead to unemployment and social unrest. For example, trees are being chopped down for fuel on a regular basis. Climatic disruption in recent times, followed by salinity intrusion, shrinking farmlands and crop losses, has added to the woes of the people of the country. Bangladesh, with the world's highest density of population, is fast losing arable land due to growing industrialization and rapid encroachment of human habitat on farming areas. 8000 hectares of farm land are being lost every year from its original 13 million hectares of cropland due to urbanization, industrialization, unplanned rural housing and infrastructure buildings.

Entrepreneurs are going to the remote areas of the countryside to set up factories. Agriculture accounts for only 21% of the country's gross domestic product (GDP) although the sector employs around 50% cent of the nation's workforce. *At the current rate of loss of cultivable land, there will be none left in 50 years.* If the trend is not reversed now, the country would permanently lose its food security, making its poor population more vulnerable to volatile international commodity prices. The government has banned the use of arable land for purposes other than agriculture. It has been suggested that the factories and educational institutions that have already been built should now go vertical. But the government does not have adequate staff to monitor such things.

The average farm size has been reduced to less than 0.6 hectares and 59% of inhabitants are landless, with nearly 80% of the ultra-poor living in rural areas. 80% of Bangladesh's total cultivated area is in *rice*, the staple food and a politically-sensitive product. No one seems to worry about farmland depletion and the call for ensuring optimum utilization of arable land and bringing fallow land under cultivation is only rhetoric. Focus was put on rice production, while fuel, cooking oils and pulses were imported at volatile prices. Suggestions for *diversifying crops* have been ignored by the policymakers. Government expenditure on agricultural research has been steadily declining in Bangladesh. Investing more on agricultural research is vital for Bangladesh since it is losing cropland quite fast.

The *World Trade Organization (WTO)* pointed out that in the world's poorest corners, including Bangladesh, land is getting divided through inheritance and farm sizes are getting smaller and smaller with the passing of every generation.

The probable loss of arable and residential lands through flooding would result in increase of internal and external environmental migration and strained relations between countries. Bangladeshis, on an average, spend 50% of their income on food.

In Bangladesh, the problem of economic development has so far been addressed mainly in isolation from the population issue. It is expected that the *National Population Council* will play its due role in controlling population while strict monitoring and vigilance of RAJUK and all city corporations are a must to stop unplanned development of towns and industries across the country. The nation cannot afford to lose agricultural land any further.[4]

Next, researchers already see a *collision course* between overpopulation and climate change, a collision that will have a major impact on food supplies in the world.

We don't worry much about food, especially when it is plentiful and cheap. Only when prices rise do we pay much attention to any potential problems with the food supply. In the United States food has been relatively cheap for decades—typically costing less than 10 percent of our income—so we often take it for granted.

Perhaps we shouldn't. Quite a few people these days aren't taking food for granted, and it's not just the *more than 800 million people worldwide* who don't have enough to eat, or the *more than 47 million in the U.S.* who need food assistance. Whether we'll have enough food at affordable prices has been a particular concern for many scientists and economists since price spikes in 2008 caused unrest in places such as Egypt, Bangladesh, and Haiti.

This week in Washington (22 May 2014), the *Chicago Council on Global Affairs*, which for years has been immersed in questions about food and its supply—where it comes from, what kind and how much we grow, how we use or waste it, and whether we will have enough in the years ahead—gathered to discuss solutions to what its members see as an *emerging food crisis.*

These researchers see a collision ahead: between a rising *world population* that wants to eat more high-quality food such as meat and dairy, and a *climate system* that is diminishing harvests in many areas. Storms, floods, heat waves, and droughts are occurring with increasing frequency, trimming some crop yields across the planet.

That's a problem, because we will need more harvests of the major grain crops—*rice, wheat, and corn*—in the decades ahead. Those crops are the basis of nearly all the food we eat—even meat, because we feed grains such as corn, wheat, and soy to meat animals.

How do we meet the challenge of dramatically rising food demand? Jonathan Foley, a University of Minnesota researcher, is among many seeking solutions. In the May issue of *National Geographic*, he outlines a five-step framework for **feeding 9 billion people by mid-century.** Foley's article opens an eight-month series in the magazine on the future of food.

Beside the linkage between climate change and food supplies, this week's Chicago Council meeting focuses on improving harvests in vulnerable regions such as sub-Saharan Africa and South Asia, where harvests are low or unreliable and the need for food solutions is escalating. Topics include "sustainable intensification" of agriculture, which means getting better yields without damaging the land and water; improving irrigation in Africa; and using field schools to teach improved farming techniques.

Climate change gets some attention too. The group is examining how agriculture—which is responsible for about one-third of all greenhouse gas emissions—can reduce its impact on climate through precision tillage and fertilizer use. Discussants also emphasized the need for accelerated crop research to breed more climate-resistant crops that can survive heat waves, droughts, floods, and saltwater.

The group issued a report today that calls for the U.S. to make **food security**—investments in research, education, technology, and data—**a top priority for the long-term**, especially in the face of documented climate impacts on harvests.

The **U.S. Agency for International Development** also announced an initiative to help improve the nutrition of mothers and children in developing nations. It's part of a broader program called Feed the Future that aims to help alleviate hunger by helping farmers grow more and better crops across the developing world.

USAID Administrator *Rajiv Shah* told attendees at the Chicago Council meeting Thursday that Feed the Future has lifted more than 12 million children out of poverty and improved the welfare of more than 7 million farmers.

The *United Nations* projected last year that *the world's population would reach 9.6 billion by 2050*, up from nearly 7.2 billion now. A large portion of the increased food demand in decades ahead is projected to result from rising appetites for meat; several pounds of grain are needed to grow each pound of meat.

We are entering uncharted territory. The March report by the *Intergovernmental Panel on Climate Change* highlighted the vulnerability of food supplies to rising temperatures and extreme weather in years ahead. Studies already show that yields are being damaged by rising levels of carbon dioxide, increasing temperatures, heat waves, and droughts. The 2012 Midwest U.S. *drought*, for example, damaged crop yields and drove prices up.

Growing enough food for a booming world population as the climate changes is cited often as being *among the greatest challenges to face humanity*. Yet, young people who can help meet this challenge are not easy to find. One report this week indicated that U.S. agriculture is facing a shortage of trained scientists. So not only must we grow more food, we must grow more people interested in growing more food.[8]

Do we know that already a large number or countries are buying and leasing large extensions of agricultural lands in other countries in order to grow food such as *Africa, Australia, Latin America, and Siberia*?

The world's population is soaring past 7 billion. Food prices keep spiking every few years. Freshwater supplies in plenty of areas are dwindling.

And so, in response, a slew of countries and investors — from *Chinese state corporations to Gulf sheiks to Wall Street firms* — have started buying up farmland overseas in an apparent attempt to acquire as much precious soil and water as possible. This phenomenon is known as *"land grabbing*," and it has been accelerating ever since the massive surge in grain prices back in 2007.

So how much land and water is actually being grabbed? Quite a lot, according to a big new study published in the "Proceedings of the *National Academies of Sciences*" this week. The authors find that somewhere between 0.7 percent and 1.75 percent of the world's agricultural land is being transferred to foreign investors from local landholders. That's *an area bigger than France and Germany combined.*

Big purchasers of foreign farmland include Britain, the United States, China, the United Arab Emirates, South Korea, South Africa, Israel, India and Egypt. They're mostly seeking out land in *Africa and Asia*, particularly in countries such as Congo, Sudan, Indonesia, Tanzania, Mozambique, Ethiopia and even Australia. Here is a map from the PNAS study (Proceedings of the National Academy of Sciences of the United States, in www.pnas.org) showing who's grabbing what from where. Red triangles indicate investors, green dots indicate land that's being snatched up. Note that some countries, like Russia and Brazil, are on both ends of the farmland trade.

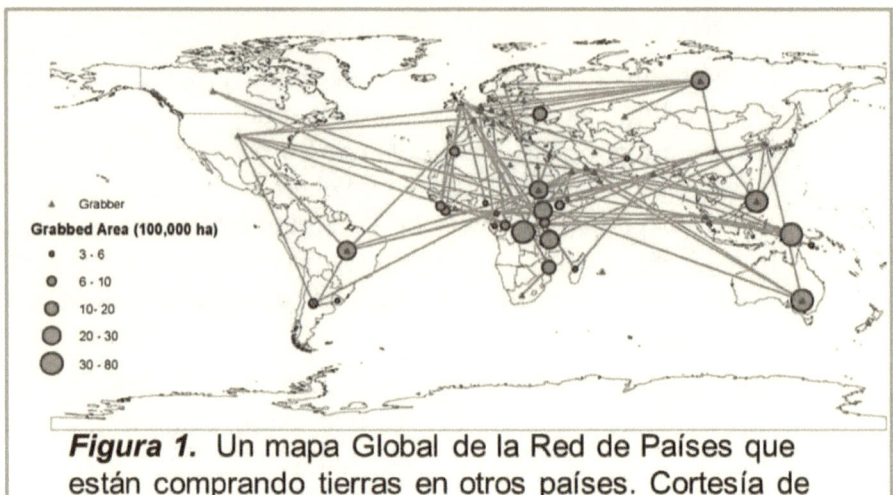

Figura 1. Un mapa Global de la Red de Países que están comprando tierras en otros países. Cortesía de National Geographic [9]

The study found that foreign investors frequently buy tracts of land that have plenty of freshwater, either from local rainfall or underground aquifers. That's the key commodity here. "This is often good agricultural land that isn't yet fully utilized," says *Paolo D'Odorico*, one of the study's co-authors. "It was being used by local farmers without modern technology, without irrigation, without fertilizer."

After the land is bought up, large commercial farms will move in and boost production to grow their own crops. One 2010 study from the **World Bank** found that about *37 percent of this "grabbed" land is used to grow food crops, 21 percent to grow cash crops and 21 percent to grow biofuels*. (For instance, some 27,400 square miles of land have been snatched up in Indonesia, largely to grow palm oil, which can be turned into biodiesel.)

Is this a problem? In the abstract, it doesn't have to be — skilled foreign investors might be able to squeeze more use out of the land than the locals can. That could, in theory, be a mutually beneficial trade. But in practice, there are a lot of concerns about how all this land is actually being acquired.

Last year, for instance, **Human Rights Watch** released a report alleging that the Ethiopian government was forcibly relocating tens of thousands of people in order to lease land to foreign investors from China and the Gulf States. "The first round of forced relocations occurred at the worst possible time of year — the beginning of the harvest," the report said. "Government failure to provide food assistance for relocated people has caused endemic hunger and cases of starvation."

D'Odorico points out that a great deal of land and fresh water is also being bought up from poorer countries that are struggling to feed themselves, such as Tanzania. "If the food being produced on this land was going to locals instead of foreigners," he points out, "it would be possible for countries like Tanzania to cut down substantially on malnourishment."

Another example: The PNAS study notes that Sudan is leasing much of its prime farmland on the banks of the Blue Nile to foreign investors who are exporting food out of the country. Meanwhile, the rest of the people in this otherwise arid country have become increasingly dependent on food aid and subsidies.

There's still an enormous amount that researchers don't know about land-grabbing, according to D'Odorico. It took years of painstaking work just to assemble data on how much land and freshwater is actually being bought up abroad. And there are many basic things that researchers can't yet detail, including where the crops grown on grabbed land actually go, or how much yields improve when foreign investors come in.

What is likely, however, is that land grabbing will become more popular in the years ahead — especially if more governments start getting nervous about securing food supplies. *Fred Pearce*, who recently investigated the phenomenon for his book "The Land Grabbers," explained the upshot in an interview with the Guardian: "*The net result is that poor farmers and cattle herders across the world are being thrown off their land. Land grabbing is having more of an impact on the lives of poor people than climate change.*"[9]

There is still agricultural land out there available for grabbing, but the **consequences are drastic** in terms of massive displacement of people, failure to provide food to those displaced people by local governments or Private Sector, four-fold rise in rice prices, and capital-rich countries and organizations having an upper hand on food distribution.

The vanishing sea resources (we're eating all the fish!)

A major problem and challenge here is that we are *eating fish high up in the food scale*, such as salmon, tuna, shark, lobster, and many others. Very large and powerful vessel fleets are grabbing the fish without allowing time and space for their populations to grow and replenish,

> Every year more than 170 billion pounds (77.9 million metric tons) of wild fish and shellfish are caught in the oceans—roughly three times the weight of every man, woman, and child in the United States. Fisheries managers call this overwhelming quantity of mass-hunted wildlife the world catch, and many maintain that this harvest has been relatively stable over the past decade. But an ongoing study conducted by *Daniel Pauly*, a fisheries scientist at the **University of British Columbia**, in conjunction with *Enric Sala*, a **National Geographic** fellow, suggests that the world catch is neither stable nor fairly divided among the nations of the world. In the study, called SeafoodPrint and supported by the Pew Charitable Trusts and National Geographic, the researchers point the way to what they believe must be done to save the seas.
>
> They hope the study will start by correcting a common misperception. The public imagines a nation's impact on the

sea in terms of the raw tonnage of fish it catches. But that turns out to give a skewed picture of its real impact, or seafood print, on marine life. "The problem is, every fish is different," says Pauly. "A pound of tuna represents roughly a hundred times the footprint of a pound of sardines."

The reason for this discrepancy is that tuna are apex predators, meaning that they feed at the very top of the food chain. The largest tuna eat enormous amounts of fish, including intermediate-level predators like mackerel, which in turn feed on fish like anchovies, which prey on microscopic copepods. A large tuna must eat the equivalent of its body weight every ten days to stay alive, so a single thousand-pound tuna might need to eat as many as 15,000 smaller fish in a year. Such food chains are present throughout the world's ocean ecosystems, each with its own apex animal. Any large fish—a Pacific swordfish, an Atlantic mako shark, an Alaska king salmon, a Chilean sea bass—is likely to depend on several levels of a food chain.

To gain an accurate picture of how different nations have been using the resources of the sea, the SeafoodPrint researchers needed a way to compare all types of fish caught. They decided to do this by measuring the amount of "primary production"—those microscopic organisms at the bottom of the marine food web—required to make a pound of a given type of fish. They found that a pound of bluefin tuna, for example, might require a thousand pounds or more of primary production.

Nations with money tend to buy a lot of fish, and a lot of the fish they buy are large apex predators like tuna. Japan catches less than five million metric tons of fish a year, a 29 percent drop from 1996 to 2006. But Japan consumes nine million metric tons a year, about 582 million metric tons in primary-production terms. Though the average Chinese consumer generally eats smaller fish than the average Japanese consumer does, China's massive population gives it the world's biggest seafood print, 694 million metric tons of primary production. The U.S., with both a large population and a tendency to eat apex fish, comes in third: 348.5 million metric tons of primary production. And the size of each of these nations' seafood prints is growing. What the study points to, Pauly argues, is that these quantities are not just extremely large but also fundamentally unsustainable.

Exactly how unsustainable can be seen in global analyses of seafood trade compiled by Wilf Swartz, an economist working on SeafoodPrint. Humanity's consumption of the ocean's primary production changed dramatically from the 1950s to the early 2000s. In the 1950s much less of the ocean was being fished to meet our needs. But as affluent nations increasingly demanded apex predators, they exceeded the primary-production capacities of their exclusive economic zones, which extend up to 200 nautical miles from their coasts. As a result, more and more of the world's oceans had to be fished to keep supplies constant or growing.

Areas outside of these zones are known in nautical parlance as the high seas. These vast territories, the last global commons on Earth, are technically owned by nobody and everybody. The catch from high-seas areas has risen to nearly ten times what it was in 1950, from 1.6 million metric tons to around 13 million metric tons. A large part of that catch is high-level, high-value tuna, with its huge seafood print.

Humanity's demand for seafood has now driven fishing fleets into every virgin fishing ground in the world. There are no new grounds left to exploit. But even this isn't enough. An unprecedented buildup of fishing capacity threatens to outstrip seafood supplies in all fishing grounds, old and new. A report by the World Bank and the Food and Agriculture Organization (FAO) of the United Nations recently concluded that the ocean doesn't have nearly enough fish left to support the current onslaught. Indeed, the report suggests that even if we had half as many boats, hooks, and nets as we do now, we would still end up catching too many fish.[10]

✳✳✳

Chapter

7

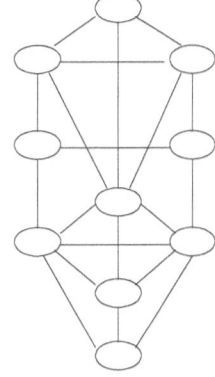

*"We tend to think of **human trafficking** as a foreign issue, not something that could happen here in our own back yards. But it's a fast-growing problem in the world, in every area, with no real defined demographic."*

--Lori   Foster,   writer.[15]

*"**Human Trafficking Awareness Day** is dedicated to raising awareness of **sexual slavery** and human trafficking worldwide. Today, there are between 21-30 million people enslaved in the world, more than at any time in human history. Every day, modern slavery can be seen: children become soldiers, young women are forced into prostitution and migrant workers exploited in the workforce. Human Trafficking Awareness Day seeks to end this slavery, return rights to individuals and make the world a safer place for all inhabitants."*

--Win Calendar.[16]

Human Trafficking, Global Network

Our planet Earth is also reaching limits in the area of *human trafficking*, that is, women, men, and children being traded for the purposes of sexual slavery, forced labor, and/or commercial exploitation by the trafficker and others. Commercial exploitation may take several forms, including providing a spouse in the context of forced marriage, or the extraction of human organs such as kidneys. Where does it occur? This type of crime against basic human rights does occur today within many countries, although it also occurs trans-nationally, that is the victims are taken by coercion from one country to another.[1] In 2004 it was estimated that human trafficking generated between $7,000 Million and $9,500 Million, and today this type of crime is one of the fastest-growing among trans-national organizations.[2]

Several prevention protocols exist today such as the *Protocol to Prevent, Suppress and Punish Trafficking in Persons* (PPSPTP), also known as the Trafficking Protocol, an international agreement under the United Nations (UN) Convention against Transnational Organized Crime (CTOC), which was ratified into force in 2003. It is the first globally, legally binding instrument against trafficking, and the only one with an agreed-upon *definition* of human trafficking and endorsed by 169 parties:

> *The recruitment, transportation, transfer, harbouring or receipt of persons by means of threat or use of force, or other forms or coercion, of abduction, of fraud, of deception, of the abuse of power or of a position of vulnerability, or of the giving or receiving of payments or benefits to achieve the consent of a person having control over another person for the purpose of exploitation. Exploitation shall include, at a minimum, the exploitation of the prostitution of others, forced labor, services of slavery, servitude, or the removal, manipulation or implantation of human organs. "Child" shall mean any person under 18 years of age.*[3]

Thanks to the United Nations (UM) Office on Drugs and Crime (UNODC) we are improving our understanding of the extent of this crime. The 2006 conflict in Lebanon saw some 300,000 domestic workers from Sri Lanka, Ethiopia, and the Philippines in a status of jobless and targets of traffickers; the global pattern of this crime has already identified 127 countries of origin, 98 transit countries, and 137 destination countries for human trafficking.[4]

Where is Human Trafficking Happening?

This criminal activity is happening in virtually every country in our planet Earth. Victims with 152 different citizenships were identified in 124 countries between 2010 and 2012. Three are the continents where most of the victims are taken to: (1) Western and Central Europe, (2) the Middle East, and (3) North America, Central America, and the Caribbean, and the UNODOC have identified as many as 510 flows into those places. Into **Western and Central Europe,** for example, there are flows of victims from South America, Sub-Sahara Africa, and East Asian countries. The flows into the **Middle East** originate in countries from Eastern and Central Europe, East Asia, South Asia (India), and from Sub-Sahara Africa. The flows of people into **North America, Central America, and the Caribbean** originate in countries in Western and Central Europe, South Asia, and East Asia, as shown below:

- Flows into Western and Central Europe:
  - South America
  - Sub-Sahara Africa
  - East Asia
- Flows into Middle East:
  - Eastern and Central Europe
  - East Asia
  - South Asia (India)
  - Sub-Sahara Africa
- Flows into North America, Central America, and the Caribbean:
  - Western and Central Europe
  - South Asia
  - East Asia

We note that the greater affluence of the destination countries; richer countries attract victims form a variety of countries.[5]

Trafficking with limited geographical reach

It has been documented that 6 in 10 of all victims have been trafficked across at least one national border, although they tend to take place within a region, say between neighboring countries. In terms of domestic trafficking, 1 in 3 trafficking cases take place in the victim's country of citizenship, and a majority of convicted traffickers are also citizens of the country where the conviction takes place. Watch out, your own countrymen are doing the human trafficking! Specifically, 64% of the convicted traffickers are nationals, 22% are foreigners from other countries nearby, and 14% are foreigners from other regions.[5]

Types of Exploitation

There are considerable differences in type of exploitation among regions, and the statistics are as follows:

- Forced labor: 40%
- Sexual exploitation: 53%
- Organ removal: 0.3%
- Other: 7%

How are these statistics distributed across regions? The statistics are as follows for the time period 2010-2012:

- Africa and Middle East:
  o Forced Labor: 37%
  o Sexual exploitation: 53%
  o Other: 10%
- Americas:
  o Forced Labor: 47%
  o Sexual exploitation: 48%
  o Other: 4%
- East Asia, South Asia, and the Pacific:
  o Forced Labor: 64%
  o Sexual exploitation: 26%
  o Other: 10%
- Europe and Central Asia:
  o Forced Labor: 26%
  o Sexual exploitation: 66%
  o Other: 8%

The total number of detected victims of forced labor has been increasing steadily from 32% in 2007 to 40% in 2011.[5]

Sex Trafficking

As many as **4.5 Million people worldwide** are impacted by sex trafficking, involving coercive or abusive situations from which it is difficult and dangerous to escape:

> *Sexual trafficking includes coercing a migrant into a sexual act as a condition for allowing or arranging the migration. It utilizes physical or sexual coercion, deception, abuse of power, and bondage incurred through forced debt. Trafficked women and children, for example, are often promised work in a domestic or service industry, but instead sometimes are taken to brothels where they are required to undertake sex work, while their passports and other identification papers are retained. They may be beaten of locked up and promised their freedom only after earning through prostitution their purchase price, as well as their travel and visa costs.*[10]

Organ Trafficking

This criminal activity can take on different forms of organized crime:

> *The victim is forced into giving up an organ of his/hers. In other cases the victim agrees to sell an organ in exchange for money, but is not paid, or paid little. Finally the victim may have the organ removed without the victim's knowledge, usually when the victim is treated for another medical problem, real or orchestrated. Migrant workers, homeless persons, and illiterate persons are particularly vulnerable to this form of exploitation. The offenders involved are: the recruiter, the transporter, the medical staff, the middlemen, and the buyers.*[11]

According to *Kevin Bales*, author of **Disposable people** (2004) "the estimates are that as many as 27 Million people in modern-day slavery may exist across the globe. In 2008 the US Department of State estimated that 2 Million children are exploited by the global commercial sex trade. In that same year, a study classified 12.3 Million persons worldwide as forced laborers, bonded laborers or sex trafficking victims. Approximately 1.39 of these persons worked as commercial sex slaves, with women and girls comprising 98%."[12]

A number of countries have been creating and funding non-government organizations to combat human trafficking. In the *United States*, for example, Derek Ellerman and Katherine Chon founded in 2002 the *Polaris Project* where callers can report and receive information on human trafficking by accessing their website (http://polarisproject.org/human-trafficking):

> *Human trafficking is a form of modern slavery, a multi-billion criminal industry that denies freedom to 20.9 Million people around the world. And no matter where you live, chances are it's happening nearby. From the girl forced into prostitution at a truck stop, to the man discovered in a restaurant kitchen, stripped of his passport and held against his will. All trafficking victims share one essential experience: the loss of freedom.*[6]

A 2013 report by the *US State Department* cites "**Russia and China** as among the worst offenders in combatting forced labor and sex trafficking, raising the possibility of US sanctions against these two countries. In 1997 alone as many as 175,000 young women from Russia, as well as from the former Soviet Union, were sold as commodities in the sex markets of the developed countries in Europe and in Americas."[13]

Beginning in 2010, *President Barack Obama* proclaimed January as National Slavery and Human Trafficking Prevention Month. In 2014 *DARPA* – a governmental organization – funded the *Memex program* with the purpose of fighting human trafficking via domain-specific search, a search capacity with the ability to reach into hidden web sites which may be involved in human trafficking and related activities.[7]

Women as Victims and Offenders

The statistics reflect both men and women as convicted offenders, with percentages of 72% and 28%, respectively, in the period 2010-2012. Women, however, comprise the vast majority of detected victims who have been trafficked for sexual exploitation. What about *victims of forced labor*? The statistics are as follows:[5]

- Africa and Middle East:
    - Men: 45%
    - Women and children: 55%
- Americas:
    - Men: 68%
    - Women and children: 32%
- East Asia, South Asia, and the Pacific:
    - Men: 23%
    - Women and children: **77%**
- Europe and Central Asia:
    - Men: 69%
    - Women and children: 31%

The *Council of Europe* became involved in 2005 adopting the *Council of Europe Convention on Action against Trafficking in Human Beings* (CETS No. 197). As of May 2016 the Convention has been ratified by 46 countries.[8] Similarly, Shri Singh, *India*'s Minister or State for Home Affairs, launched the *Anti Human Trafficking Portal* in 2014 to provide information on tracking of cases, statistics, legislation, court judgements, and rescue success stories.[9]

Feminist Perspectives on Human Trafficking

Several are the perspectives offered by *third-wave feminists* on the issues addressed above:

> *A perspective focuses on "sexualized domination which includes issues of pornography, female sex labor in a patriarchal world, rape, and sexual harassment. Feminism emphasizes sex trafficking as forced prostitution, and considers the act exploitative. Liberal feminism sees all agents as capable of reason and choice, supporting sex workers rights, and argue that women who voluntarily choose sex work as autonomous…Women from low socioeconomic class, generally from the Global South, face*

inequalities that differ from those of other sex trafficking victims, therefore feminist proponent Shelly Cavalieri advocates catering to individual trafficking victim because sex trafficking is not monolithic, and therefore there is not a one-size-fits-all intervention...Lastly, third-wave feminism promotes increasing women's agency both generally and individually, so that they have the opportunity to act on their own behalf.[14]

Chapter
8

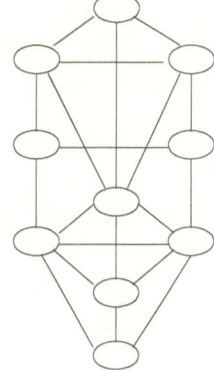

*"**Religious wars** are not caused by the fact that there is more than one religion, but by the spirit of intolerance... the spread of which can only be regarded as the total eclipse of human reason.*
--Charles de Secondat, 17th Century French philosopher.[1]

*"We have a war on women, race wars, income wars, age wars, **and religious wars**, anything you can imagine. A house divided against itself cannot stand it. And it's going to be up to us, to people, to begin the focus on the positive things, on the things that we have in common and stop listening to those who are stoking the fires of division.*
--Benjamin Carson, medical doctor, writer.[2]

Religious Wars (Islamic State)

We are killing ourselves with religious wars. During the last 5,000 years of recorded history human beings have engaged in wars over differences of Gods and their prophets here on Earth. During the Middle Ages the **Roman Catholic Church** in Europe managed to send military campaigns by the name of **Crusades** to the Middle East "to rescue the holy places" from people under Islam rules. Thousands of people died on all sides involved. Those "crusades" today would be renamed as "**terrorist attacks**" on the people and lands of the Middle East by the warlords of a Europe under Christianity. The monster of "**Islamic State**" is the latest one in our 21st century to surface, already causing thousands of deaths in multiple countries. Let us consider the facts with possibly a different perspective, my own.

In 1095, Pope Urban II proclaimed the *First Crusade* with the stated goal of restoring Christian access to holy places in and near Jerusalem. Following the First Crusade there was an intermittent 200-year struggle for control of the Holy Land, with *six more major crusades and numerous minor ones.* In 1291, the conflict ended in failure with the fall of the last Christian stronghold in the Holy Land at Acre, after which Roman Catholic Europe mounted no further coherent response in the East.

The crusaders often *pillaged* the countries through which they travelled in the typical medieval manner of supplying an army on the move. Nobles often retained much of the territory gained rather than returning it to the Byzantines as they had sworn to do. The Peoples' Crusade prompted Rhineland massacres and *the murder of thousands of Jews*. The Fourth Crusade resulted in the sack of Constantinople by the Roman Catholics, effectively ending the chance of reuniting the Christian church by reconciling the East–West Schism and leading to the weakening and eventual fall of the Byzantine Empire to the Ottomans. Nevertheless, some crusaders were merely poor people trying to escape the hardships of medieval life in an armed pilgrimage leading to Apotheosis at Jerusalem.

Criticism. After the fall of Acre in 1291, European support for the Crusades remained despite criticism by contemporaries such as *Roger Bacon* who felt the Crusades were ineffective since "those who survive, together with their children, are more and more embittered against the Christian faith." The historian *Norman Davies* summarized the case against the crusades as running counter to the Peace and Truce of God that Urban had promoted; instead they reinforced the connection between Western Christendom, feudalism, and militarism. The formation of *military religious orders* scandalized the Orthodox Christian Byzantine Greeks. The Peoples' Crusade instigated the Rhineland massacres and the massacre of thousands of Jews. In the late 19th century this episode was used by Jewish historians to support *Zionism.* Historians of the Enlightenment criticized the misdirection of the crusades. In particular they pointed to the Fourth Crusade which instead of attacking Islam attacked another Christian power—the (Eastern) Roman Empire. David Nicolle says the Fourth Crusade has always been controversial in terms of the "betrayal" of Byzantium.

Eight hundred years after the **Fourth Crusade**, *Pope John Paul II* twice expressed sorrow for the events surrounding it. In 2001, he wrote to Christodoulos, Archbishop of Athens, saying, "*It is tragic that the assailants, who set out to secure free access for Christians to the Holy Land, turned against their brothers in the faith. The fact that they were Latin Christians fills Catholics with deep regre*t." In 2004, while Bartholomew I, Patriarch of Constantinople, was visiting the **Vatican**, *John Paul II* asked, "How can we not share, at a distance of eight centuries, the pain and disgust." This has been regarded as an apology to the Greek Orthodox Church for the terrible slaughter perpetrated by the warriors of the Fourth Crusade.

In April 2004, in a speech on the 800th anniversary of the city's capture, Ecumenical Patriarch Bartholomew I formally accepted the apology. "The spirit of reconciliation is stronger than hatred," he said during a liturgy attended by Roman Catholic Archbishop *Philippe Barbarin* of Lyon, France. "*We receive with gratitude and respect your cordial gesture for the tragic events of the Fourth Crusade. It is a fact that a crime was committed here in the city 800 years ago.*"[12]

In 1492 the Catholic kings of Spain, Ferdinand and Isabella, succeeded in their conspiracy with the Dominicans, Franciscans, Jesuits, other religious orders, and some of the rich families *to overthrow the Jews from the Iberian Peninsula,* where they had been born, labored, and contributed to its society for some 700 years. The Jews were already Spanish citizens, but that was not enough, that would not do it. Those elites of the rich and powerful wanted to go beyond merely eradicating all religious competition, they also wanted the homes, properties, monies, and market infrastructure of the Jewish communities throughout the Iberian Peninsula. It was a major *series of terrorist attacks* directed at the Jewish communities. Some 50,000-80,000 Jews were thrown out of the Peninsula after confiscating and stealing all their goods and properties.

The organized religion and the elites of the powerful in Spain still wanted more property to loot and seize. These elites conducted another series of *terrorist attacks* on the *Muslim communities* in the Iberian Peninsula in the time period 1609-1613. A *total of 300,000 Muslims were thrown out of the Peninsula*, again after making sure the goods and properties were all looted and seized. They too had been Spanish citizens for over 700 years, contributing greatly and abundantly to the medical sciences, agriculture, literature, commerce, and economic well-being of everyone in the Peninsula. The Catholic Church and its elite of the rich and powerful knew of no limits to their corruption, Inquisition, hatred for other human beings, and pillage.

Since those tragic periods in the early history of our species, our political leaders in modern times continue to repeat their mistakes, mistakes that are partly responsible for the eruption of still more religious and political wars. The *First World War (1914-1918)* caused the death of over 15 Million people all over Europe, and when Germany was finally defeated the winners, England and France primarily, imposed highly humiliating surrender conditions on Germany and its people via de *Treaty of Versailles* on 28 June 1919. True, the US Senate did not ratify that treaty despite public support for it. Those humiliating conditions of the Treaty extended poverty, misery, and death among the German population during the next two decades, to the point that it made it possible for an opportunist figure like that of *Adolf Hitler to create its Nazi regime and armies*, invading country after country in Europe, the Middle East, and in Africa in the course of a Second World War (1939-1945), resulting in the death of 50-85 Million people. Yes, Adolf Hitler and his Nazi armies started that war, but I also claim that the political and military leaders of England and France need to share some responsibility for the death of those millions of people because of the severe hardships and conditions they imposed on Germany and its people with that Treaty of Versailles. We should never ignore the instincts of our species for revenge in response to extreme pain and agony.

The terrorist organization *Al-Qaeda* founded by *Osama bin Laden* and several other militants in 1988, also often reminds its followers of the attacks and persecution suffered by Muslim peoples at the hands of the *Crusaders* in early Europe, and at the hands of the powers of the West in general during wars against peoples and military groups in Iraq and Afghanistan. Initially the terror of the Crusades was imposed to "recuperate" the "*holy lands*" from the Muslim world, and in modern times the powers of the West instigated and participated in wars in order to appropriate the *rich oil fields* in the Middle East. The imposition of power structures, sabotage, pain and misery by the West powers on the Muslim world has been relentless and deep during the last 2,000 years, I would have to say. Still, the terrorist activities conducted by Al-Qaeda during attacks to the people of the USA, Spain, and other countries cannot be justified at all but, again, they speak of the instinct for revenge and opportunism of our species.

Similarly, the *Islamic State* of Iraq and Syria (ISIS) has been designated as *a terrorist organization* by the United Nations, the European Union, the USA, the United Kingdom, Australia, Saudi Arabia, Egypt, Russia, and other countries. On 29 June 2014 this group proclaimed itself to be a worldwide caliphate, claiming religious, political, and military authority over all Muslims peoples and governments worldwide. Again, countless lives are being lost today in the numerous wars and countries in which the Islamic State is participating. Again, a major confrontation between the West and the Middle East still today.

Related to this section on religious wars is the matter of land-grabbing taking place in *Palestine* by *Israeli military and government forces.* Israeli settlements are Israeli civilian communities on lands occupied by Israel during the 1967 Six-Day War, currently located on the West Bank, East Jerusalem, and in the Golan Heights. The international community considers those settlements in occupied territory to be illegal, as stated by the United Nations, the USA, and other countries. Ongoing expansion of existing settlements and outposts is criticized as an obstacle to peace in the Middle East. Having said that, we should also be cognizant of the persecution suffered by the Jewish people through the ages, during the times of the Inquisition all over Europe, and in particular the mass murder of Jews in the concentration in Germany during the Second World War. With that perspective in mind, and the perspective gained in this chapter on vanishing food resources, overpopulation, climatic change, and more, one might be able to understand that political leaders in Israel are already anticipating the drastic conditions to be met from now on, by the year 2500, over the next centuries, and are trying to secure as much land as they can for their own people, even at large costs to the Palestinian people. A "bunker" nation. **Human rights** on both sides of the conflict are being violated time and time again. Could it be that conflicts similar to the current Israeli-Palestinian conflict are already in the making in other parts of the planet? Is *a growing pattern of human rights violations* to be anticipated as a result of conflicts around the world caused by overpopulation, diminishing food resources, diminishing water resources, and climate change? Yes, planet Earth may be reaching its limits, and new forms of coexistence are needed.

Chapter

9

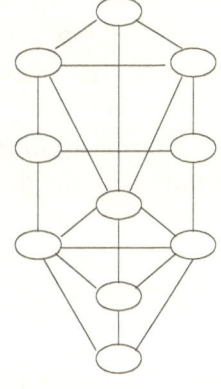

*"**Climate change** could produce a lot of misery and waste without necessarily leading to large-scale armed conflict, which depends more on ideology and bad governance than on resource scarcity."*
--**Steven Pinker**, writer, scientist[5]

*"The need to do something about **global warming** is obvious. And it's also pretty clear that the public understands the need for change and is ready to embrace it. What is missing is political will in Congress to stand up to the powerful energy companies and their well-paid lobbyists.*
--**Chellie Pingree**, politician.[6]

Climatic Change

Our high industrial productivity worldwide also has its costs. The various forms of fuel (e.g., oil, gas, electrical power, other) must burn with oxygen in order to produce motion (e.g., rotation, vertical/horizontal displacement of components) needed for our machines to operate and function, thus releasing vast quantities of CO_2 into the atmosphere. It is that CO_2 that gathers into layers high up in out atmosphere thus creating a *"**green house**" effect*, not allowing Earth heat to radiate back into space. Result: the temperature of our Earth is increasing. Let us become familiar with the current events and statistics.

More than 300 million people are already seriously affected by the *gradual warming of the earth* and that number is set to double by 2030, the report from the *Global Humanitarian Forum* warns. *"For the first time we are trying to get the world's attention to the fact that climate change is not something waiting to happen. It is impacting seriously the lives of many people around the world,"* the forum's president, former **U.N.** Secretary-General *Kofi Annan*, told CNN.

Speaking to CNN's *Becky Anderson* in London on Friday, *Annan* said the migration of people from newly uninhabitable areas presents a security issue that needs to be addressed by the United Nations Security Council. *"This is one of the reasons why I've described **climate change** as all encompassing,"* he told CNN. *"This threat to our health, this threat to food production, this threat to security. It raises political tensions, it will have people on the move -- and they are on the move -- and many more which will bring tensions."*

The report, titled *"**Human Impact Report: Climate Change -- The Anatomy of a Silent Crisis**"* comes just six months before the *United Nations Climate Conference* in Copenhagen to forge a post-Kyoto climate agreement for 2012 and beyond. Annan called on Member States to reach a "global, effective, fair and binding" outcome on climate change, as the report warned that the talks could "well be the last chance for avoiding global catastrophe." He told CNN: *"The U.S. administration has joined the mainstream about fighting climate change and that is a big step, and I hope that will also put a new momentum into the negotiations."* The report's startling numbers are based on calculations by the ***Intergovernmental Panel on Climate Change*** that the Earth's atmosphere warmed by 0.74 degrees Celsius (1.33 degrees Fahrenheit) from 1906 to 2005, with much of that increase coming in recent decades. The panel predicts that ***by 2100*** temperatures will have increased a minimum of ***two degrees Celsius*** (3.6 degrees Fahrenheit) over pre-industrial levels regardless of what's agreed in Copenhagen. "No matter what," the report concludes, *"the suffering documented in this report is only the beginning."* A rise of two degrees, it says, *"**would be catastrophic.**"*

Of the ***300,000 lives being lost each year*** due to climate change, the report finds nine out of 10 are related to "gradual environmental degradation," and that deaths caused by climate-related malnutrition, diarrhea and malaria outnumber direct fatalities from weather-related disasters. The vast majority of deaths – 99% -- are in developing countries which are estimated to have contributed less than one percent of the world's total carbon emissions. The report warns climate change threatens all eight of the Millennium Development Goals-- a set of goals agreed on by leading nations in 2000 that aim to reduce extreme poverty by 2015. The goals include eradicating hunger, reducing child mortality, and halting the spread of diseases including HIV/AIDS and malaria.

Around 45 million of the 900 million people estimated to be chronically hungry are suffering due to ***climate change***, the report says. Within 20 years that number is expected to double. At the same time food production is expected to fall, driving food prices up 20 percent. The countries considered to be most vulnerable are those in the semi-arid dry land belt that runs from the Sahara/Sahel to the Middle East and Central Asia, Sub-Saharan Africa, South and Southeast Asia, Latin America and parts of the U.S., small island states and the Arctic region. Australia is singled out as the developed country most vulnerable to the direct impacts of climate change. Over the past 15 years, the combination of rising temperature and lower rainfall has produced the worst drought in the country's recorded history.

While developed countries -- including Australia -- have committed funds to counter the impact of climate change, the Global Humanitarian Forum says developing nations need a dramatic injection of funds -- up to 100 times more than is currently available to help them adapt to the changes. The total economic cost of climate change each year is thought to ***be $125 billion,*** although the Forum warns that figure may be too conservative and doesn't take into account the impacts on "health, water supply and other shocks."[1]

International Agreements, a long Process

Several are the international agreements taking place today in order to slow down the *production of CO2* and its distribution in the atmosphere, yet some of the results are not satisfactory and many are the challenges ahead:

> When the countries which subscribed to the *Kyoto Protocol of 1997* they agreed to reduce gas emissions for several decades ahead. Next, with the objective of keeping track of the results of such objectives and other initiatives related to the climatic change, an alliance of investigative entities created a database with the name of Climate Action Tracker (CAT). The last CAT evaluation reveals a set of results that are in the category of "insufficient" mostly among the number of countries that account for 80% of the global emissions. The US plan to slow down the global climate change is considered insufficient, as is the commitment by Chile to reduce its own emissions. On the other hand, the commitment by Butan of maintaining its forest mass as it is meets of objective of small emissions.[2]

Germany, a leading energy model in Europe

This country has learned from past mistakes in modern history, and it is now leading an energy revolution replacing nuclear plants and fossil fuel with *wind and solar* technology:

> Germany is pioneering an epochal transformation it calls the *energiewende*—an energy revolution that scientists say all nations must one day complete if a climate disaster is to be averted. Among large industrial nations, Germany is a leader. Last year about 27 percent of its electricity came from renewable sources such as *wind* and *solar power*, three times what it got a decade ago and more than twice

what the United States gets today. The change accelerated after the 2011 meltdown at Japan's Fukushima nuclear power plant, which led Chancellor Angela Merkel to declare that Germany would shut all 17 of its own reactors by 2022. Nine have been switched off so far, and renewables have more than picked up the slack.

What makes Germany so important to the world, however, is the question of whether it can lead the retreat from fossil fuels. By later this century, scientists say, planet-warming carbon emissions must fall to virtually zero. Germany, the world's fourth largest economy, has promised some of the most aggressive emission cuts—by 2020, a 40 percent cut from 1990 levels, and by 2050, at least 80 percent.

The fate of those promises hangs in the balance right now. The German revolution has come from the grass roots: Individual citizens and energy *genossenschaften*—local citizens associations—have made half the investment in renewables. But conventional utilities, which didn't see the revolution coming, are pressuring Merkel's government to slow things down. The country still gets far more electricity from coal than from renewables. And the energiewende has an even longer way to go in the transportation and heating sectors, which together emit more carbon dioxide (CO_2) than power plants.

German politicians sometimes compare the energiewende to the Apollo moon landing. But that feat took less than a decade, and most Americans just watched it on TV. The energiewende will take much longer and will involve every single German—more than 1.5 million of them, nearly 2 percent of the population, are selling electricity to the grid right now. *"It's a project for a generation; it's going to take till 2040 or 2050, and it's hard,"* said Gerd Rosenkranz, a former journalist at *Der Spiegel* who's now an analyst at Agora Energiewende, a Berlin think tank. "It's making electricity more expensive for individual consumers. And still, if you ask people in a poll, "do you want the energiewende"? Then 90 percent say yes."

Why? I wondered as I traveled in Germany last spring. Why is the energy future happening here, in a country that was a bombed-out wasteland 70 years ago? And could it happen everywhere?

Wind turbines surround a coal-fired power plant near Garzweiler in western **Germany**. Renewables now generate 27 percent of the country's electricity, up from 9 percent a decade ago.[3]

In the late 1970s, when fossil fuel emissions were blamed for killing German forests with acid rain, the outrage was nationwide. The oil embargo of 1973 had already made Germans, who have very little oil and gas of their own, think about energy. The threat of *waldsterben,* or forest death, made them think harder.

Workers have been taking apart this Soviet-era nuclear power plant, near Greifswald in eastern Germany, since 1995, cleaning radioactive surfaces with steel grit so the metal can be recycled. Germany plans to shut all its reactors by 2022.

Government and utilities were pushing nuclear power—but many Germans were pushing back. This was new for them.

In the decades after *World War II*, with a ruined country to rebuild, there had been little appetite for questioning authority or the past. But by the 1970s, the rebuilding was complete, and a new generation was beginning to question the one that had started and lost the war. "There's a certain rebelliousness that's a result of the Second World War," a 50-something man named ***Josef Pesch*** told me. "You don't blindly accept authority."

Pesch was sitting in a mountaintop restaurant in the Black Forest outside Freiburg. In a snowy clearing just uphill stood two 320-foot-tall wind turbines funded by 521 citizen investors recruited by Pesch—but we weren't talking about the turbines yet. With an engineer named Dieter Seifried, we were talking about the nuclear reactor that never got built, near the village of Wyhl, 20 miles away on the Rhine River.

The state government had insisted that the reactor had to be built or the lights would go out in Freiburg. But beginning in 1975, local farmers and students occupied the site. In protests that lasted nearly a decade, they forced the government to abandon its plans. It was the first time a nuclear reactor had been stopped in Germany.

The lights didn't go out, and Freiburg became a solar city. Its branch of the Fraunhofer Institute is a world leader in solar research. Its Solar Settlement, designed by local architect Rolf Disch, who'd been active in the Wyhl protests, includes 50 houses that all produce more energy than they consume. "Wyhl was the starting point," Seifried said. In 1980 an institute that Seifried co-founded published a study called *Energiewende*—giving a name to a movement that hadn't even been born yet.

A nuclear reactor at Kalkar was finished just before the 1986 explosion at Chernobyl, Ukraine—and never used. It's now an amusement park with a ride in what would have been the cooling tower. Fear of nuclear power spurred Germany's transition.

It wasn't born of a single fight. But opposition to nuclear power, at a time when few people were talking about climate change, was clearly a decisive factor. I had come to Germany thinking the Germans were foolish to abandon a carbon-free energy source that, until Fukushima, produced a quarter of their electricity. I came away thinking there would have been no energiewende at all without antinuclear sentiment—the fear of meltdown is a much more powerful and immediate motive than the fear of slowly rising temperatures and seas.

All over Germany I heard the same story. From Disch, sitting in his own cylindrical house, which rotates to follow the sun like a sunflower. From Rosenkranz in Berlin, who back in 1980 left physics graduate school for months to occupy the site of a proposed nuclear waste repository. From Luise Neumann-Cosel, who occupied the same site two decades later—and who is now leading a citizens' initiative to buy the Berlin electric grid. And from Wendelin Einsiedler, a Bavarian dairy farmer who has helped transform his village into a green dynamo.

All of them said Germany had to get off nuclear power and fossil fuels at the same time. "You can't drive out the devil with Beelzebub," explained Hans-Josef Fell, a prominent Green Party politician. "Both have to go." At the University of Applied Sciences in Berlin, energy researcher Volker Quaschning put it this way: *"Nuclear power affects me personally. Climate change affects my kids. That's the difference."*

Global Warming, beyond our physical limits?

As human beings, how much heat can we endure conducting our daily routine? Let's take a look at some populations and regions in the planet:

If *greenhouse gas emissions* are not reduced, rising temperatures and humidity wrought by global warming could expose hundreds of millions of people worldwide to potentially lethal heat stress by 2060.

The greatest exposure will occur in populous, tropical regions such as India, Southeast Asia, the Middle East, and Africa. But even in the northeastern United States, as many as 30 million people might be exposed at least once a year to heat that could be lethal to children, the elderly, and the sick, according to the new study.

It's the first study to look at future heat stress on a global basis, says *Ethan Coffel*, a PhD candidate in atmospheric sciences at Columbia University, who presented the results at the *American Geophysical Union meeting* in San Francisco. Coffel and his colleagues used climate models and population projections to estimate how many people could face dangerous heat in 2060—assuming that greenhouse gas emissions continue to rise sharply on a "business-as-usual" course.

The findings are based on forecasts of "wet bulb" temperatures, in which a wet cloth is wrapped around a thermometer bulb. Whereas standard thermometer readings measure air temperature, a wet bulb measures the temperature of a moist surface that has been cooled as much as possible by evaporation.

On June 2015, in Pakistan, a heat wave killed more than 450 people in the port city of Karachi, where temperatures stayed around 113°F (45°C) for three days.

That reading depends on both the heat and the humidity of the surrounding air. It's generally much lower than the dry-bulb temperature, and it's a better indicator of the humid heat that humans and other large mammals find hardest to deal with.

In *India,* May 2015, temperatures rose to *120°F (50°C),* killing more than 2,300 people, and melting this street path in New Delhi.[4]

The normal temperature inside the human body is 98.6 degrees Fahrenheit, or 37 degrees Celsius. Human skin is typically at 35°C. When the wet-bulb temperature of the air exceeds that level, it becomes *physically impossible for the body to shed its own metabolic heat* and cool itself, especially by evaporating sweat. Even a fit individual would be expected to die from such heat within six hours.

Today, in 2016, even in Earth's hottest, muggiest spots, the wet-bulb temperature does not rise above 31°C. (The highest dry-bulb temperature ever recorded is 56.7°C, or 134°F.)

But a study published in October 2015 by MIT researchers found that by 2100, in Persian Gulf cities such as Abu Dhabi or Dubai, the 35°C threshold of human survival may occasionally be exceeded—again, assuming that greenhouse emissions continue to rise unabated.

Where Heat, Humidity, and People Intersect. In practice, wet-bulb temperatures below the 35°C threshold are dangerous for children, the elderly, people with heart or lung problems—or anybody actively working outside. By the 2060s, according to Coffel and his colleagues, 250 million people could be experiencing 33°C at least once a year. As many as 700 million could be exposed to 32°C. For many people, those conditions could be lethal. "You have a large portion of the world that's very densely populated and potentially at risk," says Coffel. "Populations which right now work primarily outdoors and have very little access to air conditioning. It's hard to function outdoors in those kinds of temperatures."

The MIT study concluded that wet-bulb temperatures of 32°C or 33°C could be expected to arise later this century in Mecca, for example, where they might sometimes coincide with the Hajj, when millions of pilgrims pray outdoors all day long.

But as rising temperatures push more moisture into the atmosphere, particularly near warming oceans, spells of extreme heat and humidity will become more frequent and intense in many parts of the world. Even residents of cities like New York and London could encounter future temperatures that are near the limits of what their bodies can tolerate, according to the Columbia researchers.

"Local ocean temperatures can be a really big driver for the extent of these high heat and humidity events," says co-author Radley Horton of Columbia. *"How far inland away from the coasts will we see some of these really deadly high heat and humidity events penetrate? Will this impact where people are able to live?"*

Bryan Jones, a postdoctoral fellow at the City University of New York who also studies future heat exposures but was not part of the Columbia study, said its "projections of exposure to extreme heat stress seem very reasonable. In fact, they may even be conservative, depending on how populations in West Africa, India, and Southeast Asia are distributed in the coming decades."

Heat Is Already A Big Killer. Heat already kills more people than any other form of extreme weather. In the past decade, heat waves that featured wet-bulb temperatures between 29°C and 31°C have caused tens of thousands of deaths in Europe, Russia, and the Middle East.

Last summer more than 2,300 died from extreme heat in India, where air temperatures reached 122°F. High humidity and temperatures topping 116°F also proved deadly in Egypt this year. And work stopped for several summer days in Iraq while thermometers hovered around 120°F.

Air conditioning protects those who have access to it and can afford it. The spread of high-heat-stress events is likely to produce a surge in demand, says Horton. Air conditioners don't function as efficiently in humid conditions, however—and as long as the electricity for them is generated with fossil fuels, they add to the underlying problem.

The other approach to coping with dangerous heat, Coffel says, is "reorganizing your society, like when you work outside, like giving people the day off when it's hot."

Neither air-conditioning nor staying inside is an option for other large mammals, which are affected by climbing heat and humidity in much the same way as humans. The impact on them is a "wild card," says Horton. Little research has been done so far.[4]

✳✳✳

**Part III:
A List of Missions to Carry Out**

Chapter
10

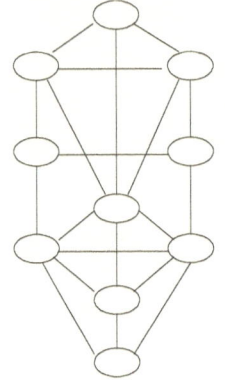

*"Ethiopia's government has been accused of forcing tens of thousands of people off their **land so it can be leased to foreign investors**. US-based Human Rights Watch says people are being forcibly relocated to new villages that lack adequate food, farmland and facilities. **Ethiopia** has already leased out more than 3.6 million hectares (8.8m acres) of land - an area the size of The Netherlands."*
--BBC News, 17 January 2012.[2]

Dr. Finley and Kathy travel to Africa

Several weeks have gone by since Kathy left the Basque Country, after meeting with Xabier for several days to continue planning the entry into the Vatican's Secret Archives. Soon after her return to Tucson she teamed up with Dr. Finley to travel to the **Democratic Republic of Congo** to do a study of land leasing and supposedly "land grabbing" by some countries as an assignment from the newly created **Council for World Peace (CWP)**.

-Hello, is that you Xabier? —It was Kathy trying to contact with Xabier after several failed attempts, phone call transfers, delays, and shifting from French to English.

-Yes! Who is this?

-It's me Xabier, it's Kathy… I'm calling from the airport at **Kinshasa**…We are waiting for some government officials to pick us up here at the airport, in the outskirts of Kinshasa.

-Kinshasa? Where is that? Are you still in Tucson, Arizona?

-Oh, sorry Xabier...No. Kinshasa is the capital of the Democratic Republic of Congo. Dr. Finley and I have just arrived and we are here in Africa for a couple of weeks only, and then return to Tucson, USA. Yes, this is the Democratic Republic of Congo, not to be confused with its neighbour, the Republic of Congo. I bit confusing, I realize, but here we are. Just wanted to let you know that we are OK, some government officials are already waiting for us, and the purpose of the trip is to do a study and report on land investments by other countries in this Republic.

-Yes, I remember now your mentioning that possible trip and study when we were in Oñati, Basque Country a few weeks ago. Yes, I remember. But why so soon such a trip?

-I will explain later, on my next call, Xabier, but basically the **Council** wants to have a clear understanding of the magnitude of China's investments in Africa, land leasing, in particular. Some reports contend that China continues to go ahead with an aggressive program of "*land grabbing*" in Africa anticipating food shortages in the future, in the next 20-25 years, while Chinese officials insist that that is not the case, and that investments on the part of China's government are much smaller. Anyway, Dr. Finley and others at the Council believe that we can conduct a few interviews with both Congo and China officials, and a few local companies, and thus arrive at an accurate study. Furthermore...

At that point a white limousine arrives in front of the main building at the *Kinshasa International Airport*.

-Sorry, Xabier, a limousine has just arrived, have to go, will call you again, tomorrow very possibly. But, very quickly, how are doing in Oñati?

-Doing fine. Members of the Vatican Eagles group are still working on the type of support they may give us as we try to enter the Secret Archives. It may take a few more days, or weeks.

-Great! Stay busy. I will call you soon. I miss you, baby.

Sure enough, three members of the **China State Farm Agri-Business Corporation (CSFAC)** and one Congo government official have arrived to pick up Dr. Finley and Kathy at the airport. Having operated in Africa since 1994, by 2016 CSFAC hosts at least 11 agricultural projects on 16,000 hectares of land in Africa, several of which were former Chinese aid projects. By 2006 there were more than 20 stated-owned and private Chinese farms in Africa. China has a large number of state-owned enterprises operating in Africa, including Angola, Congo, Nigeria, South Africa, and Tanzania involved in activities such as fishing, poultry, and grain cultivation. Are the products of these activities consumed locally or sent to mainland China? That is what the Council aims to determine.

-Dr. Finley? Very pleased to meet you! I am **Gregory Chong**, director of the CSFAC corporation, and these are my associates, Mr. Carter Shan, Ms. Fu Li, and **Mr. Eugene Mutombo** our representative of the **Democratic Republic of Congo** (DRC). Welcome to Kinshasa!

-Thank you very much! And this is Kathy Thompson, my associate from the Council for World Peace, or the CWP as we all know it.

Everyone shakes hands and together in the limousine they drive to a government building in the capital city of Kinshasa to share plans for the next weeks, including interviews with government and corporate personnel. The Chinese officials very much welcome the visit of Dr. Finley and Kathy as they hope that their study and report will testify in favor of China's position on limited land investments and local sales, as opposed to claims by other agencies of aggressive "land grabbing" on the part of mainland China.

-Yes, we are very enthusiastic so far – Stated Dr. Finley – to have a number of government officials from several countries in the global community to join us at the **Council for World Peace (CWP).** The CWP charter has been approved by many leaders, and we hope that it will be ratified by citizens in their respective countries over the following months. The main idea being that of monitoring parts of the world, meaning societies and countries in early or intermediate stages of development, for purposes of identifying "hot spots" so that all together in the planet can continue developing our societies and democracies while respecting energy, food, metal, and other resources.

-We very much agree with you and the Council, Mr. Finley – Quickly added Mr. Chong – And what are your planned activities for the next couple of weeks, and how can we be of service?

-I am going to ask my assistant, Ms. Thompson, to help us with the details of those planned activities. –Dr. Finley said with a smile, as he looked at Kathy.

-Very simple, really. Basically, we would like to conduct two types of activities: (1) be able to look at some of the officials documents, both from the CSFAC corporation, the state-owned corporation, and from the Ministry of Agriculture of the DRC, and (2) conduct a few interviews with government officials in those two agencies, and with a few local corporate people. This would be after all a first report to be published by the Council. We hope that there will be other reports in the near future. That's the plan, basically.

-And how can we be of service? – Asked Ms. Fu Li.

-It would really help if you folks would provide a list of 8-10 people in the two agencies who would participate in the interviews and at the same time bring out the relevant documents. Dr. Finley and I would also like to conduct another 4-6 interviews with local corporate personnel, independently, of course, but sharing all the relevant information with you folks.

-It makes perfect sense to all of us. – Mr. Chong said, as his associates confirmed with their smiles and slight bending of their heads.

Over the next few days Dr. Finley and Kathy conduct interviews with both Chinese and Congo officials, review contents of documents of leasing agreements, and meet in the evenings for dinners with representatives of both agencies. Many are the interviews and the documents to review. At the beginning of the second week Kathy suggests to Dr. Finley that it might be a good idea for her to begin interviews with representatives of some local corporations while he, Dr. Finley, continues reviewing those leasing documents and extracting statistics on amount of lands leased and monies invested. Dr. Finley agrees, and so Kathy makes arrangements with agricultural corporations in the vicinity of Kinshasa to meet during the day at various locations.

-How did your interviews go today? —Asks Dr. Finley as he and Kathy await for dinner service at a local restaurant.

-Very fine, very well. I did four interviews today with executives at the *Congo Horizons corporation*, just twenty minutes by taxi from hour hotel here in downtown Kinshasa. I was able to record the interviews with their permission, of course, and everything went well. Generally the executives feel that the leasing agreements with the CSFAC are in the interest of both China and the DRC.

-Would they be able to look at and confirm the statistics provided to us by the Chinese officials at the CSFAC? —Asked Dr. Finley, noticing that the waiter was coming to their table.

-I did ask that question precisely —Replied Kathy – and that is exactly what we all agreed to do tomorrow, to compare statistics, and to begin to size the total investments in land leasings by year, beginning in 1999 and all the way up to 2014. Deals and investment amounts for 2015 and 2016 would not be available yet.

-Good evening folks, are you ready to order your menus for tonight?

-Yes, thank you. What would you like to order Kathy?

-Well, I would like to order a ration of Bukari, a staple of African food, as I have been told, a mixture of corn and ground rice, and a ration of goat stew, mildly spicy, of course.

-That is an excellent choice, Miss. Will be glad to. And for you sir?

-I would like to try the chicken Moambe stew, please. It has been recommended by friends for its use of local spices, along with a small portion of vegetables, please.

-An excellent choice, sir. It should take a few minutes only, and I will then be right back. Please enjoy your cocktails and appetizers. Thank you!

Two people from Tucson, Arizona, USA, having dinner in the terrace of a restaurant in Kinshasa, in the Democratic Republic of Congo, and eating local dishes? Dr. Finley and Kathy could not believe they were enjoying such a great evening, being able to see the sunset in the distance with its tones of bright red and violet in the horizon.

The following evening, however, Dr. Finley waited for one hour for Kathy to come down from her room. He called her room from the lobby of the hotel and there was no answer. Next, he asked the clerk captain at the hotel to accompany him to Kathy's room, to knock on the door again, to enter the room, and to learn if something had happened to Kathy. Was she asleep? Had she slipped in the bath tub, fallen on the floor, and there she lying unconscious? They both entered the room and there was no sign of Kathy. She had not returned to her room that day after conducting the interviews with the local companies, as they had discussed the night before.

Fears of undesirable events began to flood Dr. Finley's head. First thing he did was to call **Gregory Chong**, the director of the CSFAC corporation.

-I understand, Dr. Finley, and it is terrible to hear that Ms. Thompson has not returned to her hotel by the end of the day... Immediately after our phone conversation I will contact our people in the Security Dept. and will ask them to initiate the search for Ms. Thompson, please be assured.

Once Dr. Finley understood that the search for Kathy had started, he decided to wait until the following morning to contact other Council officials close to him, and to call Xabier in the Basque Country as well. Yes, both Dr. Finley and Kathy knew that several international mafias operated in various African countries, that a network of such mafias were in the business of **human trafficking**, large-scale, **international human trafficking**. But they believed that their close relationship and workings with both Chinese and Congo government officials would keep them away from such danger. Maybe Kathy has been involved in a traffic accident and she lays unconscious in a nearby hospital, in the city, he also wanted to think, as a lesser tragedy.

-Hello, Xabier?

-Dr. Finley, what a pleasant surprise! How are things coming along on your trip with Kathy to the African continent, to Congo, isn't it?   --It was a long distance phone call, but Xabier still recognized Dr. Finley's voice.

-Hello, Xabier, yes, it's me… Well, I don't have good news this time, it appears Kathy has disappeared. It happened only last night, yesterday, so we still don't know what is happened, but Kathy has not returned to our hotel in Kinshana, the capital city of Congo, the Democratic Republic of Congo (DRC). We have initiated a search with the help of both Chinese and Congo government officials, so we are all working and looking for Kathy. –Dr. Finley knew of the close relationship between Kathy and Xabier and felt he needed to touch base with him.

-What!? Are you sure she is not visiting with local people while doing her interviews, or maybe in a hospital nearby. I mean, it is not like Kathy, she would have called you immediately if something wrong had happened. Right?

A moment of silence on the phone line.

-Yes, of course, Kathy would have alerted our team if anything went wrong. But…

-But what? – Asked Xabier, sensing there was more information to be said.

-Well, the possibility has been raised by some members in our team of Kathy being victim of human trafficking… That she may have been kidnapped by members of a local or international mafia involved in trafficking with human beings, and maybe they want to ask for rescue money. I know, I know, Xabier, that this sounds too outrageous, and I feel very bad about, and that is why I wanted to contact you as soon as possible to let you know that we are doing everything possible to find Kathy well and healthy!

-Human trafficking!? I thought that was happening mostly in Russia, Romania, and South Asia…

-In those countries too… In every continent too, basically. I feel it has been my mistake, in thinking that because she was accompanied by government personnel it would not occur. It's my fault, Xabier, it's my fault, I'm so sorry!

-OK, what is the next step? –Said Xabier trying to bring calm into the conversation – Are the government officials acting quickly, and how do they intend to proceed?

-Well, today *Congolese security forces* will be conducting searches in several **labor camps** adjacent to state-owned agricultural sites suspected of drug trafficking. It's a first step. Several hundred security people will be involved. I will call again tomorrow at this same phone number to keep you in the loop. As I said, we still don't know what has happened, it could be that we are imagining and complicating things, but just in case our security forces are carrying out a major search and, so, I wanted you to know.

-I hear you, Dr. Finley, and thank you for calling me. I will be waiting for your phone call tomorrow, please.

The phone conversation ended.

-I want all those 15 NGO GRAIN labor camps in the North-West part of our capital to be cordoned, secured, and searched house by house! –Comanded **Mr. Eugene Mutombo** to the leads of the security forces. Fortunately, all the 15 camps were in close proximity and so it was relatively easy to set up a cordon of security forces all around, while other security teams inspected each one of the family dwellings.

Next day, same time, Dr. Finley calls Xabier who is in Oñati, Basque Country, waiting for that phone call.

-Yes, Dr. Finley? Thank you for calling…Are there any news of Kathy?

-Hello Xabier…No, unfortunately Kathy was not found in the search carried out by the government security forces in the local labor camps. Sorry about that.

-And what about the local hospitals, did your team look into the possibility of Kathy being in one of those hospitals?

-We have also contacted the administrative offices of all 13 hospitals in this city of Kinshasa, and there is no indication of an American woman registered in the last three days.

-So what is the next step to take? –This time Xabier's voice had come down wanting to give time to Dr. Finley to talk about the next step to be carried out by the security forces. By now Xabier's head was flooded by a list of potential crimes, some realistic while others came in as would-be-products of science fiction movies. Maybe she had been drugged and she was *a sexual slave* at some labor camp. Maybe she had been kidnapped by members of an *"Islamic State"* unit in Kinshasa and they would soon be asking for a ransom in millions of dollars.

-*Mr. Mutombo* has recommended a search of a *refugee camp* located in the North-West part of the country, near the border with *Ethiopea* where would-be human traffickers might be trying to smuggle women and children for sale to rich land lords in *Saudi Arabia.*

-Ethiopia, Saudi Arabia!? –Shouted Xabier on the other side of the phone line. The way you put, Dr. Finley, this situation is already getting very serious. We have to do all we can to rescue Kathy away from those trafficking mafias!

-I know, I know, Xabier, and that is why I have also contacted some members of my team in the Council in Tucson to ask for advice, and to look for resources, resources like INTERPOL and other international agencies who…

-Dr. Finley, I need to be there and work with you on this task, really. –Xabier's voice was a bit high pitch but stable, as though he had already made up his mind about his role in this unfortunate situation – I should be there in the next two days, in Kinshasa City. You already told me you are staying at the *Pullman Kinshasa Grand Hotel*, and so as soon as my flight departs for Kinshasa from Madrid or Paris I will call you on the phone with further details.

-All by yourself, Xabier? Is someone else coming with you? From Kathy I learned that you also had a team of people working with you in the Basque Country.

-Don't know yet, but, yes, it is possible that one other person will come with me. The idea is to be there and work with you to find Kathy, no matter where she may be.

Never before had Xabier experienced such a state of anxiety, frustration, and down-to-earth pain in his guts. Well, maybe yes, one time, and that was the case when Xabier and his friends Txomin Elosetegi and Nerea Arana were members of the Ertzaintza police force in Bergara some three years ago. They were driving a van and taking some youths arrested at a demonstration in San Sebastian to police headquarters in Gasteiz-Vitoria and the van got off the road, rolled down the hill and crashed against some trees. Txomin died in that accident, Nerea was unconscious for hours, it was feared she might die, and Xabier waited during a couple of hours for help to arrive while his body and mind were disintegrating in pain. So, maybe this was a second time he was feeling such pain, impotence, and agony not being able to be close to Kathy, not being there personally to rescue her. He now finds himself in Oñati trying to decide whether he should travel alone to Kinshasa or ask a member of his team to travel with him in search of Kathy. Planning to carry out entry in the Secret Archives of the Vatican would have to wait, for sure.

Two days later, Xabier meets Dr. Finley at the Kinshasa International Airport.

-Good to see you again, Dr. Finley, and thank you for coming to the airport to pick us up... By the way, this is *Aitor Larrañaga*, a member of my team in the Basque Country. Aitor is currently quite busy helping with preparations on a couple of activities related to our attempt to enter the Secret Archives, but I was able to convince him to join us here in Kinshasa.

-Pleased to meet you, Aitor, and thanks for coming to this city of Kinshasa.

-Likewise, Mr. Finley, glad to help anyway I can.

-Any news? Did the search of the refugee camp produce any information related to Kathy's whereabouts? —Asked Xabier as he was grabbing his luggage to place it in the trunk of Dr. Finley's car.

Urban center of *Kinshasa,* capital of the Democratic Republic of Congo.

-No, not really, although tomorrow morning a group of security Chinese forces will also be joining us, that is a group from the CSFAC corporation, in order to conduct a search of a *train station* at the border with Ethiopia, some two kilometres west of the same refugee camp. Chinese officials, Congolese officials, and our team will be doing the search beginning 6:00 o'clock tomorrow morning. Yes, the idea is to get in there, surprise everyone, surround the train station, and search every train wagon. This why I am recommending –Added Dr. Finley – that we have an earlier dinner at the hotel, get some good rest, and be ready for tomorrow morning. So tonight I will be glad to share with you some historical notes about this city of Kinshasa, of course:

Formerly *Leopoldvile,* is the capital and the largest city of the Democratic Republic of the Congo (DRC). It is located on the Congo River. Once a site of fishing villages, Kinshasa is now an urban area with a 2014 population of over 11 million. It faces the capital of the neighboring Republic of Congo, Brazzaville, which can be seen in the distance across the wide Congo River. The city of Kinshasa is also one of the DRC's 11 provinces. Because the administrative boundaries of the city-province cover a vast area, over 90% of the city-province's land is rural in nature, and the urban area only occupies a small section in the far western end of the city-province.

Kinshasa is the third-largest urban area in Africa after Cairo and Lagos.[2] It is also the second-largest "francophone" urban area in the world after Paris, French being the language of government, schools, newspapers, public services and high-end commerce in the city, while Lingala is used as a lingua franca in the street. If current demographic trends continue, Kinshasa should surpass Paris in population around 2020. Kinshasa hosted the 14th Francophonie Summit in October 2012.

Residents of Kinshasa are known as *Kinois* (in French and sometimes in English) or Kinshasans (English). The city was founded as a trading post by Henry Morton Stanley in 1881. It was named Léopoldville in honor of King Leopold II of Belgium, who controlled the vast territory that is now the Democratic Republic of the Congo, not as a colony but as a private property. The post flourished as the first navigable port on the Congo River above Livingstone Falls, a series of rapids over 300 kilometres (190 miles) below Leopoldville. At first, all goods arriving by sea or being sent by sea had to be carried by porters between Léopoldville and Matadi, the port below the rapids and 150 km (93 mi) from the coast. By 1923, the city was elevated to capital of the Belgian Congo, replacing the town of Boma in the Congo estuary.

In 1965, Joseph-Désiré Mobutu seized power in the Congo in his second coup and initiated a policy of "Africanizing" the names of people and places in the country. In 1966, Léopoldville was renamed *Kinshasa*, for a village named Kinchassa that once stood near the site, today Kinshasa (commune). The city grew rapidly under Mobutu, drawing people from across the country who came in search of their fortunes or to escape ethnic strife elsewhere. In the 1990s, a rebel uprising began, which, by 1997, had brought down the regime of Mobutu. Kinshasa suffered greatly from Mobutu's excesses, mass corruption, nepotism and the civil war that led to his downfall. Nevertheless, it is still a major cultural and intellectual center for Central Africa, with a flourishing community of musicians and artists. It is also the country's major industrial center, processing many of the natural products brought from the interior.[1]

A mixed group of some 200 Congolese and Chinese officials have now cordoned the Mobutu train station, while another another 30 groups of security officials and soldiers proceed to inspect one by one each of the train wagons. Hand lamps and lanterns are being used to search the train wagons.

-Over here, quickly, over here! We have found the women and children! –The Chinese leader of one of the security groups is shouting. The team made up of Mr. Gregory Chong, Dr. Finley, Xabier, and Aitor, along with a squad of 15 Congolese soldiers approach wagon C-47. Inside the teams find 75-85 women and children sleeping on plain mattresses placed on the floor of the wagon. Some of the children begin to cry.

-Look also for any European women who may be inside the wagons, possibly drugged, unable to move or yell for help! --Shouts Mr. Chong.

Sure enough, in the other tree wagons the teams find another 135-150 women and children and, yes, there are some European women, five European women, in fact. Mr. Chong, Dr. Finley, Xabier, and Aitor quickly rush to wagon C-49 in their search for Kathy.

-No such luck, none of these women is Kathy. These European women are mostly teenagers, probably captured from families of European tourists. –Says Dr. Finley—Please, Mr. Chong, ask the search teams to continue working in the other nearby wagons, it may be that…

-Wait a minute, there is a compartment behind this wall, at the end of this wagon! --Shouts one of the security soldiers.

-Slowly, please, slowly… open that compartment, look for any signs of a handle or lock. –Commands Mr. Chong, raising his arms to make sure no force is used to open the hidden compartment. Surprise.

Three European women and one Congolese woman are found, lying on mattresses, with hands and feet tied up, and drugged. They appear to be sleeping, occasionally moving their feet.

-It's Kathy, it's Kathy! –Shouts Xabier, as he has identified Kathy and tries to help her open her eyes. He also proceeds to untie her hands and feet.

Mr. Chong orders one of his aids to call the ambulance personnel, to come to the three wagons and to begin to apply first-aid services to all the women and children. The three European and the Congolese woman are placed inside two ambulances and rushed to the nearby hospital; Xabier and Aitor are inside one of the ambulances with Kathy.

The following morning at the hospital Kathy rests on her bed, with medical and nurse personnel nearby. Xabier, Dr. Finley, and Aitor are standing nearby and occasionally sitting in chairs against the walls of the room.

-I want to thank all of you for coming to my rescue…I will be forever grateful to all of you, Mr. Chong, Dr. Finley, Xabier, and Aitor.

-You are very welcome, Kathy. –Said Dr. Finley – You were in our minds from the very beginning of this act of violence. Both the Congolese and Chinese CSFAC authorities were most supportive and determined in this effort to rescue you from the *human trafficking mafias*, and it was the deployment of their security forces that made possible your rescue, Kathy.

-Kathy, do you recall when and where you were kidnapped? Any hint at all? – Xabier felt he had to ask such question.

-No, not really… Well, maybe it all happened at one of the restaurants by the road, right after I completed my interviews… But Mr. Lemumba, my security person, was there with me, he would know. Have you talked with Mr. Lemumba?

117

-We do not know where is Mr. Lemumba; we are still investigating this case. Either he was cooperating with the human trafficking mafias, or he has also been kidnapped and is now somewhere doing forced labor. We just don't know, not yet.

-So what will be the next step? —Aitor's voice could be heard in the background. It was as though Aitor wanted to remain a quite although helpful person throughout the entire episode, but something inside of him made him speak up.

-Good question, Aitor. – replied Dr. Finley – I am going to recommend that we follow the advice of the medical personnel, and that Kathy stays in the hospital for the next couple of days under treatment and observation, with Xabier, Aitor, and three security people, while I gather the information collected to date on land investments by the Chinese CSFAC Corporation in order to mail it electronically to our Council Headquarters in Tucson, Arizona. Much of that report has been possible thanks to the cooperation and support of both Mr. Chong and Mr. Mutombo. In fact, they have also contributed statistics gathered in the last three years on human trafficking activity in the DRC and in another 11 countries in Africa; so, we will have *a second report* on that activity, as well.

-And what about Kathy? —Asked Xabier.

-Ah, yes… After those two days of rest, I propose that we all fly to Oñati, Basque Country, for all of us to regain our strength under Xabier's care and supervision! –Added Dr. Finley, as he saw Xabier smiling and applauding.

-Amen, *aurrera*! –Again, it was Aitor, also clapping along with everyone else in the room.

✳✳✳

Chapter
11

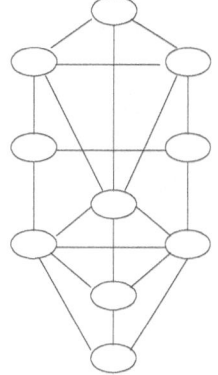

"I fell in love with her courage, her sincerity, and her flaming self-respect. And it's these things I'd believe in, even if the whole world indulged in wild suspicions that she wasn't all she should be. I love her and it is the beginning of everything.
--F. Scott Fitzgerald, on his wife, Zelda.[4]

*"**Wine** to me is something that brings people together. Wine does promote conversation and promote civility, but it's also fascinating. It's the greatest subject to study. No matter how much you learn, every vintage is going to come at you with different factors that make you have to think again.*
--Robert M. Parker, Jr., *writer.*[5]

Oñati and Laguardia, enchanted Towns

It has been two weeks since Kathy, Xabier, Dr. Finley, and Aitor finished their rescue of Kathy in Kinshasa, capital city of the *Democratic Republic of Congo (DRC)*, and now they are recuperating and getting to know the people of Oñati, Gipuzkoa, and Basque Country. Xabier and Aitor have made sure that both Kathy and Dr. Finely could rest at the **hotel Torre Zumeltzegi**, a four-star hotel in town, enjoyed great Basque cuisine, attended festivities, watched many of the folkloric dances, and even participated in some of the local fairs in the town.

-I am going to miss greatly this town of Oñati! –Said Dr. Finley, smiling and looking at Xabier, Kathy, and Aitor – I mean, I had already heard about the good food, the wines, and the way people love to sing and dance over here, but these last two weeks have provided a great experience. I would like to thank you all, an incredible experience, really.

-Well, you are very welcome, Dr. Finley. You took very good care of me and a few other friends in Tucson, Arizona, USA, so it's the least we could do. We wanted you to have a great time before you resume your new duties with the Council in Tucson.

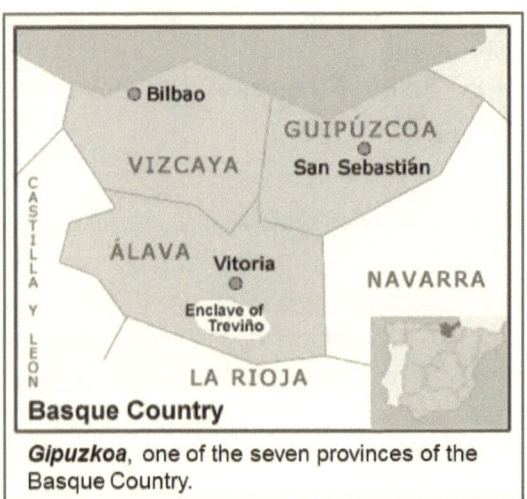

Gipuzkoa, one of the seven provinces of the Basque Country.

-Yes, there is lots of work waiting back in Tucson, for sure, just like you, Xabier, and Kathy have lots of work to do in Oñati in the next few weeks preparing the entry into the Secret Archives of the Vatican. Hopefully our friends in the *Vatican Eagles* group will soon resolve their differences so that your group here in Oñati can initiate that secret mission. By-the-way, have you heard anything from the Eagles yet?

-Not yet, Dr. Finley, but as soon as we hear from them we will give you a call in Tucson. Meantime, we would like you to come with us tonight to the main square in this town of Oñati to watch the folk dancing in which some 20 groups of young men and women will be participating. Yes, we in the middle of the Saint Michael festivities (*"San Miguel jaiak"*) this being the last week of September when the town people celebrate the town's patron saint:

> *Oñati* is a city with much history located in the province of Gipuzkoa, Basque Country, with a population of some 11,285 people, based on a green valley surrounded by tall mountains.

Among its many historical monuments, is the University of Oñati, conceived and financed in 1542 by bishop Rodrigo Mercado de Zuazola, a humanist with a vision for this town and its people. Under the patronage of the Emperor Charles I, "he dedicated all his wealth and efforts to the building of this university, which remained open from 1542 to 1901, offering degrees in Theology, Canons, Law, and Medicine. The building had a central courtyard, a ground floor with a chapel, classrooms, kitchen and refectory, and a first floor with bedrooms and the main lecture hall."

Main entrance to the old *University in Oñati*, historically the first one in the Basque Country.[3]

The city of Oñati is located in the south-east region of the province of Gipuzkoa, bordering with province of Alava, in the basin of the Deva River, and surrounded by high mountains. Neighboring cities are Arrasate-Mondragon, Bergara, Legazpia, and Eibar. Besides its urban center, the city counts with 16 neighborhoods: Arantzazu, Araoz, Uribarri, Lezesarri, Urrexola, Murguía, Olabarrieta, Berezao, Garagalza, Goríbar, Zañartu, Torreauzo, Garibai, Sancholopetegui, Zubillaga and Larraña. In the nearby fields of *Urbia* there are several archeological sites which testify to the presence of humans in pre-historic times.

A long history of internal conflicts and wars characterize this city. The Counts of Oñate had authority over this city, allowing them to collect taxes, name the city Mayor, the local priest, administer justice, and command a small army.

Group of **Dantzariak** participating at the festivities of San Miguel in Oñati, Gipuzkoa.[1]

Their place of residence was the Tower of Zumeltzegi. Castelian laws were applied to land owners and laws from the nearby kingdom of Navarra were applied to workers at the low end of the social scale. It was the Guevara family who ruled over Oñati beginning in 1149 until its incorporation into the province of Gipuzkoa in 1845. In one of those internal conflicts the troops commanded by Pedro Velez de Guevara burned the neighboring city of Arrasate-Mondragon in 1448.

Many captains and soldiers from Oñati went on to found cities in the New World, in Latin America, during the 16th and 17th centuries. As a result the city of Oñati is "sister city" to a long list of cities and territories in Latin America, including: Guadalajara, Mexico, founded by Cristobal de Oñate; Zacatecas, Mexico, also founded by Cristobal de Oñate; Chateaubernard, Argentina; and Paz, Argentina, founded by Jose Altube.[2]

Three days later Dr. Finley left for Tucson, Arizona, to continue working on his new duties as chair person for the *Council of World Peace (CWP)*. Bilbao, Frankfurt, and finally the

International Airport in Tucson; a long but not too uncomfortable flight schedule.

-So what do you suggest we do, Xabier, while we wait for the Eagles to resolve their problems? —Asked Kathy, as both completed a two hour walk to the **Aloña mountain** and were back at the lobby of the Zumetzegi hotel.

-Well, we could get some rest before we get together for dinner, and later possibly go out to see some more folk dancing at the main plaza in town, I hear some groups will be competing for a trophy —Suggested Xabier.

-And how about going up to my room in this wonderful hotel and taking a shower together? It has been a long walk after all.

Xabier could not believe his ears. Kathy was back in shape after two weeks recuperating in Oñati, and she had just invited him to her room. How could Xabier refuse such an offer? He already had something in mind along those lines, but Kathy was ahead of him, once again. Holding hands they both walked up the long staircase up to the third floor where Kathy's room was. She opened the door to her room, both entered, and Kathy placed the "**Do not disturb**" tablet on the outside door knob before locking the door.

-What a great view of the countryside you have here, one can see the entire valley, its river, and mountains! —Said Xabier as he stood in the balcony with his arms rested on the wooden frame of the balcony.

He had just uttered those words when he felt Kathy behind him, pressing her body against his body, her breasts pressing against his back, and her hands gently caressing his chest. Xabier stood still, not trying to turn around, as he knew how Kathy liked exploring the topography of his body, so he just closed his eyes and waited for Kathy to say something.

-Would you like to open up the bottle of Champaign which is cooling in the refrigerator? —Suggested Kathy, knowing well what would be Xabier's response.

-Certainly, I would be glad to do just that, but I am here captive of your charms, and cannot move. It's the spell of you voice that keeps me still, maybe.

-Well, maybe a kiss of yours could make that spell disappear. Would you like to try? –Again, suggested Kathy.

-Gently and slowly Xabier turned around until he faced Kathy in the middle of the balcony, smiling openly. Both looked at each other's eyes, with big smiles, and this time embracing each other. Xabier bent down his head slightly, Kathy's lips pushed a bit forward as they waited to meet Xabier's, and she closed her eyes. Their lips met finally, and stayed together for several seconds, a time which seemed like an eternity as both Kathy and Xabier sucked both upper and lower lips, bit each other gently, went back to sucking their lips, as their arms acted to bring their bodies even closer.

-I have waited for such a long time for this moment, woman. –Said Xabier looking at Kathy's eyes.

-Me too, Xabier. I needed to see you again, and my mind could only think of how our next encounter would be. Whether we would meet in Tucson, New York, in some country in Africa, or in Rome. I just knew that I wanted to see you again.

-Yes, I have also been waiting for the two of us to get together and, like you just said, in my mind I'm always thinking of how it would be next time we meet. Well, let's go inside and open that bottle of champagne which just happens to be waiting for us.

Inside her room Kathy retrieved the bottle from the refrigerator and gave it to Xabier to open it. Once it was open she poured over two tall glasses. They drank slowly, short sips, closed their eyes to enjoy the moment. Next, Kathy began to unbutton Xabier shirt, still smiling.

-It's hot, Xabier, don't you think so? Maybe we can take a shower together to help our bodies cool down a bit... We would have to be standing up as it is not a bathtub, it is a wide, beautiful shower surrounded with glass walls.

-I think it is a wonderful idea –Said Xabier – as he also proceeded to unbutton Kathy's shirt.

Soon both of them were standing naked in the middle of the room with the sunlight entering from the balcony and reaching their naked bodies. Yes, it was not the first time that both saw each other's bodies, and yes they had made love to each other before, but it seemed to have been such a long time ago, many months ago, and they felt as though they were going to make love for the very first time. Once inside the shower, the warm water began to run down their bodies, from her wet head down her shoulders, rushing over her ample breasts, down her slim belly and around her belly button, again rushing over her luscious butt and long thighs, all the time while she was rubbing Xabier's chest with a piece of cloth and body lotion.

Xabier also put some body lotion on his hands and began to apply it to Kathy's body, as the shower water rushed down her body. First he rubbed the lotion around her neck and shoulders, along the length of her suntanned arms, her back, around her ample breasts though ignoring her nipples for the time being, and around her beautifully shaped hips.

The world did not exist. The world outside their shower room did not exist. There was no research team in Tucson, no CDs leaked out of the Vatican, no social-political conflict in the Basque Country, no Secret Archives to enter, no planet of hominids dangerously reaching its limits… Just Kathy and Xabier looking at each other's eyes, feeling their naked bodies with their hands, fingers, and minds, hearing the water rush down their bodies, and smelling the scent of the moment.

The better part of half an hour went by, inside the shower, still standing up and kissing, until Kathy suggested they move to the living room to dry each other.

-I love many things about hotels, and one of them is these long, soft, and thick towels. –Said Kathy, as she kept on drying Xabier's shoulders.

-That, yes, and the fact that the kitchen and its refrigerator are generally so close by. --Added Xabier, also drying Kathy's back as he enjoyed watching her suntanned arms and legs.

-You must be thinking of the champagne bottle and our two glasses, right? So let's fill them up again to refresh our thirsty throats and bodies. –Next, Kathy placed her long towel around Xabier and proceeded to pull him towards the kitchen nearby, just a few feet away, and she added: I think you are resisting a bit, Xabier. Have you never made love in a kitchen?

A kitchen? Where is Kathy going with her ideas this time, Xabier was thinking, but he gladly followed her, letting her pull him towards the kitchen until they both reached the big table in the middle of it. Next, Kathy sat on one edge of the big table, still holding on to Xabier with her towel, and smiling. Xabier still standing up began to bent over her to try to kiss her lips, but Kathy slowly bent her body until she was resting with her back on the long table. It took Xabier a few seconds to realize what Kathy had in mind, but the neurons in his brain finally figured out Kathy's strategy, so Xabier proceeded to kiss and lick her body, from one end to the other. Hey, Xabier was only a man, after all, and not always able to figure the designs of a woman, especially a woman like Kathy so inclined to foreplay before jumping into the cake. So he began licking her kneecaps, left first and then the right one, moving on to her gorgeous thighs. Not only they were long and suntanned but her muscle tone was exquisite, Xabier thought. Yet, he chose not to go all the length of her thighs, and after a while he moved on to her earlobes, to the other end, as to begin a long trajectory to her belly button. Her earlobes were particularly sensitive and required his attention, something that Xabier could not understand as a man, but that he knew well, and paid due homage to both of them, kissing, licking, and slightly biting them with his teeth.

Her breasts were ample, and yet not big, though firm enough to command his care and attention, as he kissed and licked them with his wet lips, while all the time he was listening to Kathy's gentle moaning. A bit of champagne? Why not! Xabier's brain neurons had come up with such idea, so he proceeded to pour some champagne on Kathy's belly button followed by a short moan from Kathy welcoming such event. A sip here, a sip there, as Xabier drank champagne from Kathy's improvised glass, her own belly button. Pour some more champagne, and sip some more champagne. Next –as Kathy's moaning got louder and higher – Xabier got on top of the table, on top of Kathy, and flooded her with kisses, mildly sucking her lips, nose, earlobes, and chin. Minutes later it was Kathy's turn as she got on top of Xabier, taking command of events, rhythmically moving her body, biting her lower lip, and resting her hands on Xabier's shoulders to maintain her balance.

Two empty bottles of champagne later, Kathy and Xabier slowly got off the kitchen table and moved on to the living room. A long sofa in the middle of that living room was never so welcome. Both fell along the length of the sofa, holding to each other tightly, still smiling, totally exhausted.

Bright and shiny! The next morning both Kathy and Xabier went down to the hotel's eating hall for breakfast. Both were significantly hungry and thirsty.

-Thank you, Kathy, woman of my dreams.

-And I thank you, Xabier, man of my wildest desires.

-By-the-way, Kathy, I almost forgot, but a couple of weeks ago a got a call from our friend, *Emilio Beistegi*... He is the young man that we met in Tucson, you may remember, as he was doing a Masters at the University of Arizona...

-Ah, yes I remember now, he was doing a Masters in engineering if I recall well... in *systems engineering*, I believe. So what about him?

-Well, he is now in the city *San Sebastian* on his first job as an engineer, but he stopped by Oñati and he gave me the key to his house in the town of *Laguardia* in case we could get away for a few days. What do you think?

-Are you asking me if we could go to this town of Laguardia? Where is this town, and what would we be doing there?

Laguardia (Basque: *Guardia*) is a town located in the southern region of the province of Álava, Basque Country, with a population of 1,500.

The town of *Laguardia* located on a hill top with its background of mountains, Alava, *Basque Country*.[1]

Built on top of a hill, it is surrounded by a giant stone wall that the *King Sancho "the Strong"* ordered to build. There are still preserved five different entries to access the city. Their names are: Mercadal, Butchers, Páganos, San Juan, and Santa Engracia. Additionally, the streets and surroundings of Laguardia still keep a medieval atmosphere that give the city an ancient touch.

Regarding the economy, its main strength is the wine industry. Indeed, the wine is elaborated and processed in numerous wineries.

Castle **restaurant** on the town of **Laguardia**, on the "**Collado**" walk, Alava, **Basque Country**.[2]

During the Middle Ages, it appeared with names such as *Leguarda, Giardia, Guard, Guoardia, Lagarde,* and *Laguoardia* until the current name was finally fixed. Indeed, the full and complete name of the town is the town is *La Guardia de Navarra* as it was one in a long chain of fortified towns intended to guard the kingdom of Navarra and protect it from invading troops from Castile.

Laguardia has three separate neighborhoods: (1) *The Campillar*, 7.5 km from the city center, near the Ebro River, with 28 inhabitants, (2) *Laserna,* 11 km from the city center, separated from the rest of the municipality by a meander of the Ebro River, with 43 inhabitants, and (3) *Páganos*, 3.5 km away, with 87 inhabitants.

Besides its great wealth in wine harvesting and marketing, Laguardia possesses a very rich historical past.

Restaurante Marixa en **Laguardia**, with views of vineyards and lake, Laguardia, Alava, **Basque Country**.[5]

At a place called **La Hoya**, there is an important archaeological site. It is a pre-Roman settlement of Celtiberian of Berona ethnic and it covers an extensive period since the 12th century BC (before Christ) to the 2nd century BC.

As mentioned above, the core of the economy in Laguardia focuses on the world of viticulture (grape growing, **winemaking and wine industry**). Laguardia is the capital of one of the most famous wine regions of Spain, Rioja Alavesa. Additionally, both in Laguardia and its surroundings, a wine known as the *Denomination of Laguardia* is created, which has its economic advantages.

Clasical monuments and buildings everywhere in this city. **(1) The Wall**, the high walls surrounding the town are about 2 meters thick and 15 meters high; They are made of stone, with five doors that lead to the villa. (2) **The Church of Santa Maria de los Reyes**, which in the past was probably a *Templar monastery*. Next to it, there is a tower called the Tower of Santa Maria or Torre abbey (it is believed that the abbot lived there).

The tower has a remarkable Gothic facade with a portico that is conserved almost intact, indeed; the carving was finished in the 14th century and it was polychromed in the 17th. It is one of the few preserved polychrome portals in Basque Country and Spain (in Toro (Zamora) there is another one). The sizes of the archivolts represent the Apostles and the porch tells the story of the Holy Virgin.

Medieval wall of the town of *Laguardia*, showing one of its eight towers, Alava, *Basque Country*.[8]

(3) *The Church of San Juan*, which initially was built in Romanesque style and finally completed in the Gothic style. It has an attached chapel of the eighteenth century, dedicated to the Virgin of Pilar. Its bell tower belonged originally to a castle. (4) *The Hermitage of Santa María de Berberana*, Romanesque and the only church in the whole Rioja Alavesa which possesses a square apse. (5) *Plaza Mayor*, in the center of the town; tourists can find there both the new and the old town hall. The latter shows on its facade the shield of the villa and a chiming clock with automata that at 12, 14, 17 and 20 hours dance to the rhythm of a typical parade of the celebrations of the town. (6) *Renaissance Old Town Hall*, an imperial shield of

Charles V. (7) *A Capuchin convent.* (8) *Prehistoric remains* of some *dolmens* and a Celtic village in the town of La Hoya. Furthermore, there is also a Celtic pond. And (9) *the Birthplace of the fabulist Félix María de Samaniego*, a 17th century palace that houses the tourist office.

Main plaza in the town of *Laguardia*, Alava, *Basque Country*.[10]

The following day Xabier and Kathy drove in a rented car to the town of Laguardia some 80 miles south-west of Oñati. They parked the car just outside the walls of the town, next to what used to be the *pelota court* ("*pelota fronton*") and only a few feet away into a main entrance to the town's main plaza.

-That house is part of a new development, the "*La Lobera*" housing development, which you can see from here as it is only two miles away. You follow this road south, you get to the gasoline station, and continue for another mile. The development of some 20 brick and stone houses is on the left. –Said a man, a neighbor in that town of Laguardia.

Fifteen minutes later Xabier and Kathy arrived at the La Lobera development, looked for the house number given by Emilio

Beistegi, its owner, and there it was. It was a two-story brick house with a large front and back patio, surrounded by a large metal fence, and behind the house they could see the spectacular chain of mountains that Emilio had often talked about. **Three keys**. One to open the metal gate that was part of the metal fence, a walk of thirty feet to reach a second metal door in front of the main wooden door to the house, and a third key to open that wooden main door itself. Once inside the house Xabier and Kathy found a wide and long hall on the first floor with a door on their right to a large dining room with a long dining table and 20 chairs all around it; the main kitchen with an American refrigerator in it, a large window, and a door to a patio under a roof for barbeque meals; a large living room with two long sofas covered in dark green leather, and a fireplace. A fireplace!? Yes, a metal fireplace in black with a long smoke tube crossing the wide living room; a bathroom with sink and shower; a store room with lots of kitchen equipment brought in from the USA; and a door opening to a large garage, with a large metal door which opened up-and-down as if the place was a warehouse, and plenty of power tools. Obviously that guy Emilio liked using shop tools, metal and wood, to fix things around the house.

A long wooden staircase leading to the second floor in that house, beginning at the end of the long hall. Once on the second floor there were a main bedroom with its own bathroom, with a bath tub, toilet, sink, and bidet; another central rest area with two large chairs; a large office with two desks, four book cases, and a large window with a lake and the chain of mountains in the background; one second bedroom with two individual beds; and a third bedroom with a large bed, wooden wardrove, a wall table with mirror, a large sofa and two chairs, all with Japanese decoration. Ahh, yes, the entire house is full of paintings, some having Emilio as their artist and author, while others bought by Emilio in his travel to other countries.

-I can't believe my eyes! –Said Kathy, after seeing the house, in and out. –And all this property surrounded by a few neighbors and plenty of vineyards, with a lake, and a beautiful chain of mountains in the background. Green-green vineyards and blue-blue skies.

-Hey, if Emilio had told us about this house back in Tucson, we would have taken better care of him! Right, Kathy?

-Well, we were all OK with each other, for sure, but this house is spectacular. The wooden staircase and the paintings all over the house are most impressive. –Insisted Kathy, also impressed and laughing.

They continued looking at the rooms, viewing closer the paintings on the walls, porcelain figures from various countries shown in the long hall. Back in the kitchen they noticed there were two shelves full of food supplies, including flour to make *American pancakes* and three bottles of strawberry syrup.

-How about if we make some pancakes, have some coffee, and next we walk up to the town to see its people and houses? Who knows, we might even meet some of Emilio's relatives!

-It sounds great to me! –Answered Kathy realizing that it was still early in the morning.

One hour later both Xabier and Kathy started their walk to the town, only 10-15 minutes away. Beautiful countryside. Soon a gasoline station and a car showroom appeared on the left of the walking path, and the big and impressive Hotel Villa de Laguardia on their right, the scene for a wedding that day. Still going up hill they saw five apartment buildings, the four-star Hotel Amelibia, and the five-star Hotel and Restaurant Marixa. They had reached the East side of the wall with its main entrance. As they walked through that entrance they began to sense that they were entering a medieval city, something from the 15th century, buildings with thick walls, thick wooden house doors, with flowerpots hanging from balconies and full or colorful flowers. Soon they entered the town's main plaza, a big square with an enormous building on the left which happened to be the town's City Hall, five big arches with benches, and the *luxurious Hotel Parajes* in front of them, also in that main plaza. Any coffee shops and bars? Coffee shops, bars, and restaurants everywhere! Five buses loaded with tourists had arrived a few minutes earlier so the inside of the town was thriving with couples and families from every corner of the Basque Country.

Xabier and Kathy decided to have a glass of wine and two *"pintxos"* (*appetizers*) at the **Arbulu bar**, a place which Emilio had also mentioned and owned by his cousin Manolo and his wife Mertxe. The bar's counter was full with some 20 varieties of *pintxos*, individual rations of meat, chicken, and seafood set on small pieces of bread with a toothpick. Fresh from the kitchen and exquisite! Some more walking through the streets of Laguardia. The **Information Office** for tourists managed by Pilar, Maribel, y Zurine, three beautiful and intelligent young ladies; a **bakery** with delicious breads owned and managed by Marije and Paco, also cousins of Emilio; a **vegetable store** full of ripe fruits from all nearby gardens, owned and managed by Elena and Jose Mary, and their sons Eduardo and Miguel, also all cousins of Emilio. Two more glasses of wine and two *pintxos*. As they kept walking they followed a group of tourists and their guide towards the **Hotel El Castillo** just outside the town's walls, magnificent for its tower and excellent cuisine, and along the one-mile long trail named **El Collado** where tourists can see the countryside for miles without end, including some 20 other towns nearby. Two hours later they observed how the tourists were entering the various restaurants in the Villa of Laguardia. It was lunch time!

-It looks like it is lunch time in this town! Maybe we should also be heading back to our house at La Lobera. –Suggested Xabier.

-I agree, feeling a bit hungry too after all this walking and talking with the people in this beautiful town. Can we find our way back?

Forty five minutes later they were back at the brick house in the new compound La Lobera. One key, a second key, a third key and inside the house. Both Xabier and Kathy had tasted the town's wine, the pintxos, got to meet many people for the first time, and now they were back at the brick house for meal they would prepare themselves with the food supplies already available at the house. Or so they thought.

-Maybe we can change our clothings, make our stay more comfortable. Can you come up with me to the second floor? –Asked Kathy, already with pink cheeks in her face as a result of that wonderful wine.

They had already walked half of the wooden staircase, when they had to turn right to continue going up, and it was then that Kathy's left knee bent and she fell to a rectangular space in the middle of the staircase. Immediately Xabier bent his legs to help Kathy straighten out, but... Surprise!

-We don't have to get up, Xabier, stay here with me... I would love to sip some of that red wine that you still keep in your lips.

On the staircase? Immediately that thought crossed Xabier's mind, as he positioned himself next to Kathy. Yes, both were a bit drunk, but on the staircase? Kathy pulled him down gently and their lips met. It was a long kiss. Kathy smiled and went on to unbutton Xabier's shirt, and had just ondone his belt when Xabier kissed her again. Soon pieces of clothing began to fall down the ladder to land on the floor of the long hall. Lunch would have to wait, as they both were busy undressing and kissing. Xabier took a few seconds to look at the walls in that long hall and it seemed as though all the people in those paintings were looking at the two of them, and only at them and smiling. Weird and yet a wonderful feeling!

✳✳✳

Chapter

12

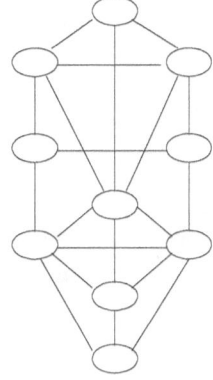

*"Given that the Archives are estimated to house 53 miles of books, there are sure to be some intriguing finds inside. But why would an institution as powerful as the Roman Catholic Church feel **the need to keep these documents secret?** Are they afraid of what might happen if the public should learn of certain information?*

--The Vatican Secret Archives Conspiracy[10]

*"On the morning of September 29, 1978, Pope John Paul I was found dead, sitting up in his bed, after only 33 days in office. Although Vatican officials claimed the 65-year-old pope died of a heart attack, there was never an autopsy, **and at the time, the Vatican definitely had ties to organized crime.** Sure enough, in 1982, Vatican Bank president Father Paul Marcinkus resigned from his post after a series of scandals exposed the bank's ties to the Mafia. Eventually, the bank had to repay more than $200 million to its creditors."*

--10 Secrets of the Vatican exposed[11]

Planning the entry into the Secret Archives

It was the first day of September, and as the invited guests arrived they entered the *Romulus and Remus* conference room in the **Hotel Foro Romano**. Still a bright day with blue skies for that time of the year, and being about 10:00 o´clock in the morning most of the guests had already had breakfast. A man in a dark suit waited until all the guests were seated and then he spoke.

137

-Good morning, my name is **Father Donovan**, David Donovan, and I would like to welcome you all to **Rome**, the eternal city, for this important meeting, a meeting that we all have been preparing for, it seems for ever, for a good number of months at least. Some of you already know each other very well, and you will get to know everyone else in the course of the meeting, of course. Please feel free to ask any questions as we go along.

-Good to see you again, Father Donovan...Can you talk about the security precautions being taken to conduct this meeting? By-the-way, my name is **Xabier** Elurmendi.

-Hi, Xabier, good to see you again, and I'm glad you brought up the subject of security measures. Yes, this is a secured room, meaning there are no hidden radio or TV recorders, and all conversations and decisions will be strictly confidential, meaning only those of you present will know about them. As you know we are here to share information on means to enter the **Secret Archives of the Vatican.**

A silence could be felt all over the room. Father Donovan continued.

-Present here today are members of the group **Secret Eagles of the Vatican**, members of the **Circle of Women**, and a few members of the **Council for World Peace** (CWP). Nobody else. I'm going to ask **Ms. Emily Connelly**, with us today, of the Circle of Women, to remind us about her reasons to learn more about documentation inside the Secret Archives. Emily?

-Thank you, Father Donovan, it's good to be here today. Our organization has the name of *Circle of Women*. It has existed for thousands of years in most civilizations in the Western world, though we have a "*more structured memory*" of events in that time period during the last three thousand years only. Our main purpose has been and it is today to look after the well-being of our sisters in society, a mostly male-dominated society, as I know you realize. For thousands of years women have subsisted as second entities, serving men, doing house chores, rearing children, etc. not being able to participate in decision-making, not able to hold public offices of any type. Blamed for draughts, diseases, and plagues by the priests in many cultures and religions. It has been only in the last one thousand years that we have managed to emerge into our own, able to care for ourselves, enter centers of learning in larger numbers, able to begin to claim our place in society, side by side with men, our neighbors, our brothers, fathers, and husbands…Not as servants, but as equals in search of a future. Equality is our driving force.

A second arm rises to ask another question.

-Hi, Emily, and what information you are hoping we find inside the Secret Archives? Yes, my name is **brother Luis Mendes**, from Santa Catarina, Rio de Janeiro.

-Well, are early sisters were also at the Getsemane meeting, the garden of Gethsemane, and probably met with Jesus, the man, the prophet, where he talked about the *"two complementary and enlightened spheres"*, as Jesus and the sisters around him called them. That early design called for two spheres, the two churches, if you will, one church integrated and directed by men, and one church integrated and directed by women, in order to attain equality among men and women from the very beginning. Those would be the long-lost Gethsemane Gospels or **Gethsemane Codex**. –Said Emily as she looked around, looking at everyone in the eyes, smiling.

-If I may add a comment –That was **Dr. Finley**, standing up to address the group – that information shared by Emily with us was also part of the contents of the two CDs which were delivered to my research team at the University of Arizona, in the USA, by someone, not knowing today who might be that person or organization. So, many of us believe there could be information inside the Vatican which talks about the early design of the Christian Church, a design which considered a better balance of power among men and women in the Christian Church. Thank you!

-So, those Gethsemane Gospels could be the ones that escaped the burning furnace of **Bishop Irenaeus** in the 2nd Century AC (After Christ)? –This time it was Father Donovan asking the question.

-Exactly! – Suggested Emily – Those gospels may have survived Irenaeus' plot to design the early Church to his likings and own interests. We believe that the "lost" Gethsemane Gospels or

Codex may contain information to help advance the cause of women for the benefit of all mankind.

-The contribution of women to our society could be larger, adding stability to our global society already threatened by a number of serious events. As we stand out today in this global society we may be seeing *a planet Earth reaching its limits*. – And this time it was *Kathy*, sitting next to Xabier and Dr. Finley, who contributed her comment.

By then the twelve people attending this meeting by invitation were participating with questions and comments. It was time for Father Donovan to get into the matter of how to get inside the underground fortress that protects the Secret Archives.

-Very good, I suggest the time has arrived to talk about *how* we plan to get inside the Secret Archives. Yes, I know that we have talked about this project for a long time and that some ideas have been communicated. Still, it is a major challenge. No person has gotten to date inside the Archives without the consent of the administrators in the Vatican. I'm going to ask *Brother Walter Altuna* to refresh our memories about how the Secret Archives are administered and guarded. Brother Altuna?

-Thank you, Father Donovan, I'll be glad to do so. The current administrators of the Secret Archives are Cardinal *Sergio Pagano*, as Prefect, and *Jean-Louis Bruges*, as Cardinal Archivist. The care and maintenance of the documents is carried out by three laboratories of restauration, photography, and copying. Now, we have to tackle this challenge in several phases, I believe. The phase that I have been responsible for is that which addresses how to get in and out of the Archives. Cardinal Pagano and Cardinal Bruges are just that, administrators, and they do not stand in front of any entrance to the Archives. There is, however, the important matter of the *Swiss Guards* who play a major role in the custody of the Archives. We have found out, however, that *Cardinal Reggio Boccasini* is the person between Cardinal Pagano and the Swiss Guards. Most important is that Cardinal Boccasini is suspected of being a *pedophile*... Yes, a pedophile, and that is where several of us in the Eagles group are betting. We propose that we *blackmail this man*: He let us inside the Secret Archives to take a few photos of some documents, nothing else, and we do not bring out the matter of his being a pedophile or not with the news media. Simple as that.

-There is also a **Plan B**. –Father Donovan added with a smile. –This time I'm going to ask Ms. Emily Connelly to tell us all about it. Emily?

-Will be glad to explain it, Father Donovan –Said **Emily**, as she stood up from her seat – We have been quite lucky really, we might say, because we have with us *a sister* in the *Circle of Wise Women* who used to work in the Secret Archives themselves years ago. As I have said before, our organization has existed for hundreds of years, and we have sisters of the Circle who have played roles in many critical points of our societies, including government structures, hospitals, universities, and military organizations, to mention a few. So, a team of three sisters will participate in Plan B: two of them dressed as sisters of a religious order, and the third one as a young and glamorous student lady. This team will ask for a list of documents from the Archives, the archivist that day will open the door to the study room where our three sisters will be waiting, next the young lady will fake a moment of great satisfaction, of ecstasy, at receiving the documents to complete her Master's degree and will faint on the spot; the archivist rushes to the floor to attend our beautiful student, and while the door to the elevator is still open one of the two sisters and the team provided by Father Donovan will go down the elevator to enter the Secret Archives. That sister already knows the labyrinth of doors leading to the Archives and, yes, the entry will take place just before closing the Archives for that day. The team would then have the entire night to search for the Gethsemane Codex. The following morning our sister will make use of her knowledge of the time routine used to open up the Archives to get the team out. It should work, we believe.

-And where inside the Secret Archives do we search for and find the *Gethsemane Gospels*? I mean such place is supposed to be dozens of miles long with bookshelves, and wardrobes full of documents. – Asked Xabier, having waited patiently to ask such question.

-Good question – Replied Brother Altuna – and we have spent a great deal of time considering the places where such a document could be held, by now possibly in paper format, copied over and over during the first three centuries, and translated from *Aramaic* into early and medieval Latin. We believe it could be within one of the wooden wardrobes of the *"Diplomatic Floor"*, forgotten and ignored. We don't believe such document would be found on a shelf with a square label which reads "Gethsemane Codex", not at all. It would have to be on a wooden wardrobe, one of a few dozen wardrobes, compared with the thousands of shelves that exist lined up one after the other for miles.

-Thank you, Emily, and thank you Father Donovan –It was Kathy with one more question – Both of you have talked about a team, a team that goes inside the Archives. How many people in that team are we talking about?

-That is also a most important matter –Replied Father Donovan – and that is why we have asked **Father Thomas Paulson**, of the University of Oxford, to work on the makeup of such a team. He is a historian on documents of the Church. Father Paulson?

-Thank you, Father Donovan. Three teams, actually, made up of two people each. This way each team will be able to concentrate on a section of the wardrobes, one person opening cardboard boxes filled with documents, and the second person taking photographs of those portions of the documents believed relevant. We have identified the number or wardrobes and the order of inspection of each wardrobe by sections in the "index" of the Archives and their geographical distribution in the same. A total of ten hours to get the job done.

Dr. Finley raised his right arm.

-What about other documents that the three teams may consider relevant in their search? I mean, documents about agreements between the Vatican and dictators during the First and Second World Wars, specifically agreements between Pope Pius XII and the dictators Hitler, Mussolini, and Franco on matters of money, concentration camps and the genocide of Jewish people, for example. Likewise, documents and decisions made by the Church during the Inquisition years, moneys loaned or received during the days of the Ambrosiano Bank. This is a great opportunity to learn about decisions which have shaped our modern societies, in my opinion.

-Yes, Dr. Finley, you are right, indeed, and that is why the three teams already have a list of related events, such as the ones you have mentioned and more. That is also why I am asking each one of us here today to give a list of related items to Father Paulson, during the next couple of hours, before we complete our meeting – Father Donovan looked at each one present at the meeting, and with a smile he added –Great! I will then ask everyone to follow me to the next room to celebrate this meeting with lunch in this wonderful *Hotel Foro Romano*!

Chapter

13

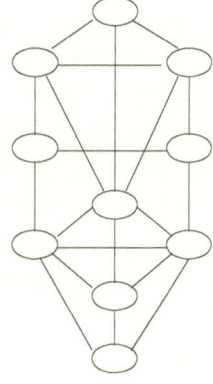

*"Where we are going as a species is a big question. **Human evolution** certainly hasn't stopped. Every time individuals produce a new zygote, there's a reshuffling and recombination of genes. And we don't know where all of that is going to take us.*
--**Donald Johanson**, scientist, writer.[11]

*"Hominid and human evolution took place over millions and not billions of years, but with **the emergence of language** there was a further acceleration of time and the rate of change.*
--**William Irwin Thompson**,
philosopher.[12]

Human Evolution, reaching its end?

While Kathy and Xabier have been busy collaborating with Dr. Finley and members of the Vatican Eagles in the analysis of documents from the Vatican Secret Archives, Aitor has stayed in Oñati carrying on with this university studies. There he has met Sharon, an American student who is about to begin a year of studies at the ***University of the Basque Country*** (*Euskal Herriko Unibertsitatea, EHU; Universidad del Pais Vasco, UPV*) in order to continue learning two more languages: German and Euskera. Aitor is a student from the local town of Arrasate-Mondragon, Gipuzkoa, and is taking courses at Mondragon Unibersitatea (MU). Both met at MU's library, and a few weeks later Aitor calls Sharon on the phone to invite her to visit together a museum in Burgos, Spain. Let us listen in:

Sharon (S): ¿Atapuerca? The *Atapuerca museum* in Burgos? What's happening in that famous museum these days?

Aitor (A): Well, as you know, it's a first-class museum in the world where they have many exhibits with fossils and a bunch of artefacts on the origins of humans in our planet, the evolution of the species, the types of hominids that existed, and very specially the evolution of humans. It's only at a distance of one-hour drive from Bilbao, so I thought you might be interested in this short trip, in seeing the heat fields on the road, and …

Sharon: Ohh, yes, I would love to go there! Of course, I love the idea! In the last few weeks we've had a lot of work at the university, with projects and exams, so I'm ready for a change of menu. Did you mention the origin of life on the planet? Are we talking about new discoveries or something like that?

Aitor: Uhh,… yes, exactly! In the last 30-40 years there have been an incredible number of scientific discoveries, an explosion of discoveries, I would say, that bring out a lot of information on a number of themes, from life-saving drugs in medicine and their treatment of diseases, advances in the engineering of airplanes and trains, the origins of the universe, and social intelligence, to the origin of humans in our planet.

Sharon: Why in the last 30-40 years only, as you say, and why not earlier? As human beings we have been doing things for thousands of years.

Aitor: Yeah, but I'm talking about the new Technologies. The discovery of *radiocarbon-14*, a radioactive isotope of carbon, in particular, made it possible to date fossils, bones, so that today we are able to determine if a sample of bones is 300 years old, 30,000 years old, or more.[1]

Sharon: ¿Ahh, really? So how does it work?

Aitor: As I understand it –a very basic understanding, nothing else-- all animal bones contain a radioactive carbon isotope that emits protons and neutron with a known frequency rate. A very high frequency and emission when the bones are first generated, and that later such emission decreases as the years go by. So, by measuring the rate of emission of that isotope in bones the scientists can determine the age of bones, in thousands and even millions of years.

Sharon: *No kidding*! That's fantastic! Are you saying that today we can determine the age of those bones and skulls which we have kept in boxes in museums all over the world for hundreds of years? I mean, we kept them in boxes out of curiosity, but we did not know what else to do with them, really.

Aitor: Exactly. It is because of this and related technologies that now we know that the **Neanderthals** lived in Europe and parts of Asia for some 300,000 years, until they became extinct only some 40,000 years ago.

Sharon: That's incredible! It's a piety we cannot do something like that with other things.

Aitor: What do you mean?

Sharon: I mean that in the case of *languages* of the world, it would great if we could somehow see inside a language, observe things, structures, syntax characteristics, for example, and the somehow be able to deduce its age in thousands of years, its place of origin, things like that.

Aitor: Yes, it's an interesting idea. But if that is not possible, what is it that linguists can do today in order to determine the origin of languages, their age, etc. And since we are at it, for how long have humans been able to talk, to have a language? 10,000 years? 25,000 years?

Sharon: For a longer period of time, much longer, but still a short time in the scale of human evolution. In my department of languages at the UPV they tell us that according to **Noam Chomsky**[2], the world-famous American linguist, we human beings acquired the capacity to speak and use a language some 60,000 years ago in Africa. According to Chomsky solar radiation altered the ADN of a single individual, only one, in Africa 60,000 years ago, and then that man or woman began to make sound with his mouth, to combine sounds and make words.

Aitor: Are you telling me that solar radiation made some changes in the DNA of a human being, and that those changes produced a change in the physiology of the mouth, the pharynx, the throat and all of that?

Sharon: Yes, that's what Chumsky is saying.

Aitor: In that case it ought to be possible to investigate and determine when that alteration of the mouth and throat occurred in humans with the use of radiocarbon-14, and whether those changes also happened to the Neanderthals and other hominids. Would you not say so?

Sharon: Right, that's a good question. But what are we going to do about Atapuerca, the visit to the museum?

Aitor: Ahh, yes... Going back to Atapuerca. We know that there were some 6-8 migration waves of early humans that originated in Africa, left Africa, and eventually managed to spread over Europe and Asia, and later over the other continents in the course of the last 2 million years, basically.

Sharon: From Africa?

Aitor: Yes, the scientific evidence points to Africa, north-east Africa, the Ethiopian region specifically, as the origin of the human species, the "*hominids*." From that region of Africa evolved the **Homo Ergaster**, one of the first hominid groups, possibly crossing the strait between the African continent and today's Saudi Arabia.

Sharon: So what did that Homo Ergaster look like?

Aitor: It is believed that he looked like today's modern man, pretty much. Same physical structure, same height, although possibly more robust and stronger, with wide hips, and with arms and legs like today's modern man. He lived and evolved over a period of some 1.4 million years, until 400,000 years ago.

Sharon: Hey, that's cool. Very impressive.

Aitor: Next came out the **Homo Erectus**. This next hominid, a descendant of the Homo Ergaster, came out of Africa some 1.6 million years, finally got to the regions of East Asia and Australia, and lived until some 300,000 ago. Strong, about 6 feet (1.8 meters) tall, with a pronounced and strong jaw. Its bones have been found in Africa, China, Indonesia, and in parts of Europe.

Sharon: There were probably several reasons why those hominids decided to extend beyond the African continent. How many people, hominids, are we talking about, how many left Africa?

Aitor: The scientists talk about a few dozens of families, only, of 2-3 hundred families that left Africa, who crossed the strait, and walked towards Europe and Asia.

Sharon: And next, who followed them? Were there other migration waves, other waves of hominids that followed?

Aitor: In 1962 scientists discovered in Atapuerca the remainings of **Neanderthals**, direct descendants of Homo Ergaster, it is believed, who lived on regions of Western Europe and Asia for a period of some 300,000 years. A relatively long period of time. And then they became extinct, with the last families lasting until 20,000-40,000 years ago, Atapuerca being one of their last colonies in the European continent.

Sharon: Yeah, lately we hear a lot about the Neanderthals. What did they look like?

Aitor: The Neanderthals were also very robust, physically strong, white skin, and red hair, generally. Well, they had black skin and curly black hair when they first came out of Africa 300,000 years ago, but after living thousands of years in the cold regions of Europe and Asia, part of their DNA changed, and they lost much of their body hair. Their bodies needed the sunlight to warm up and survive in those cold regions, so they covered their bodies with clothes and consequently lost their body hair. Skin pigmentation was also lost to better absorb sunlight in their bodies, so they acquired a lighter complexion. Those DNA changes gave them a light complexion needed to better absorb solar radiation, and the clothing made it possible to maintain heat within their bodies. They adapted to their surroundings, so they survived. Biology, physics, and chemistry, pure and simple.

Sharon: And what happened to the thousands and possibly millions of Neanderthals, why did they become extinct?

Aitor: The scientific community still does not know exactly the causes of their extinction. Some scientists believe that some of the Neanderthals mixed with individuals and families of Homo Sapiens Sapiens as these were coming out of Africa. Still other scientists believe that they got into a slow process of extinction, but do not know the causes of that process.

Sharon: Maybe these last two groups of hominids eventually learned to live together and they intermarried. When does the Homo Sapiens Sapiens first appear in the map?

Aitor: Palaeontologists say that 40.000-60.000 years ago they left Africa and began to spread throughout the continents.

Sharon: Really? That recently?

Aitor: Yes, that recently, relatively speaking. We must remember, as we said earlier, that it all began with a few dozen families of Homo Sapiens Sapiens crossing the "pond" from Africa to Saudi Arabia and then to the European continent.

Sharon: It must have been a very risky and dangerous venture, but at the same time very interesting, among other things, I'm thinking.

Aitor: What do you mean?

Sharon: Well, I'm trying to visualize that very first time, 40,000 years ago, in some place in Europe, when the Homo Sapiens Sapiens with black skin and black curly hair met their "cousins", the Neanderthals with white skin and red hair. Did their jaws "fall to the ground", got scared, and ran away from each other, of did they meet and had a big feast together to celebrate the occasion? Did we throw arrows at each other, or did we welcome each other and celebrated with a big feast?

Aitor: I get it! It must have been a big surprise on both sides! So, do I stop by with my car to pick you up this Saturday morning, say 10 o'clock, to drive and get to Atapuerca?

Sharon: *It sounds great to me!*

We have begun a voyage of discovery. To look at the scientific discoveries of the last 20-30 years in a number of areas, an analysis of each one in terms of specific criteria, the results, and then to conduct a synthesis of the types of knowledge and evidence found in those results. The language and culture of a group of human beings is part of the multi-dimensional composition of such group, I propose. Therefore, the development and evolution of those two components has a direct effect on the success, or luck of it, of the group's evolution. Why do some groups evolve successfully while other groups dwindle and eventually disappear, either because they lose their language, their culture, identity, or simply become extinct for a variety of reasons?

We examine the evolutionary trajectory of the hominids, the most recent group of hominids, **Homo Sapiens Sapiens**. What factors determined that one class of hominids would out live another class of hominids?

The beginnings of our capacity to speak, to learn and use a language. Did it happen 10,000 years ago, 20,000 years ago, or 5 million years ago?

To become aware and realize that *all human races* in the planet belong to the same class of hominids, the Homo Sapiens Sapiens, and that this class of hominids originated in *Africa*, mother Africa, from the north-eastern part of Africa, specifically from the Ethiopia regions, as the latest scientific discoveries point to. We Basques do no come from place A in the planet, Galicians do not come from place B in the planet, Tibetans do not come from place C in the planet, Chinese do not come from place D in the planet, and so forth, and instead we all come from the same ancestors, from Africa.

To continue learning and understanding about the number of factors that influenced the successful evolution of humans. Was it physical strength? Was it intelligence? Was it the complexity of some social models over other social models?

The Time Scale of the Evolution

A quick look at the timeline of evolution of the Earth, our own planet, and that of all the species, as shown on *Table 1*, might help us begin to understand the fragility of our own species in the planet.

Table 1. Timeline of Human Evolution

*Millions
of Years Ago:*   *Event:*

5000	The Earth is created (Big-bang theory).
4500	By then the surface of the Earth has cooled down, mostly.
4500-3800	**Hadean** period. Life begins at sea.
3800-2500	**Archean** period. Beginning of photosynthesis process.
2500- 600	**Proterozoic** period. Abundance of oxygen in the atmosphere.
540- 490	**Cambrian** period. "Pikaia", first "fish" with a spinal chord, the origin of all mammals
299- 200	95% of all species disappear.
200- 150	**Jurasic** period. Both "cold-blooded" and "warm-blooded" animals begin, first brids, first plants with flowers.
299- 200	95% de las especies desaparecen.
5-7	*Homo Ergaster,* common ancestro of all homo species and chimpancés.
0.3	*Neanderthals* our of Africa, into Europe and Asia (300,000 years ago).
0.04-0.6	*Homo Sapiens Sapiens* out of Africa (40,000-60,000 years ago). Families of this Group spread over the five continents. All human races in the planet today belong to this group.

*Thousands
of Years
In the Future:*   *Event:*

¿? - ¿?	Extinction of *Homo Sapiens Sapiens.*

How long ago? The Earth formed 4,500 million years ago, according to the "big-bang" theory. Yes, a very long time ago, it's nearly impossible to consider the magnitude of such long period of time. A big ball of fire rotating around the sun in our galaxy. Then, during the next 500 million years the Earth continued to cool down, the surface continued to cool down only, that is. Some time "shortly", 4,500-3,800 million years ago, during the Hadean period, *life began at sea*. Another 1,300 million years had to go by for the photosynthesis process to come into place, replacing carbon dioxide with oxygen. The abundance of oxygen in the planet made it possible for a rich variety of life to evolve on earth and under the seas. The *"pikaia"* shows up, the first "fish" with *a spinal chord*, the primal ancestor of all mammals in the planet. Next, between 5 and 7 million years ago, the hominid *Homo Ergaster* appears, and becomes the common ancestor to all hominids, as shown on **Table 1** and **Figure 2**. *Homo Erectus*, a branch of Homo Ergaster, moves out of Africa and spreads throughout East Asia and Australia during the 1.4 million years, to become extinct only in modern times. A second branch, the Homo *Neanderthals* leaves Africa about 300,000 years ago and spreads throughout parts of western Europe and Asia and, again, becomes extinct in modern times, only 30,000-20,000 years ago. Still a third branch, that of *Homo Sapiens*, had prospered in Africa during the last 400,000 years, and only 50,000 years ago left Africa, initially reached Europe and the Middle East, and eventually managed to populate all the five continents. Today, all human races belong to that third branch, now called the *Homo Sapiens Sapiens* group.

Observing that the appearance and existence of modern man, Homo Sapiens Sapiens, is but a mere point in the scale of time and evolution of our planet and, realizing how numerous have been and how quickly materialize new socio-political conflicts with catastrophic potential in the last 2,000 years, it is tempting to think that our extinction awaits in the near future. In the next 1,000 years? In the next 5,000 years? In the next 20,000 years? The way we are going about it right now, the extinction date would be somewhere in that range, I would venture to say. We are not having much success in putting together better social, cultural, economic, and political models capable of anticipating and avoiding catastrophic events worldwide, some of us would say. In which case, what species would be next in reaching and claiming hegemony, supremacy in the planet. The insects? The cockroaches? The Tibetan Rabbit?

The Evolution of the Species in the Planet

The ancestors of the modern primates, our "cousins", were small and ate insects: lemurs and adapids, predominantly, as shown on **Figure 1** in the context of the last 100 million years.[5]

Boyd and **Silk (2003)** share with us part of their understanding of the circumstances in the planet during those last 100 Million years:

"In order to understand the evolutionary forces that influenced the development of the first primates we need to consider two ítems. First, what types of animals existed at the time upon which natural selection would operate? Second, what type of animal would most likely succeed in its evolution?...The plesiadapiforms varied in size, from very small and looking like a shrew, to larger animals like a marmot, and although most of these species are known today due to their teeth, they were very likely four-legged, solitary, and nocturnal...The *Eocene period* (some 55-35 million years ago) was more humid and hotter that the preceding Pelocen period, with large tropical forests covering much of the planet... In those Eocenic primates we can see for the first time characteristics of modern primates... The oldest hominoids were members of the Precunsal gender. That gender includes five species that go from the size of a macaque (10 kgs.), to the size of an obo monkey (38 kgs.). The oldest fossils found in Losidok, north of Kenya, go back 27 million years, while other fossils found in Africa date back to times as recent as 17 million years ago." [5]

Do we humans come from different places in the planet, and from different morphologic models? Again, scientific discoveries in the last 30 years tell us the following:

"A dramatic change in the morphology of the hominids took place during the glacial period. Some 100,000 years ago the globe was inhabited by a collection of hominids morphologically similar: Neanderthals in Europe, other robust hominids in east Asia, and humans a bit more modern in the Middle East... ***30 years ago*** a majority of paleoanthropologists would have given the same answer: the robust hominids from the end of the Superior Pleistocene were part of the same species (Homo sapiens archaic), from which gradually evolved the modern morphology that we have in the planet today.

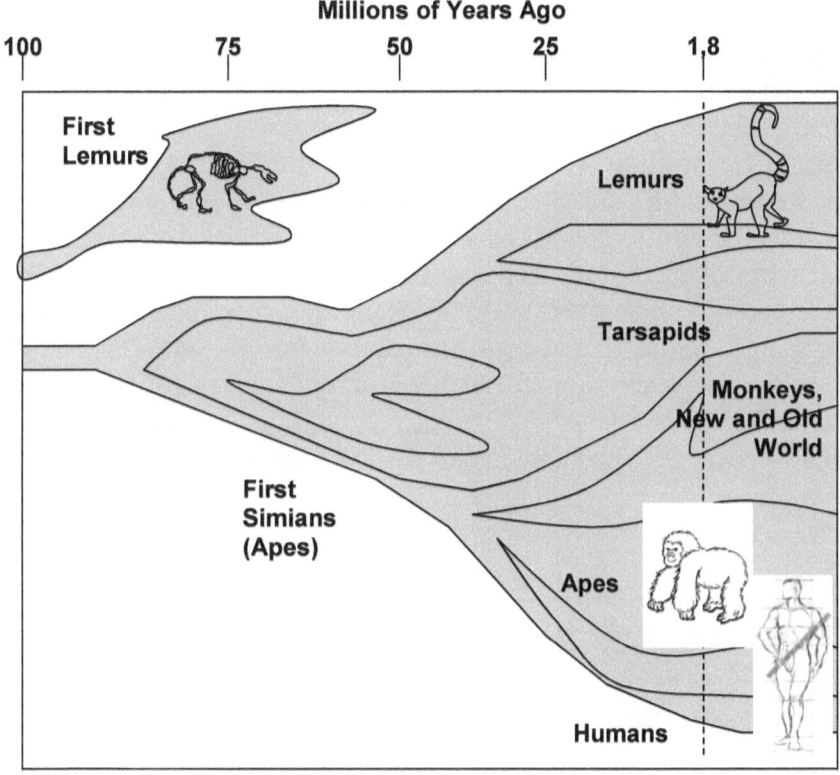

Figure 1. Evolution of the Species in the Planet. [5]

That idea was baptized with the name of ***multi-regional hypothesis***... The ***new evidence***, however, point to genes from an African population between 200,000 and 100,000 years ago that gave shape to the modern morphology. The individuals that carried these genes later spread all over Africa, giving birth to a large number of populations with modern morphology but genetically diverse. Then, some 50,000 years ago, ***a few individuals from one*** *of those populations* left Africa and spread all over the globe, replacing the other populations of hominids with relatively little genetic content in them... A great deal of the information comes from the genes that reside inside the ***mitochondria***...genes that are *inherited via the females* only."[6]

A rich genetic variety in the Homo Sapiens Sapiens that originated from one population in Africa some 50,000 ago, as illustrated in **Figure 2.** We summarize then, saying that the hominid group called ***Homo Ergaster*** originated in Africa 1.8 million years ago, and spread to several regions in that continent and the Middle East. Next, a genetic variety of that group, the ***Homo Erectus***, left Africa 1.6 million years and extended throughout Asia and the Australian continent. Another branch of the Homo Ergaster gives birth to the Homo Neanderthal that leaves Africa and enters Europe and parts of Euro-Asia some 400,000-350,000 years ago, and goes on to live up until 30,000-40,000 years ago, very recently, relatively speaking. Interesting and fortunately for us all, the modern hominids, another branch of the Homo Ergaster by the name of Homo Sapiens Sapiens also spreads throughout Africa, leaves Africa 50,000 years ago, and spreads all over the planet.

One more time. All races in the planet originated with Homo Sapiens Sapiens, that group of hominids made up of a few dozens of families that left Africa (area of Ethiopia) 50,000 years ago, spreading and reaching all five continents. Yes, Greeks, Tibetans, Galicians, Germans, Catalans, Russians, Native Americans,

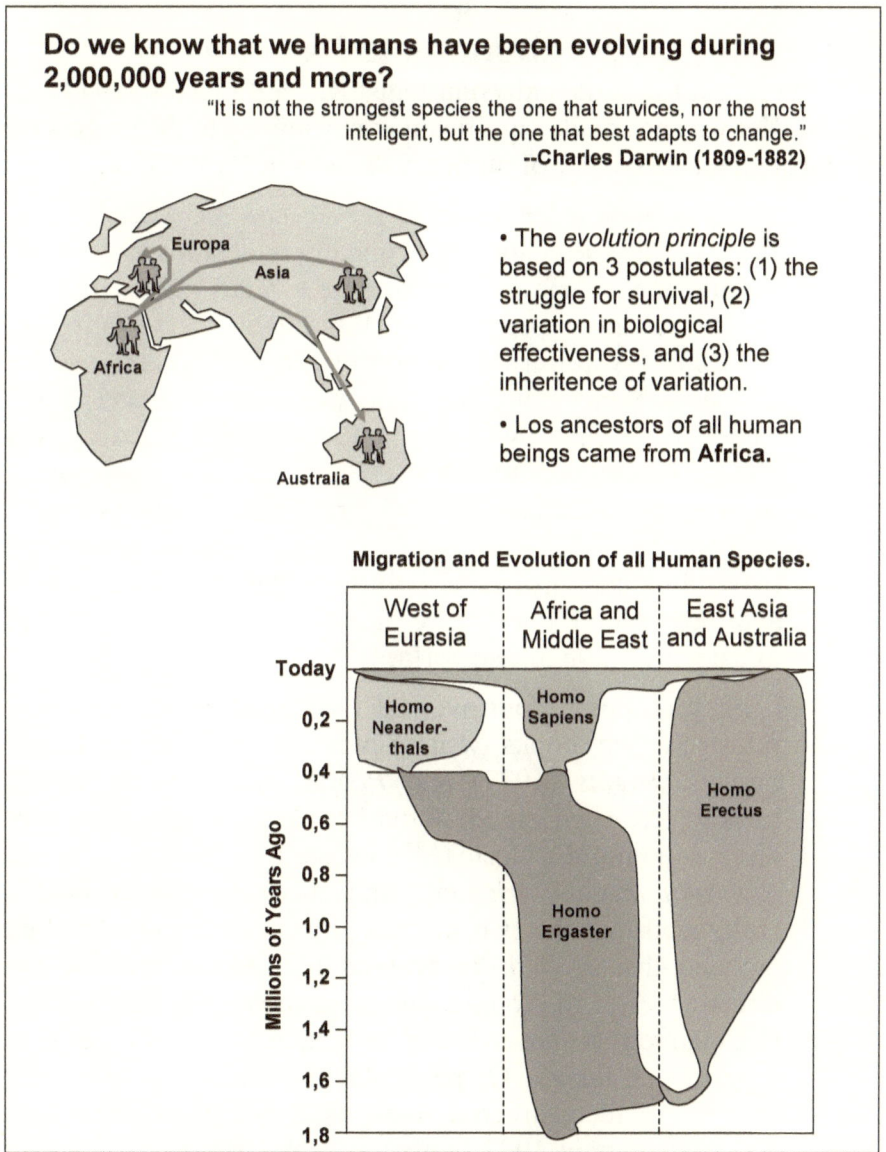

Figure 2. Migration of the Hominids out of Africa.

Basques, Rumanians, Jews, Spaniards, Irish, Palestinians, Moais… all. We all have our roots in Africa, we all come from Africa. *Our ancestors were all of dark skin, with black and curly hair. Let us review our beliefs and perspectives in order to reflect this incredible and marvellous scientific reality.*

Leakey's contributions to Palaeontology

In recent times the palaeontologist Richard Leakey (1944, Nairobi, Kenya-) has made significant contributions to the origins of man through his discovery of numerous fossils in East Africa:

> The son of noted anthropologists Louis S.B. Leakey and Mary Leakey, Richard was originally reluctant to follow his parents' career and instead became a safari guide. In 1967 he joined an expedition to the Omo River valley in *Ethiopia*. It was during this trip that he first noticed the site of Koobi Fora, along the shores of Lake Turkana (Lake Rudolf) in Kenya, where he led a preliminary search that uncovered several stone tools. From this site alone in the subsequent decade, Leakey and his fellow workers uncovered some 400 *hominid fossils* representing perhaps 230 individuals, making Koobi Fora the site of the richest and most varied assemblage of early human remains found to date anywhere in the world.

> Leakey proposed controversial interpretations of his fossil finds. In two books written with science writer Roger Lewin, *Origins* (1977) and *People of the Lake* (1978), Leakey presented his view that, some 3 million years ago, three hominid forms coexisted: *Homo habilis*, *Australopithecus africanus*, and *Australopithecus boisei*. He argued that the two australopith forms eventually died out and that *H. habilis* evolved into *Homo erectus*, the direct ancestor of *Homo sapiens*, or modern human beings. He claimed to have found evidence at Koobi Fora to support this theory. Of particular importance is an almost completely reconstructed fossil skull found in more than 300 fragments in 1972 (coded as KNM-ER 1470). Leakey believed that the skull represented *H. habilis* and that this

relatively large-brained, upright, bipedal form of *Homo* lived in eastern Africa as early as 2.5 million or even 3.5 million years ago. Further elaboration of Leakey's views was given in his work *The Making of Mankind* (1981).

From 1968 to 1989 Leakey was director of the National Museums of Kenya. In 1989 he was made director of the Wildlife Conservation and Management Department (the precursor to the Kenya Wildlife Service [KWS]). Devoted to the preservation of Kenya's wildlife and sanctuaries, he embarked on a campaign to reduce corruption within the KWS, crack down (often using force) on ivory poachers, and restore the security of Kenya's national parks. In doing so he made numerous enemies. In 1993 he survived a plane crash in which he lost both his legs below the knee. The following year he resigned his post at the KWS, citing interference by Kenyan President Daniel in the Moi's government, and became a founding member of the opposition political party Safina (Swahili for "Noah's ark"). Pressure by foreign donors led to Leakey's brief return to the KWS (1998–99) and to a short stint as secretary to the cabinet (1999–2001). Thereafter he dedicated himself to lecturing and writing on the conservation of wildlife and the environment. Another book with Roger Lewin was *The Sixth Extinction: Patterns of Life and the Future of Humankind* (1995), in which he argued that human beings have been responsible for a catastrophic reduction in the number of plant and animal species living on the Earth. Leakey later collaborated with Virginia Morell to write his second memoir, *Wildlife Wars: My Fight to Save Africa's Natural Treasures* (2001; his first memoir, *One Life*, was written in 1983). In 2004 Leakey founded Wildlife Direct, an Internet-based nonprofit conservation organization designed to disseminate information about endangered species and to connect donors to conservation efforts. He also served in 2007 as interim chair of the Kenya branch of Transparency International, a global coalition against corruption.

Leakey's wife, zoologist Meave Leakey (née Epps), conducted numerous paleoanthropological projects in the Turkana region, often in collaboration with their daughter Louise (b. 1972). In 1998 her team discovered fossil remains, more than three million years old, of a hominid that she named *Kenyanthropus platyops*. [10]

When and How Language Evolved

We already mentioned the world-famous linguist **Noam Chomsky (2012)**, who is of the opinion that language first occurred with humans 60,000 years ago, in Africa. The debate over the "when and how" about the origin of language continues today, though. All the experts coincide, however, in that language plays a crucial role in human ecology and in social behaviour. This plurality of opinions also coincides in the belief that there two main factor in the development of language: (1) de development of the larynx, and (2) the development of the brain crating cognitive capacities:

- The morphology of the human throat is different from that of the other primates.[7] The larynx and the vocal chords in humans are located in a lower position, something that improves our ability to produce a greater range of sounds. The size and shape of the tongue, and those of the chambers of the throat and mouth enable us to utter that great variety of sounds

- The grammar rules allow us to make critical and useful distinctions in those sounds. We know, for example, that many languages share some grammar rules that allow its speakers to communicate in effective and intelligible ways. Now, the order of words in a sentence also distinguishes one language from others. The "nominal syntagm" and the "verbal syntagm" of Euskera (a Pre-Indo-European language), for example, is different from its equivalents in the Indo-European languages, for example.

- The processing of language is centered in the human brain. Studies have shown that "language processing is concentrated within the left hemisphere of the brain, in the **Perisilvian Region**, in reference to its proximity to the *fissure of Silvio.* [8]

Diversity in the Planet

Languages represent an important and crucial dimension in achieving diversity in the planet, a diversity necessary towards achieving continuity of life in our planet. Such is the case with Euskera –as with every language in the planet-- a language that contributes to the goal of achieving continuity of life in our planet. This statement, I propose, has *scientific validity and value*, and it is not based on any political ideology whatsoever. Every language influences the way of thinking of each person, of his/her group and community, the alternate ways of thinking and contemplating the universe and its possibilities.

Thought and Knowledge Synthesis

We have carried out a brief review of the scientific discoveries of the last 30-40 years, particularly in the area of palaeontology, and now we can present a list of observations:

- All human races in the planet today are part of the **Homo Sapiens-Sapiens**, the last group of hominids that left **Africa** 40,000-60,000 years ago, a very short time ago in the scale of human evolution. Americans, Basques, Chinese, Catalans, Marrocans, Tibetans, Spanish, Russians, Algerians, Maoris, Eskimos, etc., we all belong to that group, we all are individuals with the same genetic content, basically, no one with significant physiological advantage over other individuals.

- "It is not the strongest species that survives, not the most intelligent, but *the one that adapts better to change*", as Charles Darwin noted. Said in other words, being strong and intelligent is a necessary condition for a group of humans but not a sufficient condition to insure survival.

- What is the relationship between *complexity* and *success* in the survival of a language? Is it a unique relationship or does

161

it have its own peculiar twists? We are aware of the complexity of some languages in some civilizations characterized by "a rudimentary technology or social organization. It has been commented that the languages of some groups with simple technology (ex., some languages of Native Americans, other) often have **expressions and representations more complex** than those in European languages.

- The human fossil discoveries of Richard Leakey and other palaeontologists have provided empirical, scientific evidence on the origins of man in **East Africa**, going back 2.5 million years. So much for divine creation, it does not exist. The human species is but one humble animal species, a speck of dust in the Universe.

✱✱✱

Chapter
14

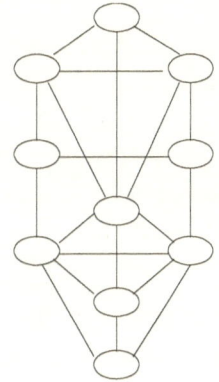

*"The Vatican needs **several hundred million dollars per year** to operate. Its many financial responsibilities include running international embassies, paying for the pope's travels around the world, maintaining ancient cathedrals, and donating considerable resources to schools, churches, and health care centers. So where does that money come from?*

--10 Secrets of the Vatican exposed.[1]

Inside the Secret Archives

It is the first Friday in the month of June, the day scheduled for the entry into the *Secret Archives* of the Vatican. The persons involved in this project have gathered in Father Donovan's room in Hotel Foro Romano. Such day was selected at the last meeting attended by some members of the Vatican Eagles group, the Circle of Wise Women, Kathy, and Xabier in the belief that it would be a very busy day at the Archives, with last-minute requests for documents by researches and the general public. Such a busy day would provide the opportunity to try such a difficult mission, or so was the hope of the planners.

-The day has arrived, *D-Day is here*, ladies and gentlemen – *Father Donovan* opened the morning meeting with these words – We have done the planning, we have gathered the people resources needed, and we have done repeated simulations of the entry into the Secret Archives and of our search for the desired documents. By now we all know each other in this project, the functions to be conducted by each person, the equipment to carry, and the protocol to follow in the event of unexpected happenings or activities.

-Any unscheduled activities or events in the last few days? – It was **Xabier** bringing up the question – Any changes in the itineraries of the Swiss guards, for example?

-I'm glad you bring up such a question, Xabier –Replied Father Donovan – I was going to alert us to the fact that Cardinal Reggio Boccasini, the main administrator of the Archives, has not been in his office in the last few days, so we were not able to talk with him, it just happened that way. It was not possible for us to **blackmail** him for his supposed pedophile activities, as he is currently doing a tour of some places in Jerusalem... some new scriptures are coming out in the Holy Land, it appears. So, that plan is out, unfortunately.

-Does that mean the team has made contact with the new administrator, and if so what are the changes to our planning? – Asked Xabier, anticipating a list of last-minute changes.

-What it means is that we are proceeding with **Plan B**, in which Sister Emily's team comes into play. That's right, Plan B will now be exercised to facilitate the entry into the Archives, everything else remains the same... three teams to enter the archives, sequence of places to look into, exit plan... Everything else remains the same. –Assured Father Donovan, using his extended arms to emphasize his words.

-We are ready – Said Sister **Emily Connelly** – We are ready and, as we have simulated repeatedly, myself and **Sister Constanza Altuna** will be dressed as nuns, while **Sister Esperanza Carlson** will be dressed as a student being the younger of the three of us. She will have to look attractive and seductive, of course. When the time comes, Sister Esperanza will faint and fall into the floor in the study room so that the archivist person will come to her rescue, thus providing the opportunity for our other three teams to enter the labyrinth of elevators and doors guided by Sister Constanza. As you may recall, Sister Constanza used to work in the Secret Archives before she joined our Circle.

Kathy has been waiting for the number of relevant questions to be asked, and feels it is now her turn.

-Is there a person in each of the three teams with knowledge of written *Aramaic* and *Latin*? I know we have talked about this requirement before, so it is just to make sure, one more time. The more fortunate ones are Xabier and I, as we only have to take photographs of the documents.

-Yes, Kathy, as a matter of fact, yes. We also talked about this item at the last meeting, and that was a major condition for being part of a team. One is the expert in Aramaic and Latin, and the other person is the photographer with his/her mini camera.

Father Donovan looked around to see if there were any more questions. He and everyone else in the room, for a total of nine people, knew about most of these questions and realized that some unexpected might happen events in this project.

-Well, then, you all know what to do. Be present and ready at the main study room of the Secret Archives this afternoon at 5:00 o'clock sharp. Go and find the *Gethsemane Codex*. You can do it! The Archives close at 6:00 PM.

That same afternoon the main study room is full of researchers, as many as 18 people, including Kathy, Xabier, the three Sisters, and the three teams.

-It's already 4:45PM… the archivist should be opening the door into the study room with the Inquisition documents, the agreement between the king of Spain and the Pope in the 16th Century… I'm getting a bit nervous –Said Xabier to Kathy.

-I know, I know. That request was made months ago, and again this morning we checked with the main archivist who said the documents would be brought into the study room at 5:00 PM, as indicated in the original request.

The minutes went by, it was 5:15PM, and the doors separating the study room from the entrance to the Secret Archives was not opening. Kathy, Xabier, and Emily were looking at each other at one on the tables in the study room, with frustration in their eyes, when a slight noise was heard and the doors opened. Two archivists, not one, showed up carrying documents. One of the archivists spoke saying softly: *"Emily Connelly, please!"*

-Two men archivists… only one archivist was supposed to come into the room! –Said Xabier to Kathy, visibly alarmed.

-Nothing to it, Xabier, we can handle it, relax and let us go ahead with the plan.

Sisters Emily and Constanza dressed in white habits and wearing glasses advanced, while Sister Esperanza, dressed as a student with an open neckline and showing cleavage, advanced too.

Our two nuns extended their arms to receive the documents while Sister Emily was saying: *"This is a great day for our student Esperanza who will now be able to prepare her Master's thesis on the Inquisition in Spain… At least that part of the story where…*

At that moment Esperanza let go an ***"Ohhh"***, and she began to fall to the floor. One of the archivists bent to try to help Esperanza, while the other archivist remained standing, still holding on to a second package of documents.

Sister Emily also rushed to the floor and while pretending to listen to Sister Esperanza's breathing, she whispered to her: *"Shake slightly your feet and show some of your thighs!"*

As soon as Sister Esperanza, dressed as an attractive student, began to show her long and beautiful thighs the second archivist bent down also trying to help. Right about then is when the three teams went through the doors leading into the Secret Archives followed by Sister Constanza. The two male archivists were now busy trying to help Sister Esperanza recover and, in fact, one of them was administering mouth-to-mouth respiration to the beautiful yet unconscious student.

The three teams are now ***inside the Secret Archives.***

-Follow me – Asked Sister Constanza – We are going down three floors in this elevator, the bottom floor, and we'll wait there until they close the archives for the night, OK?

A few minutes later the tree teams plus Sister Constanza arrived at the bottom floor.

-Please this way, follow me to the janitor's room, where I suggest we remain for the next hour until personnel has completed its shift for the day. Next, we will leave this room to begin our inspection of the wardrobes…Another thing, after 6:00 PM they shut down the air flow system, that is the fans in another part of the Vatican stop and cease pushing fresh air through the vents in the Secret Archives. No problem, we may feel a bit cloistered but there will be plenty of oxygen to breath all through the night as we do our search work.

-OK, we are all inside the janitor's room, we are safe.

-Do we begin our search on this floor, or on the first floor? – Asked **Brother Luis Mendes** in one of the teams.

-We begin our search on this third floor, as the oldest documents are here, and the centuries advance we move to the 2nd and 3rd floors, in theory. Through the centuries the Vatican has moved and rearranged documents according to different criteria, political pressures, and safety measures, but most of the early documents should be on this bottom floor, I believe. Most important, each team to set up your **GPS** so that this point, the janitor's room, is your point of reference. Most important, please do it now.

-When to take photos and when not to, how do you advice? – Asked Kathy, hoping Sister Constanza would have a recommendation.

-Shoot, shoot and shoot! I would say. That is, better to take too many photos than too few. Whenever you find a document that you believe relates to those four categories, start shooting. Also, always take photos of three or more consecutive pages, so that we later have enough text to figure out what the subject is. With your mini digital cameras and the extra memory cards that we all carry there should no limit to the number of photos we can take in nine hours, really.

-Forgive me –Said Brother Luis Mendes – but could we go over those four categories, just one more time, please?

-No problem – Replied quickly Sister Constanza – Number one are the Gethsemane gospels, either in Aramaic or Latin; number two, any agreements between the three religions, Judaism, Christianity, and Islam, most likely in Latin; number three, Inquisition papers with agreements between the Vatican and the

Spanish monarchy in the last four centuries, either in Spanish or Latin; and number four, any agreements, concordats, and documents between Pope Pius XII and the dictators Mussolini, Hitler, and Franco. Four categories to remember and look into and not any other.

-Got it!

-And if we find something very important, out of those four categories, can we still take a few minutes to photograph such document? –Yes, it was Kathy asking such question.

-Only if it is very exceptional, and that we can justify later. Time is of essence here.

-It's already 6:30 PM, we better get moving… First team with Brother Luis to go through this first corridor, wardrobes only. Second team with Kathy goes through the second corridor, and again wardrobes only. And third team with Xabier goes through the third corridor, again wardrobes only. We will meet here again in two hours, no excuses, please. I will stay with Kathy's team.

Accordingly, the first team started opening boxes and folders on the *Vatican Registries*, a section of some twelve wardrobes, containing documents of *Inocencio III, 13th and 14th centuries*. There was always the possibility that the Gethsemane papers had been stored in other later boxes. No such box reading Gethsemane Codex was expected to be found, and if those gospels existed they had to be stored in other boxes.

The second team went on to look into the *Avignon Registries* which include some 355 volumes related to the popes in Avignon, up until 1415. Letters and agreements by Clemente V and Juan XXII, both on paper and pergamino.

Next, the third team went on to look into the *Pleas Registry* ("Suplicas" registry) with some 7,400 volumes which began with Pope Clemente VI in the 14th Century, all the way up to Leon XIII. Pleas and requests by the people to the popes on a variety of subjects.

-Quiet, please –Said Sister Constanza to the two men in her team – I can hear one of the guards, probably a Swiss Guard, walking nearby. Quick get close to the wall and open that fuse box next to the wall.

Sure enough, one of the guards was just making his last round before closing the archives for the night. As he got close to the hall next to the walls of the building, he looked left and he saw Sister Constanza and the two men at the end of the hall. He made a left turn and started walking towards them.

-Just keep looking at the fuse box on the wall, pretend you are working. Everything will be OK. –She said, maintaining her own calm as best as she could.

-What are you doing here? -- Said the Swiss Guard, as he stayed a few steps away from the team and beginning to notice that it was a woman and two men.

-Oh, you did not know? Nobody told you? –Said Sister Constanza.

-Know what? What are you three doing here?

-They are almost finished. It's the **air conditioning repair team**, and I am responsible for their coming in and going out. I'm Sister Constanza, by-the-way, and they will be done in a few more minutes, I hope. Are you guys done checking the fuse box?

-Only a few more minutes, Sister. Still need to check out six more circuits, but we should be done very soon. We all want to call it a day, and go home, really.

-OK. All right, Sister, it's your responsibility. Please get these people out of the archives within the next few minutes; I still have to complete my round on this floor level.

-No problem. Thank you for stopping by. –Said Sister Constanza as she saw the Swiss Guard turn around to continue with his inspection walk. That was a close call, for sure.

Total silence along those corridors, lighted only by the small emergency red lights on the walls. With small camping white lights attached to their foreheads and the digital mini cameras the three teams worked during the next two hours.

-How was it with you guys? Were you able to inspect those wardrobes in those four categories? -- Asked Sister Constanza.

-The two of us managed to inspect all the Avignon Registries and probably took some 200-250 photos, mostly on re-structuring the Church and some early papers on the coming of the Holy Inquisition, but not totally sure. The more one reads the various pages the fewer the number of documents to inspect.

-Yes, that's a major consideration, and we need to do both, cover as many documents as possible and take photos of each sheet to be read and interpreted in our laboratory later.

During the next six hours the three teams managed to inspect and photograph documents on the three corridors. Nearly exhausted, the three teams returned to the janitor's room to carry out their exit from the Secret Archives.

-As we talked about during the rehearsal meetings, our exit is going have to take place through the *ventilation system* connecting the first floor and one of the halls adjacent to the main study room. There is another janitor's room in that hall, and that is where we will gather and wait until 8:30 AM when the visitors are allowed to come in on their way to the main study room.

The three teams take the elevator on their way to the first floor of the Secret Archives complex.

-I'm going to ask Xabier and his team to be first in crawling through the ventilation system, those 20-30 feet to get to the hall wall, just in case they find a screen they may need to remove half way through. –Said Sister Costanza looking at Xabier. –So, when the two of you are ready please go ahead. Also, please remember to press the red button on your GPS system to indicate that you have arrived and are waiting at the janitor's room, very important. The rest of us will then hear a beep in our GPS systems.

Xabier and his team mate easily removed the initial window screen and proceeded to enter the ventilation system. Xabier went in first. Fifteen minutes went by, twenty minutes. Sister Constanza and the other team members looked at each other worried.

Beep!

-Great they have made it through the ventilation system! Next team, please. Brother Luis and I will be last to make sure we place back in this first window grid —Said Sister Constanza, as she gestured for the other three team members to crawl into the ventilation system.

One hour later the first two teams had made it through the ventilation system, so Xabier and the other four team members waited for Brother Luis and Sister Constanza to arrive shortly.

Xabier and Kathy thought it was a bit peculiar that Sister Constanza had suggested that she and Brother Luis be the last ones to go through the ventilation system, but nothing else. Sister Constanza of the Circle of Wise Women did not want to leave behind any trace or suspicion of entry into the Secret Archives, they thought.

Fifteen more minutes went by. Another twenty minutes went by, and still no trace of Brother Luis and Sister Constanza. Xabier pressed the red button in his GPS, one more time. Finally, fifteen more minutes later both Sister Constanza and Brother Luis showed up. "*Yeah, we all made it through*!" someone said in a low voice. Everyone started hugging each other, five hugs for each team member.

Surprise. As Kathy embraced Brother Luis she felt she was embracing Sister Constanza again, as a slight aroma of fresh flowers was all around Brother Luis. Next, Kathy embraced Xabier and whispered in his right ear: "*Were those two, Brother Luis and Sister Constanza, having sex inside the Secret Archives while the rest of us were waiting?* And, still holding the embrace Xabier added: "*Well, someone had to be first in the Archives, the suspense, the danger, and the opportunity were there, right?*"

An hour later they could hear the first visitors walk through the hall, just outside their door, and they realized the time had arrived to mix with those visitors on their way out of the *Vatican's Secret Archives.* A day to remember.

✳✳✳

Chapter

15

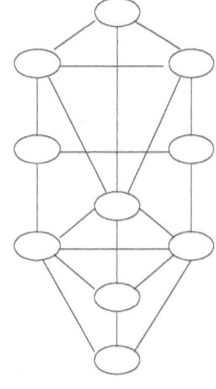

*"In the church's official annals, **Pius XII**, who died in 1958, is painted as a saintly shepherd who led his flock with great moral courage in difficult times. For many scholars, though, he is at worst the Devil incarnate, "**Hitler's Pope**", and at best a coward who refused to speak out against the extermination of Jews, gypsies and homosexuals in gas chambers, even when he had compelling evidence that it was happening, lest his words attract Nazi aggression.*

-- Religion, Rome and The Reich: The Vatican's other dirty secret.[1]

The Findings, Please

Three months have gone by since the three teams managed to get inside the *Vatican´s Secret Archives* in an effort to gather information useful to the newly created *Council for World Peace (CWP)*. Such time was required to process the thousands of photographs taken of hundreds of documents inspected by those three teams, their translation from Aramaic, Latin, 16th century Spanish, and Greek into English, by now the international language at the CWP and other collaborating organizations. During all that time Kathy, Xabier, and Dr. Finley have been in Tucson, Arizona, where the analysis of the documents was taking place. Some findings are beginning to emerge.

-Yes, I wanted the three of us to meet today because some findings are beginning to emerge, I'm happy to say. –Communicated Dr. Finley.

-Great! It has been difficult for everyone these last three months waiting for our laboratory people to go through thousands of pages from those Vatican manuscripts, their translation into English, figuring out the century when they were written, their dates, its authors, and contents. –Said Kathy, still with her arms up in the air and showing a big smile.

-Have you notified Father Donovan of the Vatican Eagles group about these findings? –Asked Xabier, showing some concern.

-No, not yet. There is still plenty of organization and cataloguing to do, but we will be able to get in touch with him a few short weeks, I believe.

-OK, so what are the findings, what things are coming out of those Vatican papers?

-Well, there are at least 30 topics, not just those 4 topics that we all set out to learn about, something we had anticipated, but the findings are beyond our expectations, really. The four topics being, as you recall: (1) the Gethsemane Codex, (2) agreements between the three religions, Judaism, Christianity, and Islam, (3) the Inquisition papers with agreements between the Vatican and the Spanish monarchy in the last four centuries, and (4) agreements and documents between Pope Pius XII and the dictators Mussolini, Hitler, and Franco. Which one would you like to hear about first?

-The Gethsemane Codex, of course. –Both Kathy and Xabier said at the same time.

-Got it. Well, we all have been very lucky that such gospel of 9 pages was located during that search in the Secret Archives, really, and not once but 5 times during that search. It appears that that gospel dating back to the 1st Century captured the attention of the early Christians, or some of the early Christians, and they ended up copying it several times, century after century. Not only that, but some of those copies ended up in different boxes so that…

-Yes, Dr. Finley, we understand now, but what are the contents, the findings, what does that gospel say? –It was Xabier asking and rushing into such question, with Kathy asserting with her head.

-Ohh, sorry, I got carried away…Some of the voices that participated in the Gethsemane Codex say that the creator, someone identified with the name of "Jesus", intended to have two Churches, one church for men, and another church for women. That within the church for men there would be a hierarchy of priests with several levels, according to their rank in the society; likewise, within the church for women there would be a hierarchy for women, identical in structure and value to that for men. No mention of bishops, cardinals, or popes at all, but that such hierarchies would contain *five levels*, with the people at the first level, followed by the priests at the second level, and so on with people of recognized status at the following levels, and last, with someone at the highest level, level four, who would be able to communicate with the Saints and Christian martyrs, including the apostles.

-Well, that coincides with the contents of the two CDs which were mailed to Dr. Finley, right here, in our research team at the University of Arizona! –Said Kathy with noticeable excitement.

-And what happened at the highest level, level five?

-From what we can tell so far, that level belonged to a person who had moved along either one of the two hierarchies, and in particular someone who could communicate with God, the "Jesus" or "Jesus Christ" that is so often mentioned in that Codex. But there was one rule that both hierarchies had to obey, which said that such person would come from one hierarchy and that upon his or her death the next person would come from the other hierarchy. What we would call today a *"woman Pope"* followed by a *"man Pope"*, followed by a "woman Pope", and so forth. That codex represents the *"lost gospel of Gethsemane"*, basically. Such structure would have helped the cause of women within the Christian Church establishment all along those centuries, the equality of women and men within the church, something that would make Sister Emily Connelly happy when she sees our report in the next few weeks, I'm sure.

-So, why was that gospel not implemented? What do we know about groups of the Church in support of this Codex, as well as groups against it? –Kathy kept asking, hoping some of that information might be coming out.

-We do know now, as a result of the findings in this project, that a group by the name of *"Guards of the Secret Oath"* has existed for centuries, a group of men determined to maintain power within the Church under the control of men, and men only. Some members of this group belonged to rich families, while other members were already individuals within the Church's hierarchy. Time and time again this group surfaces in the documents.

Xabier had been listening to this dialogue. Finally, he decided to initiate a related topic.

-It has been centuries of rivalry for the control of power and influence among the three main religions, meaning Judaism, Christianity, and Islam. Have we been able to identify any documents that point to agreements, any agreements, among these three main religions?

-Yes, as a matter of fact, yes. Our findings show that back in the *Council of Vienne* (1311-1312) in Vienne there were early writings about a potential agreement between these three religions for several reasons. For one, each religion wanted to strengthen its control and influence over its own society on its own territory: The Catholics over European territory, the Jews over Palestine territories, and the Moslems over territories in the Middle East. The Jewish people would not get their own nation-state until 1947, but already had much presence and influence in towns and cities all over Europe, as we all know. Second, these three religions already knew too much about each other, the good and the bad, and there was a common interest in each of these three not to hear criticism and condemnation from the other two religions. And third, there was a belief that through unlimited procreation one religion could outnumber the other two, basically.

-OK, I can see how those three religions could think about "cooperation", if we can call it that, at the same time that they gained time to outsmart each other. But that was then in 14th century, so what happened later with the coming of the *Holy Inquisition* in the 15th century all over Europe where the Christian establishment is killing Jews and Moslems left and right?

-From what we can tell, and after analyzing many of the documents we found, not everyone was willing to follow that agreement of "concordance", and as the **newly-formed European states** got stronger they wanted greater political control. Political control? Yes, the European states used the many prejudices within the Church to put together the criminal institution of the Inquisition to go after internal political dissidents. In Spain, for example, the monarchs Ferdinand and Isabelle of Castile requested from **Pope Sixtus IV in 1478** to institute the Inquisition with the aim of fighting political dissidents and the influence of Protestant thinkers in the peninsula. The monarchy thus would ask the Inquisition powers to go after those dissidents charging them with "heresy", and once apprehended the political system killed them, basically. In 1610, for example, the Inquisition gather the women and men considered to be dissidents, dangerous for the political order imposed in the land, but once the Inquisition got those women and men to "confess" it passed them to the Logroño political a judicial system to arrest them and burned alive to death. Similarly in England, Germany, France, and other European Countries, the Inquisition did the persecution, and arrested political dissidents and, next, they passed those political dissidents also called "heretics" to the political and judicial establishment for their execution.

-So that agreement of "cooperation" between the three religions came to an end, right? –Asked Xabier.

-No, not really, I would say. As the Catholic Church started to lose power and control in the following centuries, it recaptured the idea of "cooperation". Such was the case with the **Vatican Council II** (1962-1965) where the Church promoted "*ecumenical progress towards reconciliation*" with other Christian churches, and with Judaism and Islam, as well. Just remember, on March 2000 **Pope John Paul II** visited the *Yad Vashen* (the Israeli national holocaust memorial) in *Israel*, and went on to meet with religious and political leaders in both *Egypt* and *Jordan*, Moslem countries. We have also gathered greater detail on the "*Concordats*", those agreements between **Pope Pius XII** and the dictators Hitler, Mussolini, and Franco on matters of money, concentration camps and the genocide of Jewish people, as well.

-And what do you make out of this information, out of these "*Vatican wiki-leaks*", Dr. Finley? –Asked Kathy.

-As I said earlier, much of the documentation obtained remains to be analyzed yet, but a number of matters of great concern are beginning to take shape, matters of great concern to all of us involved in the Council for World Peace (CWP). To begin with, the determination by all these three religions to go on with high procreation rates represents a major problem to global population control and management. The current posture of the Vatican against *abortion* has a powerful negative impact on population control. With our current 7,000 Million inhabitants today, and an estimated 9,000 Million in 2050, we have a major problem in our hands and those three major religions are not helping mitigate the problem. A matter of great concern to the CWP, as we have said.

-Yes, this game of those three religions of trying to outnumber each other is a major concern, agreed. Anything came out of the Vatican papers on those agreements with the dictators Hitler, Mussolini, Franco, and others?

-Very much so –Replied Dr. Finley – We already had copies of the *Concordats* between the Vatican and those dictators, but now we also have copies of correspondence between the Vatican and those dictators prior to the Concordats themselves, to understand better how the negotiations were taking place, what favors were offered by the Vatican in exchange for money sums and tax exemption privileges that those dictators and their states would pay to the Vatican.

-Hard to believe, but most people in most countries don't know, even today, that the Vatican had negotiated those terms with so many dictators in exchange for moneys and tax exemption privileges over the last 3-4 hundred years. –Said Kathy, raising her eyebrows.

Four hours of questions and answers had gone by already. It was time to take a break for lunch or continue, so Xabier thought he would try one more question.

-I realize we need to take a break for lunch, but one more question, if I may, Dr. Finley. Has anything surfaced in these documents regarding the *origin of the human species*, as documented by **Charles Darwin** (1809-1882) and others, and what has been the position of the Catholic Church regarding this issue?

-Yes and no. Our documents show dozens of letters by many of people in the hierarchy of the Church who attended the Vatican Council I (1869-1870) and the Vatican Council II (1962-1965), asking to review the Church's stand on this issue. Letters of response insisted on the Church's posture of divine intervention, of divine creation of man, of the divine creation of all human races, ignoring the 2.0 Million year trajectory of evolution of mankind from earlier mammals. Much was at stake on that issue, however. While the Church wanted people to believe that they were all created by a God, the Church also wanted the various ethnic groups to believe they originated at different places in the planet, to mistrust each other, and to stick close to the Church for protection and salvation. That has been historically the way the Church has maintained control of its masses. Stick close to your priest hierarchy, stay away from "infidels", they are dangerous, to be feared. This has been the case, however, with all religions, not just with Christianity –Dr. Finley added – which wish all ethnic groups divided, suspicious of each other, in order to have them fear each other, in order to keep them close to its own power structure within a religions and thus maintain power over the masses. The "supernatural" over the laws of the universe. All religions are aware of the increase in **Atheism** in modern times, but refuse to address it in a formal manner during their local and international councils. We get to see only letters by members of the hierarchies of those religions outside those councils. Many of us understand that all religions are an obstacle to the attainment of peace in the global community.

-Are we all to expect more surprises coming out of those Secret Archives documents in the weeks, months ahead? –Asked Kathy, hoping to hear a specified timeframe.

-Yes, very much so. Our laboratory teams are now busy translating and reviewing those documents. Hard to tell when we will have a full report to the CWP, but the hard work in going on, and it will be ready soon.

-Will the CWP identify the entry into the Secret Archives as the means of acquiring those documents, or will it identify the earlier two CDs received by our team from an unknown person in the Vatican as the source of those documents?

-Good question –Replied Dr. Finley – We have an option there, and we will be making a decision soon.

***

Chapter
16

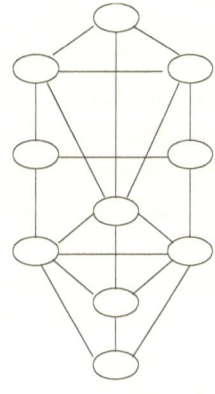

*"**Atheism** is more than just the knowledge that gods do not exist, and that religion is either a mistake or a fraud. Atheism is an attitude, a frame of mind that looks at the world objectively, fearlessly, always trying to understand all things as a part of nature."*
— **Emmett F. Fields**, American author (2014)[1]

"All thinking men are atheists."
— **Ernest Hemingway**, American author, *Farewell to Arms.*

"I cannot imagine a god that rewards and punishes objects of his creation, whose goals have been modeled by his own, a god that is only a reflection of human weakness; do not believe that people survive death, those are only ridiculous thoughts of fear or egoism."
--**Albert Einstein**, scientist.

Network of Atheist organizations

By now Kathy and Xabie are having second thoughts about the contributions of religions, if any, to the sustainability of life on Earth, a planet already at its limits at the beginning of the 21st Century. Could the absence of religion represent a cohesive force to bring together civilizations, cultures, and societies on the verge of collapse? *Atheism* is the rejection of the belief that a God or group of deities exist. Simple?

Indian Philosophy

In Indian philosophy, models of contemplative life that was not centered on deities began in the 6th century BC ("Before Christ"). Hinduism and Jainism are two such models.

Hinduism [Return]

Within this school of thought of Hindu philosophy the **Samkhya Karika** and the early **Mimansa** followings did not accept a creator-deity. They believed in a dual existence of Prakriti ("nature") and Puruscha ("spirit"), but there was no place for an Ishvara ("God") in their system, arguing that such entity cannot be proved to exist. The word *samkhya* means *empirical* or *relating to numbers*. The Samkhya system (4th century CE, "Christian Era") is called so because it enumerates' twenty five **Tattvas** or true principles, and its chief object is to effect the final emancipation of the twenty-fifth Tattva, i.e. the *Puruṣa* or soul.

> 67. *Through the attainment of perfect knowledge, virtue and the rest become devoid of their causal efficacy; yet, the Spirit continues to live for a while invested with the body, just like a potter's wheel continues to revolve (even when the potter ceases in his efforts at revolving the wheel) due to the momentum of the past impulse.* [3]

The entire Katika is full of convoluted, mystic text, with references to a long list of nature and spirit entities. **Atheistic** in nature, by contrast with Western schools of thought.

Jainism [Return]

Traditionally known as **Jain Shasan** or **Jain dharma** is an Indian religion that prescribes a path of *ahimsa*—nonviolence—towards all living beings, and emphasizes spiritual interdependence and equality between all forms of life. Practitioners believe that nonviolence and self-control are the means by which they can obtain liberation. *Asceticism* is thus a major focus of the Jain faith. The three main principles of Jainism are *Ahimsa* (Nonviolence), *Anekantavada* (Non-Absolutism) and *Aparigraha* (Non-

Possessiveness). Jainism is one of the oldest religions in the world. Jains traditionally trace their history through a succession of twenty-four propagators of their faith known as *tirthankaras* with *Rishabh* as the first and *Mahāvīra* as the last of the current era. Jainism is a religious minority in India, with 4.2 million adherents, and there are immigrant communities in Belgium, Canada, Hong Kong, Japan, Singapore, and the United States. The population of the Jain community across the world is around 6.1 million.[4]

> *I bow to the Arihants, the Conquerors,*
> *I bow to the Siddhas, the Liberated ones,*
> *I bow to the Acharyas, the Prececptors,*
> *I bow to the Upadhyays, the Teachers,*
> *I bow to all the Sages of the world,*
> *This five-fold salutation (mantra) destroys all the sins.*
> *And, of all auspicious mantras, it is indeed the foremost auspicious one.*[5]

Bowing to everyone, taking no risks, it appears. No "Gods", a religion, yes, but only as a way of living.

Buddhism [Return]

Four-hundred years before the birth of Jesus, sometime in the time period 420-380 BC, a man called *Siddhartha Gautama* was born in the town of *Lumbini*, in north-eastern *India*, today in *Nepal*. This man eventually would be known as the ***Buddha***.[4]

> ***Buddhism*** *is a non-theistic religion that encompasses a variety of traditions, beliefs and practices largely based on teachings attributed to* ***Siddhartha Gautama***, *who is commonly known as the* ***Buddha***, *meaning "the awakened one". According to Buddhist tradition, the Buddha lived and taught in the eastern part of the Indian subcontinent sometime between the 6th and 4th centuries BCE. He is recognized by Buddhists as an awakened or enlightened teacher who shared his insights to help human beings end their suffering through the elimination of ignorance and craving by way of understanding and the seeing of Dependent Origination*

and the Four Noble Truths, with the ultimate goal of attainment of the sublime state of Nirvana. Two major branches of Buddhism are generally recognized: **Theravada** *("The School of the Elders") and* **Mahayana** *("The Great Vehicle"). Theravada has a widespread following in Sri Lanka and Southeast Asia (Cambodia, Laos, Thailand, Myanmar etc.). Mahayana is found throughout East Asia (China, Korea, Japan, Vietnam, Singapore, Taiwan etc.) and includes the traditions of Pure Land, Zen, Nichiren Buddhism, Tibetan Buddhism, Shingon, and Tiantai (Tendai). In some classifications, Vajrayana—practiced mainly in Tibet and Mongolia, and adjacent parts of China and Russia—is recognized as a third branch, while others classify it as a part of Mahayana. While Buddhism is practiced primarily in Asia, both major branches are now found throughout the world. Estimates of Buddhists worldwide vary significantly depending on the way Buddhist adherence is defined. Estimates range from* **350 million to 1.6 billion,** *with 350–550 million the most widely accepted figure. Buddhism is also recognized as one of the fastest growing religions in the world."*[2]

Ancient Greece and Rome [Return]

Already during the ancient Greece and Rome period (7th century BC -5th century AD) *Atheism* was recognized , and it was used as a political tool to eliminate "enemies of the State." Let us take a brief look at two schools of thought in that period.

The Sophists [Return]

In ancient Greece, *sophists* were a category of teachers who specialized in using the techniques of philosophy and rhetoric for the purpose of teaching to young statesmen and nobility, for a fee, of course.

The Greek word *sophist* derives from the words *sophia*, and *sophos*, meaning "wisdom" or "wise" since the time of Homer and was originally used to describe expertise in a particular knowledge or craft. Gradually, however, the word also came to denote general wisdom and especially wisdom about human affairs (for example, in politics, ethics, or household management). Sophists were philosopher-teachers who traveled about in Greece teaching their students everything that was necessary to be successful in life including rhetoric and public speaking. These were useful skills, where being persuasive could lead to political power and economic wealth. Athens became the center of their activity, due to their tolerance of freedom of speech and the available wealth. Among Sophists, Protagoras, Gorgias, Prodicus, Hippias, Thrasyma chus, Callicles, Lycophron, Antiphon, and Cratylus are well known. Despite the opposition from philosophers such as Socrates, Plato and Aristotle, it is clear that Sophists had a vast influence on a number of spheres, including the growth of knowledge and on ethical political theory. Their teachings, although controversial, had a huge influence on thought in the fifth century B.C. The Sophists turned away from the theoretical natural science to the more sensible examination of human affairs and the betterment and success of human life. They explained that divine deities could no longer be the explanation of human action.[6]

Epicureanism [Return]

Epicurus (341–270 BC) was an ancient Greek philosopher, founder of the school of philosophy called *Epicureanism*. Only a few fragments and letters of Epicurus's 300 written works remain:

> For *Epicurus*, the purpose of philosophy was to attain the happy, tranquil life, characterized by ataraxia—peace and freedom from fear—and aponia—the absence of pain—and by living a self-sufficient life surrounded by friends. He taught that pleasure and pain are the measures of what is good and evil; death is the end of both body and soul and should therefore not be feared [*there is no afterlife*]; the gods neither reward nor punish humans; the universe is infinite and eternal; and events in the world are ultimately based on the motions and interactions of atoms moving in empty space.[7]

Hey, I like this guy! It is remarkable that an individual who lived 300 years before the Christian era would already have such clear and strong convictions. It would take another 2.000 years for some Western thinkers and philosophers (as in *Chapter 11*) to come to realize that the Universe is indifferent to the fate of human beings.

Middle Ages [Return]

No clear expression of Atheism is known to appear during the Middle Ages (5th -15th century DC). We should not be very surprised of this being the case, given the strong presence of both Christianity and Islam, the first fiercely assisted by the Holy Inquisition, and the second quick as well to dispose of "heretics."

Renaissance and Reformation [Return]

That is the time between the 14th and the 17th centuries, considered by many people as the bridge between the Middle Ages and Modern history. A time for new ideas, new interpretations of the Universe, a time to question old beliefs. Let us take a look at some of the most prominent thinkers of that time period.

Baruch Spinoza (1632-1677) [Return]

A Dutch philosopher, *Spinoza* was born Benedito de Espinosa in a *Sephardic Jewish family* that had settled in the city of *Amsterdam* following the expulsion of the Jews in Spain (1942) and the Portuguese Inquisition (1536):

> Attracted by the *Decree of Toleration* issued in 1579 by the Union of Utrecht, Portuguese "*conversos*" first sailed to Amsterdam in 1593 and promptly reconverted to *Judaism*. In 1598 permission was granted to build a synagogue, and in 1615 an ordinance for the admission and government of the Jews was passed. As a community of exiles, the Portuguese Jews of Amsterdam were highly proud of their identity.

> The Spinoza family ("*Espinosa*" in Portuguese) probably had its origins in Espinosa de los Monteros, near Burgos, or

in Espinosa de Cerrato, near Palencia, both in Northern Castile, Spain. *The family was expelled from Spain in 1492 and fled to Portugal.* Portugal compelled them to convert to Catholicism in 1498. Spinoza's father was born roughly a century after this forced conversion in the small Portuguese city of Vidigueira, near Beja in Alentejo. When Spinoza's father was still a child, Spinoza's grandfather, Isaac de Spinoza (who was from Lisbon), took his family to Nantes in France. They were expelled in 1615 and moved to Rotterdam, where Isaac died in 1627.

Spinoza argued that God exists, *a non-anthropomorphic God*, but that he/she is abstract and impersonal. Spinoza's system imparted order and unity to the tradition of radical thought, offering powerful weapons for prevailing against "received authority." He contended that everything that exists in Nature is one Reality (substance) and there is only one set of rules governing the whole of the reality which surrounds us and of which we are part. *Spinoza viewed God and Nature as two names for the same reality*, namely a single, fundamental substance (meaning "that which stands beneath" rather than "matter") that is the basis of the universe and of which all lesser "entities" are actually modes or modifications, that all things are determined by Nature to exist and cause effects, and that the complex chain of cause and effect is understood only in part. That humans presume themselves to have *free will*, he argues, is a result of their awareness of appetites which affect their minds while being unable to understand the reasons why they want and act as they do. Spinoza's system also envisages a God that does not rule over the universe by Providence in which God can make changes, but a God which itself is the deterministic system of which everything in nature is a part. Spinoza argues that "things could not have been produced by God in any other way or in any other order than is the case. He directly challenges a transcendental God which actively responds to events in the universe. Everything that has and will happen is a part of a long chain of cause and effect which, at a metaphysical level, humans are unable to change.

Spinoza also held that everything must necessarily happen the way that it does (deterministic). Therefore, **humans have no free will.** They believe, however, that their will is free. This illusionary perception of freedom stems from our human consciousness, experience, and indifference to prior natural causes. Humans think they are free but they "dream with their eyes open". For Spinoza, our actions are guided entirely by natural impulses.[8]

An *outcast* of both Jews and Christians, Spinoza called "God" the laws of the Universe. His teachings are also known as *"Pantheism."*

Thomas Hobbes (1588-1679) [Return]

This English philosopher is best known for his work on political philosophy, in particular because of his book *Leviathan* where he establishes his views on *social contract theory*:

> Though on rational grounds a champion of absolutism for the sovereign, Hobbes also developed some of the fundamentals of European liberal thought: the right of the individual; the natural equality of all men; the artificial character of the political order (which led to the later distinction between *civil society and the state*); the view that all legitimate political power must be "representative" and based on the consent of the people; and a liberal interpretation of law which leaves people free to do whatever the law does not explicitly forbid. He was one of the founders of modern *political philosophy* and political science. His understanding of humans as being matter and motion, obeying the same physical laws as other matter and motion, remains influential; and his account of human nature as self-interested cooperation, and of political communities as being based upon a *"social contract"* remains one of the major topics of political philosophy.
>
> Born prematurely when his mother heard of the coming invasion of the *Spanish Armada*, Hobbes later reported that

"my mother gave birth to twins: myself and fear." His childhood is almost a complete blank, and his mother's name is unknown. His father, also named Thomas, was the *vicar* of Charlton and Westport. Thomas Hobbes Sr. had an older brother, Francis Hobbes, who was a wealthy merchant with no family of his own. Thomas Hobbes, the younger, had one brother Edmund who was about two years older than he. Thomas Sr. abandoned his wife, two sons and a daughter, leaving them in the care of his brother, Francis, when he was forced to flee to London after being involved in a fight with a clergyman outside his own church. Hobbes was educated at Westport church from the age of four, passed to the Malmesbury school and then to a private school kept by a young man named Robert Latimer, a graduate of the University of Oxford. Hobbes was a good pupil, and around 1603 he went up to Magdalen Hall, which is most closely related to Hertford College, Oxford. The principal John Wilkinson was a Puritan, and he had some influence on Hobbes.

At university, Hobbes appears to have followed his own curriculum; he was "little attracted by the scholastic learning". He did not complete his B.A. degree until 1608, but he was recommended by *Sir James Hussey*, his master at Magdalen, as tutor to William, the son of *William Cavendish*, and began a lifelong connection with that family.

Hobbes came home, in 1637, to a country driven with discontent which disrupted him from the orderly execution of his philosophic plan. However, by the end of the Short Parliament in 1640, he had written a short treatise called **The Elements of Law, Natural and Politic.** It was not published and only circulated among his acquaintances in manuscript form. A pirated version, however, was published about ten years later. Although it seems that much of *The Elements of Law* was composed before the sitting of the Short Parliament, there are polemical pieces of the work that clearly mark the influences of the rising political crisis. Nevertheless, many (though not all) elements of Hobbes's political thought were unchanged between *The Elements of Law* and **Leviathan**, which demonstrates that the events of the **English Civil War** had little effect on his contractarian methodology. When in November 1640 the Long Parliament succeeded the Short, Hobbes felt he was a marked man by the circulation of his treatise and fled to Paris. He did not return for eleven years. In Paris he rejoined the coterie about Mersenne, and wrote a critique of the *Meditations on First Philosophy* of *Descartes*, which was printed as third among the sets of "Objections" appended, with "Replies" from Descartes in 1641. A different set of remarks on other works by Descartes succeeded only in ending all correspondence between the two.

During the years of the composition of **Leviathan**, Hobbes remained in or near Paris. In 1647 a serious illness disabled him for six months. On recovering from this near fatal disorder, he resumed his literary task, and carried it steadily forward to completion by 1650. Meanwhile, a translation of *De Cive* was being produced; scholars disagree over whether Hobbes translated the work himself or not. In *Leviathan*, Hobbes set out his **doctrine of the foundation of states** and legitimate governments and creating **an objective science of morality**. This gave rise to **social contract theory**. *Leviathan* was written during the English Civil War; much of the book is occupied with demonstrating the necessity of a strong central authority to avoid the evil of discord and civil war.

Hobbes was accused of **atheism**, or **of teachings which could lead to atheism.** This was an important accusation, and Hobbes himself wrote, in his answer to Bramhall's "the catching of the Leviathan" that "*atheism, impiety, and the like are words of the greatest defamation possible*". Hobbes always defended himself from such accusations. The king was important in protecting Hobbes when, in 1666, **the House of Commons introduced a bill against atheism and profaneness.** That same year, on 17 October 1666, it was ordered that the committee to which the bill was referred "should be empowered to receive information touching such books as tend to atheism, blasphemy and profaneness... in particular... the book of Mr. Hobbes called the *Leviathan*". *Hobbes was terrified at the prospect of being labeled a heretic, and proceeded to burn some of his compromising papers.* In October 1679, Hobbes suffered a bladder disorder, which was followed by a paralytic stroke from which he died on 4 December 1679. He is said to have uttered the last words "*A great leap in the dark*" in his final moments of life. He was interred within St. John the Baptist Church in Ault Hucknall in Derbyshire, England.[9]

Kazimierz Lyszczynski (1634-1689) [Return]

A Polish nobleman, landowner, philosopher, and soldier in the ranks of the Sapieha family:

For eight years he studied philosophy as a *Jesuit* and then became a *supply judge* in legal cases against the Jesuits concerning estates. Lyszczynski had read a book by Henry Aldsted entitled *Theologia Naturalis*, which attempted to prove the existence of divinity. But its arguments were so confused that Lyszczynski was able to infer many contradictions. Ridiculing Aldsted, Lyszczynski wrote in the book's margins the words "*ergo non est Deus*" ("therefore God does not exist"). Lyszczynski wrote a treatise entitled "*De non existentia Dei*" (*the non-existence of God*), which stated that *God does not exist and that religions are the inventions of man*.

This was discovered by one of Lyszczynski's debtors, *Jan Kazimierz Brzoska*, who was the *nuncio* of Brest in Poland. Brzoska, reluctant to return a great sum of money to him lent by Łyszczyński, accused the latter of being an *atheist* and gave the aforementioned work as evidence to Witwicki, bishop of Poznań. Brzoska also stole and delivered to the court a handwritten copy of *De non existentia Dei*, which was the first Polish philosophical treatise presenting reality from an atheistic perspective, and which Łyszczyński had been working on since 1674. Witwicki along with Załuski, bishop of Kiev, took up this case with zeal. The King

191

attempted to help Łyszczyński by ordering that he should be judged at Vilna, but this could not save Łyszczyński from the clergy. Łyszczyński's first privilege as a Polish noble, that he could not be imprisoned before his condemnation, was violated. The Lyszczynski case was brought before the *diet* of 1689 where he was accused of having *denied the existence of God* and having blasphemed against the Virgin Mary and the saints. He was *condemned to death* for *atheism.* The sentence was carried out before noon in the Old Town Market in Warsaw, where his tongue was pulled out followed by a *beheading*. After that, his corpse was transported beyond the city borders and cremated.

Bishop Załuski gave the following account of the execution: "*After recantation the culprit was conducted to the scaffold, where the executioner tore with a burning iron the tongue and the mouth, with which he had been cruel against God; after which his hands, the instruments of the abominable production, were burnt at a slow fire, the sacrilegious paper was thrown into the flames; finally himself, that monster of his century, this deicide was thrown into the expiatory flames; expiatory if such a crime may be atoned for.*" The treatise itself was destroyed by the *diet* but the cited *fragments that survived are as follows*:

I - We beseech you, o' theologians, by your God, if in this manner do you not extinguish the light of Reason, do you not oust the sun from this world, do you not pull down your God from the sky, when attributing him the impossible, the characteristics and attributes contradicting themselves.

II - The *Man is a creator of God*, and God is a concept and creation of a Man. Hence the people are architects and engineers of God and God is not a true being, but a being existing only within mind, being chimeric by its nature, because a God and a *chimera* are the same.

III - Religion was constituted by people without religion, so they could be worshipped although the God is not existent. Piety was introduced by the unpietic. The fear of

God was spread by the unafraid so that the people were afraid of them in the end. Devotion named godly is *a design of Man*. Doctrine, be it logical or philosophical, bragging to be teaching the truth of God, is false, and on the contrary, the one condemned as false, is the very true one.

IV - Simple folk are cheated by the more cunning with the *fabrication of God* for their own oppression; whereas the same oppression is shielded by the folk in a way, that if the wise attempted to free them by the truth, they would be quelled by the very people.

V - Nevertheless we do not experience within us and within any other such an imperative of reason, which would ensure us of a truth of divine revelation. Alas if they were present in us, then everyone would have to acknowledge them and would have no doubts and would not contradict the Writings of Moses and the Gospels - which is not true - and there would be no different congregations and their followers as Mahomet etc. Such an imperative is not known and there are not only doubts, but there are *some who deny a revelation, and they are not fools, but wise men*, who with a proper reasoning prove what? *Concluding, that God does not exist*".

During his trial, Lyszczynski claimed that the work was to be about a Catholic and an atheist having a debate, in which the Catholic would eventually win (he told the *diet* that the work would have had a different title from *De non existentia Dei*). The atheist was to speak first followed by the Catholic. He claimed that he only wrote the first half of the work (that is only the atheist's argument) and then stopped writing at the advice of a priest. In March 2014, his persona and ideas were the key theme in a public performance during the 2014 *Procession of Atheists* in Poland.[10]

Age of Enlightment [Return]

That time period of reason and light among thinkers from the 1650s to the 1780s. Men and women would meet in coffee houses, bars, salons, and Masonic lodges to question traditional thinking, the existence of Gods, and the dominant position of the Catholic Church. My words of respect, admiration, and thanks to those men and women!

Jean Meslier (1664-1729) [Return]

Here is an interesting man, a French Catholic priest "who was doing one thing but thinking another", by the name of Jean Meslier. Considered by many to mark the beginning of *"the history of true Atheism"*

> Jean Meslier was born in Mazerny in the Ardennes (**Mazerny** is a commune in the Ardennes department in northern France). He began *learning Latin* from a neighborhood priest in 1678 and eventually *joined the seminary.* He later claimed, in the Author's Preface to his *Testament*, this was done toease his parents. At the end of his studies, he took Holy Orders and, on 7 January 1689, *became priest* at Étrépigny, in Champagne. One public disagreement with a local nobleman aside, Meslier was to all appearances generally unremarkable, and he performed his office without complaint or problem for 40 years. He lived like a pauper, and every penny left over was donated to the poor.

> *Big surprise*. When Meslier died, there were found in his house three copies of a 633-page *octavo manuscript,* his *"testament"* in which the village curate denounces organized religion as *"but a castle in the air"* and theology as *"but ignorance of natural causes reduced to a system".*

> In his *Testament*, Meslier repudiated not only the God of conventional Christianity, but even the generic God of the natural religion of the deists. For Meslier, the existence of evil was incompatible with the idea of a good and wise God. He denied that any spiritual value could be gained from suffering, and he used the deist's argument from design against god, by showing the evils that he had permitted in this world. To him, *religions were fabrications fostered by ruling elites*; although the earliest Christians had been exemplary in sharing their goods, *Christianity*

had long since degenerated into encouraging the acceptance of suffering and submission to tyranny as practiced by the kings of France: injustice was explained away as being the will of an all-wise Being. *However, none of the arguments used by Meslier against the existence of God were original*, in fact, he derived them from books written by orthodox theologians in the debate between the Jesuits, Cartesians, and Jansenists: their inability to agree on a proof for God's existence was taken by Meslier as a good reason not to presume that there were compelling grounds for belief in God.

Meslier's philosophy was that of an *Atheist*. He also denied the existence of the *soul* and dismissed the notion of *free will*. In Chapter V, the priest writes, "If God is incomprehensible to man, it would seem rational never to think of Him at all". In his most famous quote, Meslier refers to a man who *"...wished that all the great men in the world and all the nobility could be hanged, and strangled with the guts of the priests."* Meslier admits that the statement may seem crude and shocking, but comments that this is what the priests and nobility deserve, not for reasons of revenge or hatred, but for love of justice and truth. *Voltaire* often mentions Meslier (referring to him as "a good priest") in his correspondence, in which he tells his daughter to "read and read again" Meslier's only work, and says that "every honest man should have Meslier's *Testament* in his pocket." However, he also described Meslier as writing "in the style of a carriage-horse".[11]

Baron d'Holbach (1723-1789) [Return]

Born *Paul Heinrich Dietrich*, he was a French-German author, philosopher, and a prominent figure during the *French Enlightment* period. He kept a salon, and was well known for his *Atheism*, his denouncing of religion, as expressed in his famous book *The System of Nature.*

D'Holbach's mother Catherine Jacobina was the daughter of Johannes Jacobus Holbach the Prince-Bishop's *tax collector* for the Roman Catholic Diocese of Speyer. His father, Johann Jakob Dietrich, was *a wine-grower*. D'Holbach wrote nothing of his childhood though it is known he was raised in Paris by his uncle Franz Adam Holbach, who had become a millionaire by speculating on the Paris stock-exchange. With his financial support, d'Holbach attended the *Leiden University* from 1744 to 1748 and went on to marry his second cousin, Basile-Geneviève d'Aine (1728–1754), on 11 December 1750. In 1753 both his uncle and his father died, leaving d'Holbach with an enormous inheritance. D'Holbach would remain wealthy throughout his life. In 1754, his wife died from an unknown disease. The following year received a special dispensation from the Pope *to marry his deceased wife's sister*, Charlotte-Suzanne d'Aine. From c. 1750 to c. 1780, Baron d'Holbach used his wealth to maintain *one of the more notable and lavish Parisian salons*, which soon became an important meeting place for the contributors to the *Encyclopédie*.

Despite his extensive contributions to the *Encyclopédie*, d'Holbach is better known today for his philosophical writings, all of which were published anonymously or under pseudonyms and printed outside of France, usually in Amsterdam by *Marc-Michel Rey*. *His philosophy was expressly materialistic and atheistic and is today categorised into the philosophical movement called French materialism*. In 1761 *Christianisme dévoilé* ("Christianity Unveiled") appeared, in which he attacked Christianity and religion in general as an impediment to the moral advancement of humanity.." *Christianity Unveiled* was followed by others, notably *La Contagion sacrée* (1768 - "The Sacred Contagion"), *Théologie portative* (1768 - "Portable Theology") and *Essai sur les préjugés* (1770 - "Essay on prejudice").

In 1770, d'Holbach published his most famous book, *The System of Nature* (*Le Système de la nature*), under the name of Jean-Baptiste de Mirabaud, the secretary of the Académie française who had died ten years previously.

Denying the existence of a deity, and refusing to admit as evidence all *a priori* arguments, d'Holbach saw the universe as nothing more than matter in motion, bound by inexorable natural laws of cause and effect. There is, he wrote "***no necessity to have recourse to supernatural powers to account for the formation of things.***" The *Catholic Church in France* threatened the Crown with withdrawal of financial support unless it effectively suppressed the circulation of the book. The authorship of his various anti-religious works did not become widely known until the early 19th century. Ironically, he was buried in the Church of Saint-Roch, Paris.[12]

David Hume (1711-1776) [Return]

A Scottish historian, economist, diplomat, and philosopher, best known for his *empiricism*:

Throughout his life Hume, who never married, spent time occasionally at his family home at Ninewells by Chirnside, Berwickshire, which had belonged to his family since the 16th century. His finances as a young man were very "slender". His family was not rich and, as a younger brother, he had little patrimony to live on. He was therefore forced to make a living somehow.

Hume attended the *University of Edinburgh* at the unusually early age of twelve (possibly as young as ten) at a time when fourteen was normal. He had little respect for the professors of his time, telling a friend in 1735 that "there is nothing to be learnt from a Professor, which is not to be met with in Books".

Aged around 18, Hume made a philosophical discovery that opened up to him "a new Scene of Thought", which inspired him "to throw up every other Pleasure or Business to apply entirely to it". He did not recount what this "Scene" was, and commentators have offered a variety of speculations. Due to this inspiration, Hume set out to spend a minimum of ten years reading and writing. He came to the verge of a ***mental breakdown***, after which he decided to have a more active life to better continue his learning.

From about 1729 he began to suffer from what a doctor diagnosed as the "***Disease of the Learned***". Hume wrote that it started with a coldness, which he attributed to a "Laziness of Temper", that lasted about nine months. Later, however, some scurvy spots broke out on his fingers. It was this that persuaded Hume's physician to make his diagnosis. Hume wrote that he "went under a Course of Bitters and Anti-Hysteric Pills", taken along with a pint of claret every day. His health improved somewhat, but, in 1731, he was afflicted with a ravenous appetite and palpitations of the heart. After eating well for a time, he went from being "tall, lean and raw-bon'd" to being "sturdy, robust [and] healthful-like".[12]

He worked for four years on his first major work, *A Treatise of Human Nature*, subtitled "Being an Attempt to Introduce the Experimental Method of Reasoning into Moral Subjects", completing it in 1738 at the age of 28. Although many scholars today consider the *Treatise* to be Hume's most important work and one of the most important books in Western philosophy, the critics in Great Britain at the time did not agree, describing it as "abstract and unintelligible". As Hume had spent most of his savings during those four years, he resolved "to make a very rigid frugality supply my deficiency of fortune, to maintain unimpaired my independency, and to regard every object as contemptible except the improvements of my talents in literature". Despite the disappointment, Hume later wrote, "Being naturally of a cheerful and sanguine temper, I soon recovered from the blow and prosecuted with great ardour my studies in the country." There, in an attempt to make his larger work more intelligible, he published the _Abstract_, as a summary of the main doctrines of the *Treatise*, without revealing its authorship.[17] However, there has been academic speculation as to who actually wrote this book.[18]

After the publication of *Essays Moral and Political* in 1744, which was included in the later edition called <u>*Essays, Moral, Political, and Literary*</u>, Hume applied for the Chair of Pneumatics and Moral Philosophy at the University of Edinburgh. However, the position was given to <u>William Cleghorn</u> after Edinburgh ministers petitioned the town council not to appoint Hume because he was seen as an <u>atheist</u>.

Hume's religious views were often suspected. It was necessary in the 1750s for his friends to avert a trial against him on the charge of heresy. However, he "*would not have come and could not be forced to attend if he said he was not a member of the Established Church*". Also, perhaps on this account, **Hume failed to gain the chair of philosophy at the University of Glasgow**. In 1749 he went to live with his brother in the country, returning to Edinburgh in 1751. It was after returning there, and as he wrote in **My Own Life**, that, in 1752, "the Faculty of Advocates chose me their Librarian, an office from which I received little or no emolument, but which gave me the command of a large library".This resource enabled him to continue historical research for *The History of England*. Hume's volume of *Political Discourses*, written in 1749 and published by Kincaid & Donaldson in 1752, was the only work he considered successful on first publication.

Eventually, with the publication of his six volumes *The History of England* between 1754 and 1762, Hume achieved the fame that he coveted. The volumes traced events from the Invasion of Julius Caesar to the Revolution of 1688, and were bestsellers in its day.

Although he wrote a great deal about **religion**, **Hume's personal views are unclear**, and there has been much discussion concerning his religious position. Contemporaries seemed to consider him to be an **atheist,** or at least un-Christian, and the Church of Scotland seriously considered bringing charges of infidelity against him.

However, in works such as *On Superstition and Enthusiasm*, Hume specifically seems to support the standard religious views of his time and place. This still meant that he could be **very critical of the Catholic Church**, dismissing it with the standard Protestant accusations of **superstition and idolatry**, as well as dismissing what his compatriots saw as uncivilised beliefs. He also considered extreme Protestant sects, the members of which he called "enthusiasts", to be corrupters of religion.

Philosopher *Paul Russell* writes that it is likely that Hume was skeptical about religious belief, but not to the extent of complete atheism. He suggests that perhaps Hume's position is best characterized by the term "irreligion", while philosopher *David O'Connor* argues that Hume's final position was "weakly deistic". For O'Connor, Hume's *"position is deeply ironic. This is because, while inclining towards a weak form of deism, he seriously doubts that we can ever find a sufficiently favorable balance of evidence to justify accepting any religious position."* He adds that Hume *"did not believe in the God of standard theism ... but he did not rule out all concepts of deity"*, and that *"ambiguity suited his purposes*, and this creates difficulty in definitively pinning down his final position on religion"[13]

Charles Bradlaugh (1833-1891) [Return]

An English political activist and possibly the most famous English *Atheist* of the 19th century:

Born in *Hoxton* (an area in the East End of London), Bradlaugh was the son of a solicitor's clerk. He left school at the age of eleven, worked as an office errand-boy, and later as a clerk to a coal merchant. After a brief spell as a Sunday school teacher, he became disturbed by discrepancies between the Thirty-nine Articles of the Anglican Church and the *Bible*. When he expressed his concerns, the local vicar, *John Graham Packer*, accused him of *atheism* and suspended him from teaching. He was thrown out of the family home and was taken in by *Elizabeth Sharples Carlile*, the widow of Richard Carlile, who had been imprisoned for printing Thomas Paine's *The Age of Reason*. Soon Bradlaugh was introduced to George Holyoake, who organised Bradlaugh's first public lecture as an *atheist*.

At the age of 17, he published his first pamphlet, *A Few Words on the Christian Creed*. However, refusing financial support from fellow freethinkers, he enlisted as a soldier with the *Seventh Dragoon Guards* hoping to serve in *India* and make his fortune. Instead he was stationed in Dublin. In 1853, he was left a legacy by a great-aunt and used it to purchase his discharge from the army.

He was President of the *London Secular Society* from 1858. In 1860 he became editor of the secularist newspaper, the *National Reformer*, and in 1866 co-founded the ***National Secular Society***, in which *Annie Besant* became his close associate. In 1868, the *Reformer* was prosecuted by the British Government for blasphemy and sedition. Bradlaugh was eventually acquitted on all charges, but fierce controversy continued both in the courts and in the press.

A decade later (1876), Bradlaugh and Besant decided to republish the American Charles Knowlton's pamphlet advocating birth control, *The Fruits of Philosophy, or the Private Companion of Young Married People*, whose previous British publisher had already been successfully prosecuted for obscenity. The two activists were both tried in 1877, and ***Charles Darwin*** refused to give evidence in their defence, pleading ill-health, but at the time writing to Bradlaugh that his testimony would have been of little use to them because he opposed birth control. They were sentenced to heavy fines and six months' imprisonment, but their conviction was overturned by the Court of Appeal on a legal technicality. ***The Malthusian League was founded as a result of the trial to promote birth control.**** He was a member of a ***Masonic lodge*** in Bolton, although he was later to resign due to the nomination of the Prince of Wales as Grand Master.

Bradlaugh was an advocate of trade unionism, republicanism, and *women's suffrage*, and he opposed socialism. His anti-socialism was divisive, and many secularists who became socialists left the secularist movement because of its identification with Bradlaugh's liberal individualism. He was a supporter of *Irish Home Rule*, and backed France during the Franco-Prussian War. In 1880 Bradlaugh was elected *Member of Parliament* for Northampton. To take his seat and become an active Parliamentarian, he needed to signify his allegiance to the Crown and on 3 May Bradlaugh came to the Table of the House of Commons, bearing a letter to the Speaker "begging respectfully to claim to be allowed to affirm" instead of taking the religious Oath of Allegiance, citing the Evidence Amendment Acts of 1869 and 1870. Speaker Brand declared that he had "grave doubts" and asked the House for its judgment. *Lord Frederick Cavendish*, for the Government, moved that a Select Committee be set up to decide whether persons entitled to make a solemn affirmation in court were also allowed to affirm instead of taking the Parliamentary oath.

Because Members had to take the oath before being allowed to take their seats, he effectively forfeited his seat in Parliament. His seat fell vacant and a by-election was declared. Bradlaugh was re-elected by Northampton four times in succession as the dispute continued. Supporting Bradlaugh were William Ewart Gladstone, T. P. O'Connor and *George Bernard Shaw* as well as hundreds of thousands of people who signed a public petition. Opposing his right to sit were the Conservative Party, the Archbishop of Canterbury, and other leading figures in the Church of England and Roman Catholic Church. On at least one occasion, Bradlaugh was escorted from the House by police officers. In 1886 Bradlaugh was finally allowed to take the oath, and did so at the risk of prosecution under the Parliamentary Oaths Act. Bradlaugh's funeral was attended by 3,000 mourners, including a then 21-years-old *Mohandas Gandhi*. He is buried in Brookwood Cemetery.[14]

Karl Marx (1818-1883) [Return]

A German journalist, revolutionary, economist, socialist, and philosopher, best known for his books on economics such as *The Communist Manifest* and *Das Kapital*:

Karl Marx was born Heinrich Marx and Henrietta Pressburg in Trier, a town then part of the Kingdom of Prussia's Province of the Lower Rhine. Ancestrally *Jewish*, his maternal grandfather was a Dutch rabbi, while his paternal line had supplied Trier's rabbis since 1723, a role taken by his grandfather Meier Halevi Marx. Karl's father, as a child known as Herschel, was the first in the line to receive a secular education; he became a lawyer and lived a relatively wealthy and middle-class existence, with his family owning a number of Moselle vineyards. Prior to his son's birth, and to escape the constraints of anti-Semitic legislation, Herschel converted from *Judaism* to the Protestant Christian denomination of Lutheranism, the predominant sect in Germany and Prussia at the time, taking on the German forename of Heinrich over the *Yiddish* Herschel.

Marx studied at the Universities of Bonn and Berlin where he became interested in the philosophical ideas of the Young Hegelians. After his studies he wrote for a radical newspaper in Cologne and began to work out the theory of the materialist conception of history. He moved to Paris in 1843, where he began writing for other radical newspapers and met *Friedrich Engels*, who would become his lifelong friend and collaborator. In 1849 he was exiled and moved to London together with his wife and children, where he continued writing and formulating his theories about social and economic activity. He also campaigned for socialism and became a significant figure in the *International Workingmen's Association.*

Marx's theories about society, economics and politics, the collective understanding of which is known as Marxism, hold that human societies progress through *class struggle*: *a conflict between an ownership class that controls production and a dispossessed labouring class that provides the labour for production*. States, Marx believed, were run on behalf of the ruling class and in their interest while representing it as the common interest of all; and he predicted that, like previous socioeconomic systems, *capitalism* produced internal tensions which would lead to its self-destruction and replacement by a new system: *socialism*. He argued that class antagonisms under capitalism between the bourgeoisie and proletariat would eventuate in the working class' conquest of political power and eventually establish a classless society, *communism*, a society governed by a free association of producers. Marx actively fought for its implementation, arguing that the working class should carry out organised *revolutionary action* to topple capitalism and bring about socio-economic change.

In late 1847, *Marx and Engels* began writing what was to become their most famous work, a programme of action for the Communist League. Written jointly by Marx and Engels from December 1847 to January 1848, *The Communist Manifesto* was first published on 21 February 1848. *The Communist Manifesto* laid out the beliefs of the new Communist League. Proceeding on from this, the *Manifesto* presents the argument for why the Communist League, as opposed to other socialist and liberal political parties and groups at the time, was truly acting in the interests of the proletariat to overthrow capitalist society and to replace it with socialism. One of Marx's comments on religion:

> *Religious suffering is, at one and the same time, the expression of real suffering and a protest against real suffering. Religion is the sigh of the oppressed creature, the heart of a heartless world, and the soul of soulless conditions. It is **the opium of the people**. The*

abolition of religion as the illusory happiness of the people is the demand for their real happiness. To call on them to give up their illusions about their condition is to call on them to give up a condition that requires illusions.

Following the death of his wife, Jenny, in December 1881, Marx developed a catarrh that kept him in ill health for the last 15 months of his life. It eventually brought on the bronchitis and pleurisy that killed him in London on 14 March 1883. He died a stateless person; family and friends in London buried his body in Highgate Cemetery, London, on 17 March 1883. There were between nine and eleven mourners at his funeral. Several of his closest friends spoke at his funeral, including *Wilhelm Liebknecht* and **Friedrich Engels**. Engels's speech included the passage:

On the 14th of March, at a quarter to three in the afternoon, the greatest living thinker ceased to think. He had been left alone for scarcely two minutes, and when we came back we found him in his armchair, peacefully gone to sleep, forever. [15]

Friedrich Nietzsche (1844-1900) [Return]

A German philologist , philosopher, cultural critic, a poet, and a compower. He wrote several works critical of religion, morality, contemporary culture, philosophy, and science.

Nietzsche's key ideas include perspectivism, the **Will to Power**, the "**death of God**", the *Übermensch* ("**Superman**") and eternal recurrence. One of the key tenets of his philosophy is the concept of "life-affirmation," which embraces the realities of the world in which we live over the idea of a world beyond. It further champions the creative powers of the individual to strive beyond social, cultural, and moral contexts. Nietzsche's attitude towards religion and morality was marked with **Atheism,** psychologism, and historism; he considered them to be human creations loaded with the error of confusing cause and effect.[16]

Atheist Feminism

A movement that advocates feminism within *atheism*. Atheist feminists also oppose religion as a main source of female oppression and inequality, believing that the majority of the religions are sexist and oppressive to women. Hey, let us give space, time, and our attention to our brave women!

Ernestine Rose (1810-1892)

An American Atheist feminist, an abolitionist, and a major figure behind women's rights movement in 19th century USA:

> She was born in Piotrków Trybunalski, *Russia-Poland*, as *Ernestine Louise Polowsky*. Her father was a wealthy *Rabbi* and her mother the daughter of a wealthy businessman. At the age of five, Rose began to "question the justice of a God who would exact such hardships" at the frequent fasts that her father performed. As she grew older, she began to question her father more and more on religious matters, receiving only, "A young girl does not want to understand the object of her creed, but to accept and believe it." in response. By the age of fourteen, she had completely rejected the idea of female inferiority and the religious texts that supported that idea.

> When she was sixteen her mother died and her father, without her consent, betrothed her to a young Jew who was a friend of his. Rose, not wanting to enter a marriage with a man she neither chose nor loved, confronted him, professing her lack of affection towards him and begging for release. However, Rose was a woman from a rich family, and he denied her plea. Rose traveled to the secular *civil court*, where she pleaded her case herself. The courts ruled in her favor, not only freeing her from her betrothal, but ruling that she could retain the full inheritance she received from her mother. Although she decided to relinquish the fortune to her father, she gladly took her

freedom from betrothal. She returned home only to discover that in her absence her father had remarried, ***to a sixteen-year-old girl.***

Rose then traveled to Berlin, where she found herself hampered by an **anti-Semitic law** that required all non-Prussian Jews to have a Prussian sponsor. She appealed directly to the king and was granted an exemption from the rule. She traveled to Belgium, the Netherlands, France, and finally England. Her arrival in England was less than smooth, however, as the ship in which she was sailing wrecked. Although Rose did make it to England safely, all her possessions had been destroyed, and she found herself destitute. In order to support herself, she sought work as a teacher in the languages of German and Hebrew and she continued to sell her room deodorizers. While in England, she met *Robert Owen*, a Utopian socialist, who was so impressed by her that he invited her to speak in a large hall for radical speakers. In spite of her limited knowledge of English, the audience was so impressed that from then on her appearances were regular. She and Owen were close friends, and she even helped him to found the *Association of All Classes of All Nations*, a group that espoused human rights for all people of all nations, sexes, races and classes. During her time there she also met *William Ella Rose*, a Christian jeweler and silversmith, an Englishman and an "Owenite". They were soon married by a civil magistrate, and both made it plain that they considered the marriage a civil contract rather than a religious one.

In May 1836 the Roses emigrated to the United States, where they later became **naturalized citizens** and settled in a cozy house in New York city in 1837. The Roses soon opened a small "Fancy and Perfumery" store in their home, where Rose sold her perfumed toilet water and William ran a silversmith shop.

Rose soon began to give lectures on the subjects that most interested her, joining the "Society for Moral Philanthropists" and traveling to different states to espouse her causes of the **abolition of slavery**, religious tolerance, public education and *equality for women*. Her lectures were met with controversy. When she was in the South to speak out against slavery, one slaveholder told her he would have "*tarred and feathered her if she had been a man*". When, in 1855, she was invited to deliver an anti-slavery lecture in Bangor, Maine, a local newspaper called her "*a female Atheist... a thousand times below a prostitute*." When Rose responded to the slur in a letter to the competing paper, she sparked off a town feud that created such publicity that, by the time she arrived, everyone in town was eager to hear her. Her most ill-received lecture was likely in Charleston, West Virginia, where her lecture on the evils of slavery was met with such vehement opposition and outrage that she was forced to exercise considerable influence to even get out of the city safely.

In the winter of 1836, Judge Thomas Hertell submitted a *married women's property act* to the legislature of New York city to investigate methods of improving the civil and property rights of married women, and to allow them to hold real estate in their own name. When Rose heard of this resolution, she drew up a petition and began to solicit names in support of it. In 1838, this petition was sent to the state legislature in spite of it only having five names. This was the *first petition ever introduced in favor of rights for women*. During the following years, she increased both the number of petitions and the number of signatures. In 1849, these rights were finally won. Rose was elected president of the *National Women's Rights Convention* in October, 1854, in spite of objections that she was an *atheist.* Her election was heavily supported by Susan B. Anthony, who declared that, "every religion – or none – should have an equal right on the platform". Although she never seemed to attach any importance to her Jewish background, in 1863 Rose had a published debate with *Horace Seaver*, the abolitionist editor of the Boston Investigator, whom she accused of being anti-Semitic. In her later years, after a six month trip to Europe, she attempted to stay away from platforms and controversy. Within 6 months, she made the closing address at the nationwide **Women's Rights Convention**. However, her health once again took a downward turn, and on June 8, 1869, she and her husband set sail for England. *Susan B. Anthony* arranged a farewell party for them, and the couple received many gifts from friends and admirers, including a substantial amount of money. After 1873, her health improved, and she began to advocate women's suffrage in England, even attending the Conference of the Woman's Suffrage movement in London and speaking in Edinburgh, Scotland at a large public meeting in favor of woman's suffrage. She died in England in 1892.[17]

Elizabeth Cady Stanton (18 15-1902) [Return]

Among the most prominent people to publicly advocate for *Feminism* as well as *Atheism* in the 1800s were Elizabeth Cady Stanton and Matilda Joslyn Gage.

> *Elizabeth Cady Stanton* was an American social activist, abolitionist, and leading figure of the early women's rights movement. Her *Declaration of Sentiments*, presented at the Seneca Falls Convention held in 1848 in Seneca Falls, New York, is often credited with initiating the first *organized women's rights and women's suffrage movements* in the United States.

> Before Stanton narrowed her political focus almost exclusively to *women's rights*, she was an active abolitionist with her husband, *Henry Brewster Stanton* and cousin, *Gerrit Smith*. Unlike many of those involved in the women's rights movement, Stanton addressed various issues pertaining to women beyond voting rights. Her concerns included women's parental and custody rights, property rights, employment and income rights, divorce, the economic health of the family, and *birth control*.

> After the *American Civil War*, Stanton's commitment to female suffrage caused a schism in the women's rights

movement when she, together with *Susan B. Anthony*, declined to support passage of the Fourteenth and Fifteenth Amendments to the United States Constitution. *She opposed giving added legal protection and voting rights to African American men while women, black and white, were denied those same rights.* Her position on this issue, together with her thoughts on organized Christianity and women's issues beyond voting rights, led to the formation of *two separate women's rights organizations* that were finally rejoined, with Stanton as president of the joint organization, approximately twenty years after her break from the original women's suffrage movement.

In 1885 Elizabeth wrote an essay entitled "*Has Christianity Benefited Woman?*" arguing that it had in fact hurt women's rights, and stating, "*All religions thus far have taught the headship and superiority of man, [and] the inferiority and subordination of woman. Whatever new dignity, honor, and self-respect the changing theologies may have brought to man, they have all alike brought to woman but another form of humiliation*". In 1895 she wrote *The Woman's Bible*, revised and continued with another book of the same name in 1898, in which she criticized religion and stated "*the Bible in its teachings degrades women from Genesis to Revelation.*" She died in 1902. The right to vote was won for American women in 1920, and after that feminism of all types in America largely lay *dormant* until the 1960s.[18]

Matilda Gage (1826-1898) [Return]

A *Native American* activist, and abolitionist, a prolific writer, and *freethinker*, "born with a hatred of oppression."

Matilda Gage spent her childhood in a house which was used as a station of the *Underground Railroad*. She faced prison for her actions under the *Fugitive Slave Law of 1850* which criminalized assistance to escaped slaves. Even though she was beset by both financial and physical (cardiac) problems throughout her life, her work for women's rights was extensive, practical, and often brilliantly executed.

Gage became involved in the women's rights movement in 1852 when she decided to speak at the *National Women's Rights Convention* in Syracuse, New York. She served as president of the *National Woman Suffrage Association* from 1875 to 1876, and served as either Chair of the Executive Committee or Vice President for over twenty years. During the 1876 convention, she successfully argued against a group of police who claimed the association was holding an illegal assembly. They left without pressing charges.

Gage was considered to be **more radical** than either Susan B. Anthony or Elizabeth Cady Stanton (with whom she wrote *History of Woman Suffrage*). Along with Stanton, she was a vocal critic of the *Christian Church*, which put her at odds with conservative suffragists such as *Frances Willard* and the *Woman's Christian Temperance Union*. Rather than arguing that women deserved the vote because their feminine morality would then properly influence legislation, she argued that they deserved suffrage as a "natural right."[19] Despite her opposition to the Church, Gage was **in her own way deeply religious**, and she joined Stanton's Revising Committee to write **The Woman's Bible**:

"If language has any meaning, we have in these texts a plain declaration of the existence of the feminine element in the life, equal in power and glory with the masculine. The heavenly Mother and Father! "God created man in his own image, male and female." Thus Scripture, as well as science and philosophy, declares the eternity and equality of sex, the philosophical, without which there could have been no perpetuation of creation, no growth or development of the animal, vegetable, or mineral kingdoms, no awakening nor progressing in the world of thought. The masculine and feminine elements, exactly equal and balancing each other, are essential to the maintenance of the equilibrium of the universe as positive and negative

electricity, the centripetal and centrifugal forces, the laws of attraction which bind together all we know of this planet whereon we dwell and of the system in which we revolve."[20]

Anne Nicol Gaylor (1926-) [Return]

An American Atheist feminist, co-founder of *Freedom From Religion Foundation* in 1976 with her daughter, Annie Laurie Gaylor.

Aside from promoting atheism in general, her *atheist feminist activities* include writing the book "*Woe To The Women: The Bible Tells Me So*", first published in 1981, which is now in its 4th printing. This book exposes and discusses sexism in the Bible. Furthermore, her 1997 book, "*Women Without Superstition: 'No Gods, No Masters,'* was the first collection of the writings of historic and contemporary *female freethinkers*. She has also written several articles on religion's harm to women. She wrote the book *Abortion Is a Blessing* and edited *The World Famous Atheist Cookbook*. In 1985 Gaylor received the Humanist Heroine Award from the *American Humanist Association*, and in 2007 she was given the *Tiller Award* by NARAL Pro-Choice America.

Anne Nicol was born to Jason Theodore and Lucy Edna (Sowle) Nicol on November 25, 1926, near Tomah, Wisconsin. Her mother died when Anne was two years old. Anne graduated from high school at age 16 and earned an *English degree* from the *University of Wisconsin–Madison* in 1949. She married Paul Joseph Gaylor the same year, and they had four children. Gaylor started the first private employment agency in Madison, Wisconsin, which she sold in 1966. She then became editor of the *Middleton Times-Tribune*. Her husband died of brain cancer in 2011, and she moved into a retirement home outside of Madison in 2012.

In 1967, while editor of the *Times-Tribune*, Gaylor wrote an editorial calling for *legalized abortion* in Wisconsin. She later joined the Association for the Study of Abortion, the

Wisconsin Committee to Legalize Abortion, and *Zero Population Growth*. In 1970 first-trimester abortions were legalized in Wisconsin, and she began the Zero Population Growth Referral Service to refer women to abortion providers. However, there were still few doctors who provided abortions in the state, so Gaylor often referred women to Mexico and New York. She also served on the Board of Directors of NARAL, now known as NARAL Pro-Choice America.

Gaylor, along with University of Wisconsin chemistry professor *Robert West*, founded the *Women's Medical Fund* to expand the services provided by the ZPG Referral Service. The organization was incorporated as a nonprofit in 1976. It provides small grants (on average about $200) to women who are unable to pay the full costs of their abortions. Funding comes from individual donors and foundation grants. In the past the Fund advertised its services, but now referrals come directly from abortion clinics. The organization is run entirely by volunteers, with no paid staff, and Gaylor answers many of the referral calls herself. It has paid out nearly $3,000,000 to abortion providers on behalf of patients. In 2009 the organization paid out $162,202 to its clients, and Gaylor took about 800 phone calls. By 2010, Gaylor had written checks to help pay for 18,986 abortions.

While working on abortion rights issues, Gaylor felt the need to address what she saw as the root cause of *women's oppression: religion.* She felt that the existing women's rights organizations were not confronting this issue, so she founded the *Freedom From Religion Foundation (FFRF)* in 1976, along with her daughter Annie Laurie Gaylor and the late John Sontarck. She served as the president and executive director until her retirement in 2005. The group is currently headed by her daughter, *Annie Laurie Gaylor*, and son-in-law, *Dan Barker*. She currently works as a consultant for the FFRF and holds the position of president emerita. While she was president the group grew from three to over 19,000 members in all 50 U.S. states and Canada.

FFRF is a nonprofit organization that promotes the separation of church and state and educates the public on matters relating to *atheism, agnosticism, and nontheism*. Under her leadership, the foundation was involved in several high-profile legal cases, including one that ended the teaching of Christian doctrine in a Tennessee public school and another that overturned a law that made Good Friday a state holiday in Wisconsin. Gaylor produced the *first atheist commercials that ever aired on television, on Madison's Channel 3*. She also appeared on television and radio programs such as *Crossfire,* Larry King's radio show, and *Oprah Winfrey*'s *A.M. Chicago*.[21]

Ayaan Hirsi Ali (1969-) [Return]

A Somali-born American (formerly Dutch) activist, writer, and politician. She is known for her views *critical of female genital mutilation* and of   Islam, while   supportive   of *women's rights and atheism*.

Hirsi Ali is the daughter of the Somali politician and opposition leader *Hirsi Magan Isse*. She and her family left Somalia in 1977 for Saudi Arabia, then Ethiopia, and later settled in Kenya. In 1992, Ali sought and obtained political asylum in the Netherlands. Following graduate work, she published articles on her political views and spoke in support of *Muslim women*, becoming *an atheist*. In 2003, Hirsi Ali was elected a member of the House of Representatives (the lower house of the Dutch parliament), representing the People's Party for Freedom and Democracy (VVD). A political crisis related to the validity of her Dutch citizenship led to her resignation from parliament, and indirectly to the fall of the second Balkenende cabinet in 2006.

In 2005, Hirsi Ali was named by *Time* magazine as one of the *100 most influential people in the world*. She has also received several awards, including a free speech award from the Danish newspaper *Jyllands-Posten*, the

Swedish Liberal Party's Democracy Prize, and the Moral Courage Award for commitment to conflict resolution, ethics, and world citizenship. Hirsi Ali has published two autobiographies: in 2006 and 2010.

She collaborated on a short movie with *Theo van Gogh*, entitled *Submission* (2004). *Critical of Islam*, it provoked controversy, and death threats were made against each of the two. Van Gogh was assassinated later that year by a Dutch Muslim.

Hirsi Ali emigrated to the United States, where she was a fellow of the *American Enterprise Institute*. She founded the women's rights organisation, *the AHA Foundation*. She became a naturalized US citizen in 2013 and that year was made a *fellow* at the Kennedy Government School at Harvard University, and a member of The Future of Diplomacy Project at the Belfer Center. She is married to British historian and public commentator Niall Ferguson.[22]

Ophelia Benson (1944-) [Return]

An American author, editor, blogger, and *Atheist* feminist. An editor in the website *Butterflies and Wheels*, and former editor of The *Philosopher's Magazine*.

Her books and website defend objectivity and scientific truth against the threats to rational thinking posed by *religious fundamentalism*, pseudoscience, wishful thinking, postmodernism, relativism and "the tendency of the political Left to subjugate the rational assessment of truth-claims to the demands of a variety of pre-existing political and moral frameworks".

Benson was born in *New Jersey* and attended university in the USA before working in a variety of jobs, including being a *zookeeper* for several years, before becoming an author. In 2004 Benson co-authored *The Dictionary of Fashionable Nonsense* with *Jeremy Stangroom*. It is a satire on post-modernism, modern jargon and anti-rationalist

215

thinking in contemporary academia. The Times Literary Supplement said *"With wit and invention, Benson and Stangroom take us through the checklist argot that so often litters postmodern texts."*

In 2006 Benson and Stangroom published **Why Truth Matters**, which examines the "spurious claims made for creationism, Holocaust denial, misinterpretation of evolutionary biology, identity history, science as mere social construct, and other 'paradigms' that prop up the habit of shaping our findings according to what we want to find". In 2009 Benson co-authored **Does God Hate Women**? with Stangroom. The book explores the oppression of women in the name of religious and cultural norms and how these issues play out both in the community and in the political arena.[23] Her own words in an interview with The *Freethinker Magazine*:

Freethinker (*FT*): How would you describe your personal philosophy?
Ophelia Benson (*OB*): I'm not sure I really have anything as grand as a personal philosophy, I think I have more of a methodology. It could be boiled down to not wanting to be taken for a sucker, or in more philosophical language, to a dislike of bullshit. I hate dishonest manipulative language of all sorts, and I spend a lot of time sniffing it out and then making fun of it. But on the affirmative side, I am in favour or a lot of things, if that adds up to a philosophy. It might be more what the philosopher *Rebecca Goldstein* in her novel *The Mind-body Problem* called a mattering map. Freedom and autonomy matter to me, as do rights. So do poetry, music, starry nights. Like *Richard Rorty* trying to unite Trotsky and wild orchids, I'm not sure how to connect the two, so I just put them on the mattering map.

FT: Is it true that your upcoming book, **Does God Hate Women**?, was turned down by the first publisher because in was too critical of **Islam**?
OB: Yes, a publisher did turn it down for that compelling reason. It wasn't exactly the first publisher since it never

actually accepted it, but it was very interested, got Jeremy [Stangroom, the co-author] in to have a chat etc. I live six thousand miles away or I would have gone along for the chat too, whether they'd invited me or not. They said they'd decided not to publish it because one mustn't criticize *Islam.*

FT: How did you feel about that at the time?
OB: A mix of amusement and disgust, I think, amusement at the docile predictability, disgust at the crawling. I also felt even more convinced that the book was needed, precisely because a publisher would turn it down for such a reason.

FT: Does God hate women?
OB: The God of most of the people who think there is a God certainly hates women. The God of some of them hates women with a weirdly obsessive neurotic hostility, so weird and petty and obsessive that one wonders what this god would make women for if it hates them so much. If it wants them covered up all the time, why didn't it make them out of a bale of cloth? If it doesn't want men looking at them, why didn't it make men without any eyes? [24]

State Atheism [Return]

And now we come to a deplorable phase in the history of Atheism, that of *state atheism*, characterized by a reign of terror, the killing of millions of people at the hands of some thinkers, politicians, military personnel, and plain dictators bent on changing the social and economic system of their respective countries. They traded one form of terror for another, using state-mandated atheism as a weapon to change society. Many lessons-to-be-learned from this dark, criminal, and sad period in the history of mankind. Never again must we allow the redeeming values of atheism to be used as tools to impose any type of ideology.

Vladimir Lenin (1870-1924) [Return]

Vladimir Ilyich Ulyanov *(Lenin)* was a Russian communist revolutionary, politician, a political theorist, and an Atheist.

He served as head of government of the ***Russian Soviet Federative Socialist Republic*** from 1917 and of the ***Soviet Union*** from 1922 until his death. Under his administration, the Russian Empire was replaced by the Soviet Union; all wealth including land, industry and business was nationalized. Based in ***Marxism***, his political theories are known as ***Leninism***.

Born to a wealthy middle-class family in Simbirsk, Lenin gained an interest in revolutionary leftist politics following the execution of his brother *Aleksandr* in 1887. Expelled from Kazan State University for participating in anti-Tsarist protests, he devoted the following years to a ***law degree*** and to radical politics, becoming a Marxist. In 1893 he moved to St Petersburg, and became a senior figure in the Russian Social Democratic Labour Party (RSDLP). Arrested for sedition and ***exiled to Siberia*** for three years, he married *Nadezhda Krupskaya*, and fled to Western Europe, where he became known as a prominent party theorist. In 1903, he took a key role in the RSDLP schism, leading the ***Bolshevik faction*** against Julius Martov's Mensheviks. Briefly returning to Russia during the ***Revolution of 1905***, he encouraged violent insurrection and later campaigned for the ***First World War*** to be transformed into a Europe-wide proletariat revolution. After the 1917 February Revolution ousted the Tsar, he returned to Russia.

Lenin, along with ***Leon Trotsky***, played a senior role in orchestrating the ***October Revolution in 1917***, which led to the overthrow of the Provisional Government and the establishment of the Russian Socialist Federative Soviet Republic. Lenin was elected to the position of the head of government by the All-Russian Congress of Soviets. Under Lenin's leadership the new government nationalized the estates and crown lands. ***Homosexuality and abortion were*** *legalized, being Lenin's Russia the first country in the world to establish both of these rights*. Free access was being given to both abortion and birth control. *No-fault divorce was also legalized*, along with universal *free healthcare* and free education being established. The Bolsheviks fought in the Russian Civil War during which Lenin's government carried out the *Red Terror. The civil war resulted in millions of deaths.* Lenin supported world revolution and immediate peace with the Central Powers, agreeing to a punitive treaty that turned over a significant portion of the former Russian Empire to Germany. The treaty was voided after the Allies won the war. In 1921 Lenin proposed the New Economic Policy, a mixed economic system of state capitalism that started the process of industrialisation and recovery from the Civil War. In 1922, the Russian SFSR joined former territories of the Russian Empire in becoming the Soviet Union, with Lenin as its head of government. Only 13 months later, after being incapacitated by a series of strokes, Lenin died at his home in Gorki.

After his death, there was a struggle for power in the Soviet Union between two major factions, namely *Stalin's* and the Left Opposition (with *Trotsky* as de facto leader). Eventually, Stalin, whom Lenin distrusted and wanted removed came to power and eliminated any opposition.

Lenin remains a controversial and highly divisive world figure. Historian J. Arch Getty has remarked that "Lenin deserves a lot of credit for the notion that the meek can inherit the earth, that there can be a political movement based on social justice and equality". Lenin had a significant influence on the *international Communist movement* and was one of the most influential and controversial figures of the 20th century. Admirers view him as a champion of working people's rights and welfare while critics see him as dictator who carried out mass human rights abuses: one of his biographers *Robert Service*, says he, "*laid the foundations of dictatorship and lawlessness. Lenin had consolidated the principle of state penetration of the whole society, its economy and its culture. Lenin had practised terror and advocated revolutionary amoralism."* *Time* magazine named Lenin one of the 100 most important people of the 20th century, and one of their top 25 political icons of all time; remarking that "for decades, Marxist–Leninist rebellions shook the world while Lenin's embalmed corpse lay in repose in the Red Square". Following the dissolution of the USSR in 1991, reverence for Lenin declined among the post-Soviet generations, yet he remains an important historical figure for the Soviet-era generations.[25]

Mao Zedong (1893-1976) [Return]

Also known as Mao Tse-Tung, he was a Chinese communist revolutionary, a political theorist, and a main figure in the implementation of "state Atheism" in mainland China.

> The founding father of the *People's Republic of China* (ROC), which he governed as Chairman of the Communist Party of China from its establishment in 1949 until his death in 1976. His Marxist-Leninist theories, military strategies and political policies are collectively known as Marxism-Leninism-Maoism or Mao Zedong Thought.
>
> Born the son of a wealthy farmer in Shaoshan, Hunan, Mao adopted a Chinese nationalist and anti-imperialist outlook in early life, particularly influenced by the events of the Xinhai Revolution of 1911 and May Fourth Movement of 1919. Mao converted to Marxism-Leninism while working at *Peking University* and became a founding member of the *Communist Party of China* (CPC), leading the Autumn Harvest Uprising in 1927. During the Chinese Civil War between the Kuomintang (KMT) and the CPC, Mao helped to found the *Red Army*, led the Jiangxi Soviet's radical land policies and ultimately became head of the CPC during the Long March. The KMT is also known as the Chinese Nationalist Party, the "Nationalists"; Generalissimo *Chiang Kai-shek*, assumed the leadership of KMT after the death of Sun Yat-

sen, the founder of KMT, in 1925. Although the CPC temporarily allied with the KMT under the United Front during the Second Sino-Japanese War (1937–45), after Japan's defeat China's civil war resumed and in 1949 Mao's forces defeated the Nationalists who withdrew to *Taiwan*.

On October 1, 1949 Mao proclaimed the foundation of the *People's Republic of China* (PRC), a single-party state controlled by the CPC. In the following years Mao solidified his control through land reforms and through a psychological victory in the Korean War, and through campaigns against landlords, people he termed "counter-revolutionaries", and other perceived enemies of the state. In 1957 he launched a campaign known as the *Great Leap Forward* that aimed to rapidly transform China's economy from an agrarian economy to an industrial one, which also led to widespread famine estimated to have resulted in up to 45 million deaths through starvation and other causes. In 1966, he initiated the Great Proletarian Cultural Revolution, a program to remove "counter-revolutionary" elements of Chinese society that lasted 10 years and which was marked by violent class struggle, widespread destruction of cultural artefacts and unprecedented elevation of Mao's personality cult and which is officially regarded as a "severe setback" for the PRC. In 1972, Mao welcomed US president *Richard Nixon in Beijing*, signaling a policy of opening China, which was furthered under Deng Xiaoping's rule in China.

A controversial figure, Mao is regarded as one of the most important individuals in modern world history.ws Supporters credit him with modernising China and building it into a world power, *promoting the status of women*, improving education and health care, and increasing life expectancy as China's population grew from around 550 to over 900 million during the period of his leadership. He is also known as a theorist, military strategist, poet, and visionary. In contrast, *critics consider him a dictator who severely damaged traditional Chinese culture, perpetrated systematic human rights abuses, and who is responsible for an estimated 40 to 70 million deaths* through starvation, forced labour and executions, ranking his tenure as the top incidence of genocide in human history.

Mao's private doctor reported on his personal hygiene. *He never brushed his teeth*, preferring to rinse out his mouth with tea and chew the leaves. By the time of his death, his gums were severely infected and his teeth were coated with green film, with several of them coming loose. Rather than bathe, he had a servant rub him down with a hot towel; according to at least one account, he went a quarter-century *without taking a bath*. Biographer *Peter Carter* described Mao as having "an attractive personality" who could for much of the time be a "moderate and balanced man", but noted that he could also be ruthless, and showed no mercy to his opponents. This description was echoed by Sinologist *Stuart Schram*, who emphasised Mao's ruthlessness, but who also noted that he showed no sign of taking pleasure in torture or killing in the revolutionary cause. *Lee Feigon* considered Mao "draconian and authoritarian" when threatened, but opined that he was not the "kind of villain that his mentor Stalin was". *Alexander Pantsov and Steven I. Levine* claimed that Mao was a "man of complex moods", who "tried his best to bring about prosperity and gain international respect" for China, being "neither a saint nor a demon." They noted that in early life, he strived to be "a strong, willful, and purposeful hero, not bound by any moral chains", and that he "passionately desired fame and power". *Carter* noted that throughout his life, Mao had the ability to gain people's trust, and that as such he gathered around him "an extraordinarily wide range of friends" in his early years.[26]

Enver Hoxha (1908-1985) [Return]
The socialist leader of *Albania*, one of the smallest and poorest countries in Europe, from 1944 until his death.

Albania under *Enver Hoxha* became, in 1967, the first (and to date only) formally declared *"atheist state"*, going far beyond what most other countries had attempted, completely prohibiting religious observance, and systematically repressing and persecuting adherents. The right to religious practice was restored in the fall of communism in 1991. He was chairman of the Democratic Front of Albania and commander-in-chief of the armed forces from 1944 until his death. He served as Prime Minister of Albania from 1944 to 1954 and at various times served as foreign minister and defence minister as well.

Hoxha was born in Gjirokastër, a city in southern Albania (then under the Ottoman Empire) that has been home to many prominent families. He was the son of Halil Hoxha, a Bektashi Tosk *cloth merchant* who travelled widely across Europe and the United States and Gjylihan (Gjylo) Hoxha. Fourteen years before Enver set off for France to study, his father brought him to seek the blessing of Baba Selim of the Zall Teqe. The baba did not refuse the request of the petitioner and made a benediction over the boy. At age 16, Enver Hoxha helped found and became secretary of the Students Society of Gjirokastër, which protested against the monarchist government of *Zog I*. After the government closed the Society, he moved to Korçë, continuing his studies in a French secondary school. There he learned French history, literature and philosophy. In this city he read for the first time the *Communist Manifesto.*

The 40-year period of Hoxha's rule was politically characterized by the *elimination of the opposition*, prolific use of the death penalty or long prison terms of his political opponents and evictions from homes where their families lived and their internment in remote villages that were strictly controlled by police and the secret police (*Sigurimi*). His rule was also characterized by Stalinist methods to destroy his associates who threatened his own power. Economically, during his period, *Albania became industrialised and saw rapid economic growth, as well as*

223

unprecedented progress in the areas of education and health. He focused on rebuilding the country which was left in ruins after World War II, building Albania's first railway line, eliminating adult illiteracy and leading Albania towards becoming agriculturally self-sufficient.

Albania, being a predominantly **Muslim European country**, largely due to Turkish influence in the region, had, like the Ottoman Empire, identified religion with ethnicity. In the Ottoman Empire, Muslims were viewed as Turks, Orthodox Christians were viewed as Greeks, and Roman Catholics were viewed as Latins. Hoxha believed this was a serious issue, feeling that it both fueled Greek separatists in North Epirus and that it also divided the nation in general. The Agrarian Reform Law of 1945 confiscated much of the church's property in the country. Catholics were the earliest religious community to be targeted, since **the Vatican was seen as being an agent of Fascism and anti-Communis**m. In 1946 the **Jesuit Order** and in 1947 the Franciscans were banned. *Decree No. 743* (On religion) sought a national church and forbade religious leaders from associating with foreign powers.

The Party focused on **atheist education in schools**. This tactic was effective, primarily due to the high birthrate policy encouraged after the war. During holy periods such as Lent and Ramadan many forbidden foods (dairy products, meat, etc.) were distributed in schools and factories, and people who refused to eat those foods were denounced. Starting on 6 February 1967, the Party began a new offensive against religion. Hoxha, who had declared a "Cultural and Ideological Revolution" after being partly inspired by China's Cultural Revolution, encouraged communist students and workers to use more forceful tactics *to promote atheism*, although violence was initially condemned.

According to Hoxha, the surge in anti-religious activity began with the youth. The result of this "spontaneous, unprovoked movement" was the **closing of all 2,169 churches and mosques in Albania. State atheism became** *official policy*, and Albania was declared the world's first atheist state. Religiously based town and city names were changed, as well as personal names. During this period religiously based names were also made illegal. The *Dictionary of People's Names*, published in 1982, contained 3,000 approved, secular names. In 1992, *Monsignor Dias*, the Papal Nuncio for Albania appointed by *Pope John Paul II*, said that of the three hundred Catholic priests present in Albania prior to the Communists coming to power, only thirty survived. All religious practices and all clergymen were outlawed and those religious figures who refused to give up their positions were arrested or forced into hiding.

Hoxha suffered a heart attack in 1973 from which he never fully recovered. In increasingly precarious health from the late 1970s onward, he turned most state functions over to Ramiz Alia. In his final days he was a *wheelchair user* and was suffering from diabetes, which he had suffered from since 1948, and cerebral ischemia, which he had suffered from since 1983. On 9 April 1985, he suffered a massive ventricular fibrillation. All efforts to reverse it failed, and he died early on the morning of 11 April 1985. Hoxha's death left Albania with *a legacy of isolation and fear of the outside world.* Despite some economic progress made by Hoxha, the country was in economic stagnation; Albania had been the poorest European country throughout much of the Cold War period. Following the *transition to capitalism in 1992*, Hoxha's legacy diminished, so that by the early 21st century very little of it was still in place in Albania. [27]

Modern Atheism [Return]

In this section we learn about *Modern Atheism*, a movement in progress mostly in the USA, England, Kenya, and other countries. Its leaders have learned to appeal to the *legal system* in efforts to stop Bible reading in public schools and to consolidate the separation of Church and State, as the Constitutions of those countries aim to guarantee for its citizens. It is an atheism that does not use force, military means, or fear to counter act the forces of organized religion, yet it is seen by some people as "aggressive" in nature and means.

Madalyn Murray O'Hair (1919-1995) [Return]

An American atheist activist, founder of *American Atheists*, and the organization's president from 1963 to 1986.

> O'Hair is best known for the *Murray v. Curlett* lawsuit, which led to a landmark **Supreme Court ruling ending official Bible-reading in American public schools** in 1963. This came just one year after **the Supreme Court prohibited officially sponsored prayer in schools** in *Engel v. Vitale*. After she founded the American Atheists and won *Murray v. Curlett*, she achieved attention to the extent that in 1964 *Life* magazine referred to her as "*the most hated woman in America*".

> In 1941, she married *John Henry Roths*. They separated when they both enlisted for **World War II** service, he in the United States Marine Corps, she in the Women's Army Corps. In April 1945, while posted to a cryptography position in Italy, she began a relationship with an officer, **William J. Murray**, a married Roman Catholic, who would refuse to divorce his wife. She divorced Roths, adopted the name Madalyn Murray, and gave birth to a boy whom she named William J. Murray III (nicknamed "Bill").

> In 1949, Murray completed a bachelor's degree from Ashland University. In 1952, she received an LL.B. *law degree* from the then unaccredited South Texas College of Law; however, she failed the bar exam and never practiced law. On November 16, 1954, she gave birth to her second son, Jon Garth Murray, fathered by her boyfriend *Michael Fiorillo*. She and her children traveled by ship to Europe, planning on defecting to the Soviet embassy in Paris and residing in the Soviet Union, due to that nation's promotion of **state atheism**. However, the USSR denied them entry. Murray and her sons returned to Baltimore, Maryland in 1960.

Murray filed a lawsuit against the Baltimore City Public School System in 1960, in which she asserted that it was unconstitutional for her son William to be required to participate in *Bible readings* at Baltimore public schools. In this litigation, she stated that her son's refusal to partake in the Bible readings had resulted in *bullying* being directed against him by classmates, and that administrators condoned it. After consolidation with *Abington School District v. Schempp,* the lawsuit reached the Supreme Court of the United States in 1963. The Court voted 8–1 in Schempp's favor, which effectively *banned mandatory Bible verse recitation at public schools in the United States*. Prayer in schools other than Bible-readings had already been ended in 1962 by the Court's ruling in *Engel v. Vitale.*

O'Hair appeared on the *Donahue Show* several times, including the first episode in 1967, following her appearance on the show Donahue himself said she was unpleasant and mocked him off camera for being a Catholic, although after O'Hair's death Donahue described her message of atheism as "Very Important." She also appeared on the show again in March 1970 debating with Preacher *Bob Harrington* "The Chaplain of Bourbon Street". Harrington also made a vinyl record on O'Hair entitled "10 Reasons why Madalyn Murray O'Hair Must Be Stopped." In the record Harrington ranted that Atheism "Isn't American".

Following her arrival in Austin, Texas, O'Hair founded *American Atheists*, "*a nationwide movement which defends the civil rights of non-believers, works for the separation of church and state and addresses issues of First Amendment public policy*". She acted as the group's first chief executive officer, the public voice and face of atheism in the United States during the 1960s and 1970s. In a 1965 interview with *Playboy Magazine*, she described religion as "a crutch" and an "irrational reliance on superstitions and supernatural nonsense".

In the same *Playboy* interview, O'Hair gave a long list of incidents of harassment, intimidation, and even death threats against her and her family for her views. She read several profane letters she received in the mail, with content including one that said (referring to the conversion of Paul the Apostle on the road to Damascus), "May Jesus, who you so vigorously deny, change you into a Paul." In response, O'Hair told the interviewer, "Isn't that lovely? Christine Jorgensen had to go to Sweden for an operation, but *me* they'll fix with faith, painlessly and for nothing." She stated that she left Baltimore because of persecution from Baltimore residents, including receipt of mail containing photos smeared with feces, the strangulation of her son Jon Garth's pet kitten and the stoning of her home by neighborhood residents, which she believed had caused her father's fatal heart attack.

She filed several lawsuits on issues over which she felt that the United States Constitution was **violated by a collusion of church and state.** One was against the city of Baltimore, demanding that it assess and collect taxes on property owned by the Catholic Church. O'Hair founded an atheist radio program in which she criticized religion and theism, and a television show she hosted, *American Atheist Forum*, was carried on more than 140 cable television systems. In the 1990s, American Atheists amounted to O'Hair, her son Jon Murray, her granddaughter Robin Murray O'Hair, and a handful of support personnel. (Robin, the daughter of William Murray, was adopted by Madalyn. William had not seen nor spoken to any of them in many years.) The trio lived together in O'Hair's large home. They went to the office together, took vacations together, and returned home together.

Her legacy. Madalyn Murray's lawsuit largely led to the removal of compulsory Bible reading from public schools in the United States, amongst other lasting and significant effects. Until the lawsuit, it was commonplace for students to participate in many types of religious activities while at school, including religious instruction itself. Nonreligious students were compelled to participate in such activities and were not usually given any opportunity to opt out. The Murray suit was combined with an earlier case, so the Court might have acted without Murray's intervention. With the success of the lawsuit, the intent of the Constitution with regard to the relationship between church and state again cam e under critical scrutiny and has remained there to this day. The success of O'Hair's lawsuit led to subsequent lawsuits by *Mormon and Catholic families* in Texas in 2000 to limit compulsory prayer at school-sponsored football games.

In 1995 she was *kidnapped, murdered and mutilated*, along with her son Jon Garth Murray and granddaughter Robin Murray O'Hair, by David Roland Waters, a convicted felon out on parole, and fellow career criminals Gary Karr and Danny Fry.[28]

Christopher Hitches (1949-2011) [Return]

A British-American author, *Atheist*, polemicist, debater, and journalist. He was also noted for his position against all religions, religious institutions, the Vietnam War, nuclear weapons, and racism.

He contributed to several books and newspapers, including *New Statesman*, *The Nation*, *The Atlantic*, *London Review of Books*, *The Times Literary Supplement* and *Vanity Fair*. *Hitchens* was the author, co-author, editor and co-editor of over thirty books, including five collections of essays, on a range of subjects, including politics, literature and religion. A staple of *talk shows* and lecture circuits, his confrontational style of debate made him both a lauded and controversial figure. Known for his contrarian stance on a number of issues, Hitchens excoriated such public figures as Mother Teresa, Bill Clinton, Henry Kissinger, Diana, Princess of Wales, and Pope Benedict XVI.

A noted critic of religion and an *antitheist* he said that a person "*could be an atheist and wish that belief in god were correct*", but that "*an antitheist, a term I'm trying to get into circulation, is someone who is relieved that there's no evidence for such an assertion"*. According to Hitchens, *the concept of a god or a supreme being is a totalitarian belief that destroys individual freedom, and that free expression and scientific discovery should replace religion as a means of teaching ethics and defining human civilisation*. His anti-religion polemic, New York Times Bestseller, *God Is Not Great: How Religion Poisons Everything,* sold over 500,000 copies.

Hitchens was born in Portsmouth, Hampshire. His parents, *Eric Ernest Hitchens* (1909–87) and *Yvonne Jean Hitchens*, met in Scotland when both were serving in the Royal Navy during World War II. His mother was *Jewish*, and kept that fact a secret. It wasn't until late 1987 that Hitchens learned he was Jewish by birth (though he became *a lifelong atheist*). He said, "My initial reaction, apart from pleasure and interest, was the faint but definite feeling that I had somehow known all along." His mother was a "Wren" (a member of the Women's Royal Naval Service), and his father an officer aboard the cruiser HMS *Jamaica*, which helped sink Nazi Germany's battleship *Scharnhorst* in the Battle of the North Cape. His father's naval career required the family to move a number of times from base to base throughout Britain and its dependencies, including in Malta.

In the 1960s, Hitchens joined the political left, drawn by his anger over the Vietnam War, nuclear weapons, racism, and oligarchy, including that of "the unaccountable corporation". He expressed affinity with the politically charged countercultural and protest movements of the 1960s and 1970s.

Hitchens was *bisexual* during his younger days, until he claimed his looks *"declined to the point where only women would go to bed with me."* While at Oxford he claimed to have had sexual relations with two male students who would later become Tory ministers during the Premiership of Margaret Thatcher.

Hitchens said that organized religion is *"the main source of hatred in the world, violent, irrational, intolerant, allied to racism, tribalism, and bigotry, invested in ignorance and hostile to free inquiry, contemptuous of women and coercive toward children"*, and that accordingly it "ought to have a great deal on its conscience". He often spoke about his efforts to champion the word 'antitheist' as he expressed his position that it was a relief that there is no evidence for a 'celestial North Korea'. Atheism was a word not strong enough to encompass his feelings about the immoral conundrum that the existence of a deity would necessarily imply. In *God Is Not Great*, Hitchens said that:

God Is Not Great, rendered Hitchens a major advocate of the *"New Atheism" movement*, and he also was made an Honorary Associate of the *National Secular Society*. Hitchens said he would accept an invitation from any religious leader who wished to debate with him. He also served on the advisory board of the Secular Coalition for America, a lobbying group for atheists and humanists in Washington, DC. In 2007, Hitchens began a series of written debates on the question "Is Christianity Good for the World?" with Christian theologian and pastor, Douglas Wilson, published in *Christianity Today* magazine. This exchange eventually became a book by the same title in 2008. During their book tour to promote the book, film producer Darren Doane sent a film crew to accompany them. Doane produced the film **Collision: Is Christianity GOOD for the World?**, which was released on 27 October 2009. On 4 April 2009 Hitchens debated William Lane Craig on the existence of God at Biola University.

In February 2006, Hitchens helped organise a pro-Denmark rally outside the Danish Embassy in Washington, DC in response to the Jyllands-Posten *Muhammad cartoons* controversy. Hitchens was accused by *Bill Donohue* of the Catholic League for Religious and Civil Liberties of being particularly anti-Catholic. Hitchens responded "when religion is attacked in this country ... the Catholic Church comes in for a little more than its fair share". Hitchens had also been accused of anti-Catholic bigotry by others, including Brent Bozell, Tom Piatak in *The American Conservative*, and UCLA Law Professor Stephen Bainbridge. In an interview with *Radar* in 2007, Hitchens said that if the **Christian right's agenda** were implemented in the United States "*It wouldn't last very long and would, I hope, lead to civil war, which they will lose, but for which it would be a great pleasure to take part.*" When Joe Scarborough on 12 March 2004 asked Hitchens whether he was "consumed with hatred for conservative Catholics", Hitchens responded that he was not and that he just thinks that "**all religious belief is sinister and infantile**".

In February 2010, Christopher Hitchens was named to the Honorary Board of distinguished achievers of the *Freedom From Religion Foundation*. In June 2010, Hitchens was on tour in New York promoting his memoirs *Hitch-22* when he was taken into emergency care suffering from a severe pericardial effusion and then announced he was postponing his tour to undergo treatment for **esophageal cancer.** He announced that he was undergoing treatment in a *Vanity Fair* piece entitled "Topic of Cancer". Hitchens said that he recognized the long-term prognosis was far from positive, and that he would be a "very lucky person to live another five years".

In April 2011, Hitchens was forced to cancel an appearance at the **American Atheist Convention**, and instead sent a letter that stated, "*Nothing would have kept me from joining you except the loss of my voice (at least my speaking voice) which in turn is due to a long argument I am currently having with the specter of death.*" He closed with "And don't keep the faith." **The letter also dismissed the notion of a possible deathbed conversion**, in which he claimed that "redemption and supernatural deliverance appears even more hollow and artificial to me than it did before." Hitchens died on 15 December 2011 at the University of Texas MD Anderson Cancer Center in Houston. According to Andrew Sullivan, his last words were "*Capitalism,* *downfall*." In accordance with his wishes, his body was donated to medical research. [29]

Richard Dawkins (1941-) [Return]

An English ethnologist, evolutionary biologist, Atheist, and writer. He is an *emeritus fellow* of New College, Oxford, and was the University of Oxford's Professor for Public Understanding of Science from 1995 until 2008.

> Dawkins came to prominence with his 1976 book *The Selfish Gene*, which popularized the gene-centred view of evolution. Dawkins is an *atheist*, a patron of the British Humanist Association, and a supporter of the Brights movement.[6] He is well known for his criticism of creationism and intelligent design. In his 1986 book *The Blind Watchmaker*, he argues against the watchmaker analogy, an argument for the existence of a supernatural creator based upon the complexity of living organisms. Instead, he describes evolutionary processes as analogous to a *blind* watchmaker.

> He has since written several popular science books, and makes regular television and radio appearances, predominantly discussing these topics. In his 2006 book *The God Delusion,* Dawkins contends that a supernatural creator almost certainly does not exist and that religious faith is a delusion—"a fixed false belief". As of January 2010, the English-language version had sold more than two million copies and had been translated into 31 languages. Dawkins founded the *Richard Dawkins Foundation for Reason and Science* to promote *the teaching of evolution* and to counteract those who advocate classroom programs against evolution.

> Dawkins was born in Nairobi, Kenya on 26 March 1941. He is the son of Jean Mary Vyvyan (née Ladner) and Clinton John Dawkins (1915–2010), who was an agricultural civil servant in the British Colonial Service in Nyasaland (now Malawi). Dawkins considers himself English and currently lives in Oxford, England. Having

been born in Kenya, he is a British citizen. His father was called up into the King's African Rifles during World War II; he returned to England in 1949, when Dawkins was eight. His father had inherited a country estate, Over Norton Park in Oxfordshire, which he turned into a commercial farm. Both his parents were interested in *natural sciences*; they answered Dawkins's questions in scientific terms.

Dawkins describes his childhood as "*a normal Anglican upbringing*". He was a Christian until halfway through his teenage years, at which point he concluded that the *theory of evolution* was a better explanation for life's complexity, and ceased believing in a god. Dawkins states: "*the main residual reason why I was religious was from being so impressed with the complexity of life and feeling that it had to have a designer, and I think it was when I realised that Darwinism was a far superior explanation that pulled the rug out from under the argument of design. And that left me with nothing.*" In his scientific works, Dawkins is best known for his popularisation of *the gene as the principal unit of selection in evolution*. This view is most clearly set out in his books:

> *The Selfish Gene* (1976), in which he notes that "all life evolves by the differential survival of replicating entities".
> *The Extended Phenotype* (1982), in which he describes natural selection as "the process whereby replicators out-propagate each other".

Critics of Dawkins's approach suggest that taking the gene as the unit of *selection* (a single event in which an individual either succeeds or fails to reproduce) is misleading; the gene could be better described, they say, as a unit of *evolution* (the long-term changes in allele frequencies in a population). In *The Selfish Gene*, Dawkins explains that he is using George C. Williams's definition of the gene as "that which segregates and recombines with appreciable frequency." Another common objection is that a gene cannot survive alone, but must cooperate with other genes to build an individual, and therefore a gene cannot be an independent "unit". In *The Extended Phenotype*, Dawkins suggests that from an individual gene's viewpoint, all other genes are part of the environment to which it is adapted.

Dawkins's book *The Greatest Show on Earth: The Evidence for Evolution* expounds the evidence for biological evolution, and coincided with Darwin's bicentennial year. Dawkins coined the word *meme* (the behavioural equivalent of a gene) as a way to encourage readers to think about how Darwinian principles might be extended beyond the realm of genes. Indeed, it was intended as an extension of his "replicators" argument, but it took on a life of its own in the hands of other authors such as *Daniel Dennett* and *Susan Blackmore*. These popularisations then led to the emergence of *memetics*, a field from which Dawkins has distanced himself.

Dawkins's *meme* refers to any *cultural entity* that an observer might consider a replicator of a certain idea or complex of ideas. He hypothesised that people could view many cultural entities as capable of such replication, generally through exposure to humans, who have evolved as efficient (although not perfect) copiers of information and behaviour. Because memes are not always copied perfectly, they might become refined, combined, or otherwise modified with other ideas; this results in new memes, which may themselves prove more or less efficient replicators than their predecessors, thus providing a framework for a hypothesis of *cultural evolution* based on memes, a notion that is analogous to the theory of biological evolution based on genes.

Dawkins is a prominent critic of *creationism* (the religious belief that humanity, life, and the universe were created by a deity without recourse to evolution). He has described the *Young Earth* creationist view that the Earth is only a few thousand years old as "a preposterous, mind-shrinking falsehood", and his 1986 book, *The Blind Watchmaker*, contains a sustained critique of the argument from design, an important creationist argument. In the book, Dawkins argues against the watchmaker analogy made famous by the 18th-century English theologian William Paley via his book *Natural Theology*, in which Paley argues that just as a watch is too complicated and too functional to have sprung into existence merely by accident, so too must all living things—with their far greater complexity, be purposefully designed. Dawkins shares the view generally held by scientists that **natural selection is sufficient** *to explain the apparent functionality and non-random complexity of the biological world*, and can be said to play the role of watchmaker in nature, albeit as an automatic, nonintelligent, *blind* watchmaker.

He has ardently opposed the inclusion of **intelligent design** in science education, describing it as "not a scientific argument at all, but a religious one". He has been referred to in the media as "Darwin's Rottweiler", a reference to English biologist *T. H. Huxley*, who was known as "Darwin's Bulldog" for his advocacy of **Charles Darwin's evolutionary ideas**. He has been a strong critic of the British organization Truth in Science, which promotes the teaching of **creationism** in state schools, and he plans through the **Richard Dawkins Foundation for Reason and Science** to subsidize schools with the delivery of books, DVDs, and pamphlets that counteract their (Truth in Science's) work, which Dawkins has described as an "educational scandal".

Dawkins sees education and consciousness-raising as the primary tools in opposing what he considers to be religious dogma and indoctrination. These tools include the fight against certain stereotypes, and he has adopted the term *bright* as a way of associating positive public connotations with those who possess a naturalistic worldview. He has given support to the idea of a free thinking school, which **would not indoctrinate children in atheism or in any religion but would instead teach children to be critical and open-minded**. Inspired by the consciousness-raising successes of **feminists** in arousing widespread embarrassment at the routine use of "he" instead of "she", Dawkins similarly suggests that phrases such as "Catholic child" and "Muslim child" should be considered as socially absurd as, for instance, "Marxist child", as he believes that children should not be classified based on their parents' ideological or religious beliefs.

Dawkins suggests that atheists should be proud, not apologetic, stressing that atheism is evidence of a healthy, independent mind. He hopes that the more atheists identify themselves, the more the public will become aware of just how many people actually hold these views, thereby reducing the negative opinion of atheism among the religious majority. Inspired by the *gay rights movement*, he founded the ***Out Campaign*** to encourage atheists worldwide to declare their stance publicly and proudly. He supported the UK's first atheist advertising initiative, the *Atheist Bus Campaign* in 2008, which aimed to raise funds to place atheist advertisements on buses in the London area.[30]

New Atheist Movement, Latest [Return]

More insight into this modern, new Atheistic movement. A social and political movement in favour of *atheism* and *secularism* promoted by a collection of modern atheist writers who have advocated the view that "*religion should not simply be tolerated but should be countered, criticized, and exposed by rational argument wherever its influence arises*." Such collection of writers is represented in particular by Richard Dawkins, Christopher Hitchens, Sam Harris, and Daniel Dennett, and Ayaan Hirsi Ali.

New Atheism lends itself to and often overlaps with secular humanism and antitheism, particularly in its criticism of what many New Atheists regard as the *indoctrination of children* and the perpetuation of ideologies. There is uncertainty about how much influence the movement has had on religious demographics worldwide. In England and Wales, as of 2011 the increase in atheist groups, student societies, publications and public appearances coincided with the non-religious being the largest growing demographic, followed by *Islam* and Evangelicalism. This trend in the growth of non-religion preceded the New Atheist movement.

The 2004 publication of *The End of Faith: Religion, Terror, and the Future of Reason* by *Sam Harris*, a bestseller in the US, marked the first of a series of popular bestsellers. Harris was motivated by the events of September 11, 2001, which he laid directly at the feet of *Islam*, while also directly criticizing *Christianity* and *Judaism*. Two years later Harris followed up with *Letter to a Christian Nation*, which was also a severe criticism of Christianity. Also in 2006, following his television documentary *The Root of All Evil?*, Richard Dawkins published *The God Delusion*, which was on the *New York Times* bestseller list for 51 weeks.

In a 2010 column entitled *Why I Don't Believe in the New Atheism*, Tom Flynn contends that what has been called "New Atheism" is neither a movement nor new, and that what was new was the publication of atheist material by big-name publishers, read by millions, and appearing on best-seller lists. These are some of the significant books in the field of New Atheism:

- *The End of Faith: Religion, Terror, and the Future of Reason* by Sam Harris (2004)
  - *Atheist Manifesto: The Case Against Christianity, Judaism, and Islam* by Michel Onfray (2005)
  - *Infidel* by Ayaan Hirsi Ali (2006 in Dutch, English translation 2007)
  - *The God Delusion* by Richard Dawkins (2006)
  - *Breaking the Spell: Religion as a Natural Phenomenon* by Daniel Dennett (2006)
  - *God: The Failed Hypothesis – How Science Shows That God Does Not Exist* by Victor J. Stenger (2007)
  - *God Is Not Great: How Religion Poisons Everything* by Christopher Hitchens (2007)

- *Godless: How an Evangelical Preacher Became One of America's Leading Atheists* by Dan Barker (2008)
- *The God Argument* by A. C. Grayling (2013).

During a public discussion featuring *Richard Dawkins, Christopher Hitchens, Sam Harris*, and *Daniel Dennett*, the group of prominent atheists were jokingly referred to as the "*Four Horsemen of the Non-Apocalypse*", a humorous reference to the Four Horsemen of the Apocalypse mentioned in the Book of Revelation in the Bible.

While The Four Horsemen are arguably the foremost proponents of the New Atheism, there are a number of other current, notable New Atheists including: Lawrence M. Krauss (author of *A Universe from Nothing*), Jerry Coyne (*Why Evolution is True* and complementary blog which specifically includes polemics against topical religious issues), Greta Christina (*Why are you Atheists so Angry?*), Victor J. Stenger (*The New Atheism*), Michael Shermer (*Why People Believe Weird Things*), David Silverman (President of the American Atheists), Ibn Warraq (*Why I Am Not a Muslim*), Matt Dillahunty host of the Austin-based webcast and cable-access television show *The Atheist Experience*, and others.

The New Atheists write mainly from a **scientific perspective**. Unlike previous writers, many of whom thought that science was indifferent, or even incapable of dealing with the "God" concept, Dawkins argues to the contrary, claiming the "God Hypothesis" is a valid scientific hypothesis, having effects in the physical universe, and like any other hypothesis can be tested and **falsified**. New atheism is politically engaged in a variety of ways. These include campaigns to reduce the influence of religion in the public sphere, attempts to promote cultural change (centring, in the United States, on the mainstream acceptance of atheism), and efforts to promote the idea of an '**atheist identity**'. Internal strategic divisions over these issues have also been notable, as are questions about the diversity of the movement in terms of its gender and racial balance.

Criticisms. *Cardinal William Levada* believes that **New Atheism** has misrepresented the doctrines of the church. Cardinal *Walter Kasper* described New Atheism as "aggressive", and he believed it to be the primary source of discrimination against Christians. In a *Salon* interview, intellectual provocateur *Chris Hedges* argued that **New Atheism propaganda is just as extreme as that of Christian right propaganda**. Some commentators have accused the New Atheist movement of **Islamophobia**. *Wade Jacoby* and *Hakan Yavuz* assert that "*a group of 'new atheists' such as Richard Dawkins, Sam Harris, and Christopher Hitchens*" have "*invoked Samuel Huntington's 'clash of civilizations' theory to explain the current political contestation*" and that this forms part of a trend toward "*Islamophobia [...] in the study of Muslim societies*". **William W. Emilson** argues that "the 'new' in the new atheists' writings is not their aggressiveness, nor their extraordinary popularity, nor even their scientific approach to religion, rather it is their attack not only on militant Islamism but also on **Islam** itself under the cloak of its general critique of religion".

Noam Chomsky, the prominent linguist, has said that Harris, Dawkins and Hitchens are "religious fanatics" and that in their quest to bludgeon society with their beliefs about secularism, they have actually adopted the state religion, one that, though void of prayers and rituals, demands that its followers blindly support the whims of politicians. Toronto-based journalist and commentator on Mideast politics, *Murtaza Hussain*, has alleged that leading figures in the New Atheist movement "have stepped in to give a veneer of scientific respectability to today's politically-useful bigotry".[31]

Demography and Statistics of Atheism [Return]
In this section I propose we take a look at the demographics of Atheism in the world, the difficulties in attempting to make such an assessment with statistics, and how these statistics are changing.

A 2012 poll on the **demographics of atheism** by *Gallup International*, featuring over 50,000 respondents worldwide, recorded that 13% of those interviewed said they were "*convinced atheists*". Other studies have concluded that *atheists* comprise anywhere from 2% to 8% of the world's population, with *irreligious* individuals adding a further 10% to 20%. *In Scandinavia and East Asia, and particularly in China, atheists and the nonreligious are the majority*. Globally, atheists and the nonreligious are concentrated in Asia and the Pacific with over 76% of all the irreligious or nonreligious residing in those regions. In *Europe*, the nonreligious make up 12.5% of the population and in *North America* they make up 5% of the population. In Africa and South America, atheists are typically in the single digits.

Discrepancies exist among sources as to how atheist and religious demographics are changing. Social scientific assessment of the extent of "atheism" in various populations is problematic. First, in most of the world outside of East Asia most populations are believers in either a monotheistic or polytheistic system. Consequently questions to assess non belief often take the form of any negation of the prevailing belief rather than an assertion of positive atheism and these would then be accounted accurately to rising "atheism". According to the 2012 Gallup International survey, *the number of atheists is on the rise across the world*, with religiosity generally declining. However, other global studies have indicated that global atheism may be in decline due to irreligious countries having the *lowest birth rates* in the world and religious countries having higher birth rates in general.

Statistical difficulties. Statistics on atheism are often difficult to represent accurately for a variety of reasons. Atheism is a position compatible with other forms of identity. *Some atheists also consider themselves Agnostic, Buddhist, Hindu, Jains, Taoist, or hold other related philosophical beliefs*. Some, like Secular Jews and Shintoists, may indulge in some religious activities as a way of connecting with their culture, all the while being atheist. Therefore, given limited poll options, some may use other terms to describe their identity. Some politically motivated organizations that report or gather population statistics may, intentionally or unintentionally, misrepresent atheists. Survey designs may bias results due to the nature of elements such as the wording of questions and the available response options. Also, many atheists, particularly former Catholics and former Mormons, are still counted as Christians in church rosters, although surveys generally ask samples of the population and do not look in church rosters. A negative perception of atheists and pressure from family and peers may also cause some atheists to disassociate themselves from atheism. Misunderstanding of the term may also be a reason some label themselves differently.

According to a 2011 Gallup poll, *more than 9 in 10 Americans say "yes" when asked the basic question "Do you believe in God?"*; this is down only slightly from the 1940s, when Gallup first asked this question. However, when given the choice to express uncertainties, the percentage of belief in God drops into the 70% to 80% range. Overall, *Americans* who profess no religion or self-identify as atheist or agnostic are more likely to be white or Asian and less likely to be black or Hispanic, as compared to the general adult population in U.S. Men are more likely to be atheists and less religious than women. 55 percent of atheists in America are under age 35, while 30 percent are 50 and over (compared to 37 percent of the total population). As a group, agnostics are older than atheists, though still younger than the general population. Irreligion in *South America* had increased for a period of 30 straight years, and it had a growing status in all countries in the first decade of the 21st century:

- Uruguay: 17.2% atheist or agnostic; 23.2% "believing in God but without religion"
- Argentina: 11.3% "indifferent towards religion" (including agnostic and atheists)
- Chile: 25% non-religious

- Ecuador: 7.94% atheist and 0.11% agnostic
- Brazil: 8.0% non-religious
- Colombia: 3% atheists, 12% atheists or agnostics
- Peru: 1.4% non-religious as of 1993
- Paraguay: 1.1% non-religious
- Venezuela: 8%

Europe. According to a ***2010 Eurostat Eurobarometer poll***, 51% of European Union citizens responded that "they believe there is a God", whereas 26% answered that "they believe there is some sort of spirit or life force" and 20% that "they do not believe there is a spirit, God, nor life force". Results were widely varied between different countries, with 94% of Maltese respondents stating that they believe in God, on the one end, and only 16% of Czechs stating the same on the other.

Next, Statistics on levels of religion and atheism in the following countries in the European Union, as shown on ***Table 1***. [32]

Table 1. Eurobarometer Poll 2010

Country	"I believe there is a God"	"I believe there is some sort of spirit or life force"	"I don´t believe there is any sort of spirit, God, of life force"
Malta	94%	4%	2%
Romania	92%	7%	1%
Cyprus	88%	8%	3%
Greece	79%	16%	4%
Poland	79%	14%	5%
Italy	74%	20%	6%
Ireland	70%	20%	7%
Portugal	70%	15%	12%
Slovakia	63%	23%	13%
Spain	59%	20%	19%
Lithuania	47%	37%	12%
Luxembourg	46%	22%	24%
Hungary	45%	34%	20%
Austria	44%	38%	12%
Germany	44%	25%	27%
Latvia	38%	48%	11%
United Kingdom	37%	33%	25%
Belgium	37%	31%	27%
Bulgaria	36%	43%	15%
Finland	33%	42%	22%
Slovenia	32%	36%	26%
Denmark	28%	47%	24%
Netherlands	28%	39%	30%
France	27%	27%	40%
Estonia	18%	50%	29%
Sweden	18%	45%	34%
Czech Rep	16%	44%	37%
EU27	**51%**	**26%**	**20%**

Thought and Knowledge Synthesis [Return]

My own observations on the thinkers presented above:

- A remarkable thinker, **Baruch Spinoza** did not believe in the anthropomorphic God of both Jews and Christians and, instead, he saw the laws of the universe as the closest entity to call "God." It is also interesting and impressive to realize that even though he predated *Charles Darwin* by 200 years, *Spinoza* already believed that **man has no free will**, given that his actions are dictated to a great extent by his physical and mental impulses, impulses that reflect his/her own evolutionary processes developed through millions of years. One of my favorite philosophers while I was growing up in my teenage and adult years.

- Though his contributions to **social contract theory** are well founded and recognized in political philosophy, **Thomas Hobbes'** status as an atheist person is confusing if not questionable, due to his own ambivalence on the subject. Yes, his writings were interpreted by many as "leading to atheism", but time and time again he made statements to preclude his being labeled a "heretic." Great thinker on social contract theory, but not a leading figure on atheism, I would say.

- Truly a remarkable and brave thinker is this **Kazimierz Lyszczynski,** clear in his convictions about the non-existence of God, a God created by man, as he asserted in his treatise *De non existentia Dei* (**The non-existence of God**). Punished by the Catholic Church in a most horrifying, terrorist, and criminal manner, pulling his tongue, burning his hands in slow fire, and then throwing him into the flames. So much to say for the good nature of the Catholic Church, again.

- That French priest, **Jean Meslier**, "was doing one thing but thinking another", performing services as a priest but writing his Atheistic "testament." He lived to be 65 years old, and I wonder if he ever felt he needed to keep his mask as a "priest" so he could later receive some sort of a pension from the church. There may be many priests in his situation, I often think. ¿What is a priest to do when he is well into his years, possibly approaching retirement, and realizes that all that religion, the church, and god is but a fantasy? ¿Say so, denounce religion and the church as a farce and lose his retirement pension from the church?

- I cannot find anything new in *d'Holbach's writings.* His *atheistic views* of the universe quickly remind us of *Spinoza's* natural laws, one hundred years earlier. It is peculiar, though, that he was buried within a church. Also, I find it interesting that this man, the owner of a salon in Paris, would find the time to write so extensively. Hey, the man knew how to organize his time and money, cheers to the man!

- *Ambiguity* is the word that I would use to define *David Hume*'s work on religion, the existence of god, and his discussions on the "afterlife." The man wanted to play it safe, stay alive in the face of a very powerful and sanguineous Catholic Church in Scotland at the time. He was considered by some to be an *Atheist*, though I would rather call him an *Agnostic*, at best. On the other hand, he did make worthwhile contributions to economics in areas of private property, inflation, and foreign trade, to the point that some consider that "Hume created the *first economic model*." High on economics, not very notable on Atheism.

- Politically he is remembered best as an advocate of trade unionism, republicanism, and for his support of women's suffrage in the conservative England of his time. Most important to me was his personal and public stand on *his right to be an Atheist* within the political system, a long struggle for his convictions. *Charles Bradlaugh* did not contribute to any writings on Atheistic thinking, but significantly enough he was a co-founder of the *National Secular Society*, a British campaigning organization that promotes *secularism* and the *separation of Church and State*.

- Recognized as a great political thinker, a co-founder of sociology, an economist, and a philosopher, *Karl Marx*, occupies a highly visible chair in the realm of free thinkers.

When it came to religion, he quickly dismissed it as *"the opium of the masses"*, giving it a very minimum of his personal effort and openly professed **Atheism** throughout his life. Yes, also a co-founder of **modern communism**, a major social upheaval early in the 19th century and during much of the 20th century. Marx was certain that communism would mean the success of the working class over capitalism, and yet we have come to observe that communism was a social and economic **experiment that lasted 50 years only** and that it is now gone, a thing of the past. We human beings are a bit more complicated than Marx may have thought of, apparently, given that no matter what group of people we employ to build a new society, a few within that group will eventually build a hierarchy to try to exploit, live better off than the rest in the group.

- As a man of many talents, **Nietzsche** wrote on many subjects as an independent thinker, and in none of them he chose to identify himself with an earlier school of thought or project, *Buddhism* being the exception. I have not been able to find any of his thinking to be totally new, though I recognize he gained recognition for the statement *"God is dead"* in one of his writings, *Thus Spoke Zarathustra*. Still, I agree with his need to "re-invent" life in an Atheistic world, as an experience worth living, and to do away with the *nihilism* of earlier thinkers. Unfortunately his poor mental health interfered with his critical thinking. A brave man who fought *anti-Semitism* and ill will against *homosexuality*.

- Being a woman and coming from a Jewish family, it is most commendable that 16-year old **Ernestine Rose** began to question religion and reject the concept of woman's inferiority in relation to man in society. She was not a writer, and she did not create new philosophical models, but she was among the most active and influential **Atheist** women in the USA and England in favor of women's rights, against slavery, in favor of the *feminist movement*. Rose was elected president of the **National Women's Rights Convention** in 1854.

- An incredibly strong person in her convictions, **Elizabeth Cady Stanton**, went on to become one of the most influential and pioneering women in the areas of *women's suffrage and rights, abolition of slavery*. Most amazing and daring is her writing of *The Woman's Bible* with other prominent women, where they defied the writings in the Old Testament and the New Testament, writings by men obsessed with the creation of hierarchy of men only, over all other men and all women. A major step, in my opinion, towards **Atheism**, the promotion of equality among women and men, and an understanding of mankind's presence in our planet, its finite existence now and never again.

- It cannot be said that **Matilda Gage** was an Atheist person, because she had religious beliefs of her own, but she would have been considered so at the time given her strong posture against Christianity, its church, its hierarchy of only men, and her defense of women's rights. I give her all possible credit and merit because in her time and condition as a woman the need for reform of laws and the creation of new ones to abolish slavery, recognize women's right to property and vote, was more important than promoting Atheism, I would say. Go for the basic things in life first, I say, next decide on religion or its avoidance.

- An extremely intelligent and brave woman, **Anne Nicole Gaylor**, greatly advanced the condition of American women through her leadership and effort promoting legalized abortion, her denunciation of religion as a cult against women's rights and equality. Her organization, *Freedom from Religion Foundation*, empowers some 19,000 members in the USA and Canada in their search for human dignity, gender equality, and service to the community. Not just an Atheist, but an **Atheist** person involved in service to the community and the nation.

- Again, intelligence, courage, and commitment would have to be the words to begin to describe **Ayaan Hirsi Ali,** a *Somali-born American* **Atheist,** and feminist activist. She is also unique and brave because she converted from a religion,

Islam in her case, to Atheism, a major feat in her own early society and culture. Today her attributes are highly valued as an associate at the *American Enterprise Institute (AEI)*, an organization that promotes separation of Church and State, limited government, and a strong Private Sector.

- Truly a remarkable person, **Ophelia Benson**, for decades has defended women's rights, intelligence, and value in society against religious fundamentalism, organized religions, and human stupidity in general on a large number of issues. A *feminist and an atheist*, this person deserves the highest praise for her dedication and effort using the mass media wisely to denounce oppression of women by all religions, especially through the use of interviews, a very effective means of communication. My greatest respects to this outstanding American thinker for her valuable services to the community!

- Much has been written and said about **Vladimir Lenin**, a principal figure in the transformation of the Russian Empire into the Soviet Union, beginning in 1917. I chose to include him in this list of prominent figures in history not because he was a philosopher, but because he was an Atheist, one of the first Atheist in modern "*state Atheism*." During much of the history of the Russian Empire of the Tzars the Russian people suffered at the hand of rich families, a hierarchy of nobility, a hierarchy of the Church in conspiracy with the nobility. A major change was in the making. He was convinced that the social change needed was in the form of a revolution, a revolution that would overthrow the rich and powerful, the owners of the means of production, the overthrow of the ruling Church, and its replacement with the ruling of the proletariat, the poor. Millions of people died or were murdered in the process, in achieving that major social change. The absence of religion in the administration of the new state gave rise and meaning to "state Atheism." Was state Atheism the answer to all problems? No, certainly not. It simply replaced the old hierarchy of power administrators with another hierarchy of power administrators. An experiment that lasted the better part of 50 years, as I mentioned earlier, an experiment that failed. Human nature is much more complicated. It must be said, however, that Lenin set the basis for industrializing the vast mother Russia, a capacity that later, during the Second World War, would enable the Russian people to defeat and repel Hitler's Nazis, with the help of the American people.

- The importance of **Mao Zedong** in the transformation of mainland China from a gigantic rural and agricultural extension of peoples and lands into a modern industrial complex is most significant. In some ways an experience similar to that of Vladimir Lenin in Russia, Mao Zedong, appeared at the right moment as China was about to undergo major social, economic, cultural, and political changes. Interesting enough, his "state Atheism" is having a longer longevity than that of Lenin in Russia, starting in 1919 and still going strong in the People's Republic of China (ROC). The experiment of "*state Atheism*" and communism in the ROC still goes on today, by contrast. Some of us feel that such longevity may be due in part to China's ability to consider and to **adopt forms of modern capitalism** in its industrial complex and multi-ethnic, multi-cultural societies.

- After briefly reviewing the development and legacy of "state Atheism" in the two largest societies at the beginning of the 20th century, I also wanted us to review the experience of Albania, one of the smallest and poorest countries in Europe, along that road under the leadership of **Enver Hoxha**. In these three cases the gains made in transforming their agrarian societies into industrial complexes resulted in the persecution and ultimate death of millions of people. **To what extent was the death of those millions of people the result in part of "state atheism"**? We may never know for sure. *What appears to be certain is that forced "state Atheism" is not the answer either to poor societies in our planet aspiring to a better life.* Infrastructures of power, whether directed and implemented by religious, governmental, or forced "Atheist state" hierarchies generally result in massive loss of life, and not in a deeper understanding of the trajectory of the human species over millions of years, not in an appreciation of the fragility of our existence in the planet. Is this experience and realization of potential value in the search for future development of Atheism? I propose to consider this question in the following chapters.

- Her story speaks of personal courage, determination, knowledge of the American institutional system and set of laws in the country, the USA, but also of opposition to her views and vision by many citizens, her controversial appearances on TV, Radio, and other mass media. *Madalyn Murray* did achieve a most significant breakthrough for Atheism in the USA through her use of the legal system in wining her lawsuit, *Murray v. Curlett*, which led to a landmark *Supreme Court ruling ending official Bible-reading in American public schools* in 1963. The US Constitution guarantees religious freedom, freedom to have and practice a religion of your choice, or the absence of religion, something that I happen to agree with, very much so. Without doubt, the USA continues to be one of the countries in the world where most religions flourish today. Her legacy is a tribute and a service to the community. The crime against Ms. Murray and her family members was perpetrated by a band of criminal men, and not by the American people, I would say.

- In *Christopher Hitchens* we definitely find a new type of Atheism, one that is not content with simply not believing in the existence of God, but one that passionately enumerates all the misery, destruction, and malefic use of power made by all religions, specially Judaism, Christianity, and Islam through the ages. Yes, he sought the eye and the ear of the media in the form of TV, Radio, talk shows, and books, with the debate as a main vehicle, and approach that I support. Not the imposition of parental beliefs on children who have to reached the age of reasoning, but reasoning, debate, and posture taking among adults.

- In *Christopher Hitchens* we definitely find a new type of Atheism, one that is not content with simply not believing in

251

the existence of God, but one that passionately enumerates all the misery, destruction, and malefic use of power made by all religions, specially Judaism, Christianity, and Islam through the ages. Yes, he sought the eye and the ear of the media in the form of TV, Radio, talk shows, and books, with the debate as a main vehicle, an approach that I support. Not the imposition of parental beliefs on children who have yet to reach the age of reasoning, but debate, posture taking, and reasoning *among adults*. Have we noticed how all religions gain in numbers by imposing their beliefs on the minds of young children, from the moment they are born?

- *Richard Dawkins* comes to us as an Atheist via his studies and work in the area of *evolutionary biology*, rather than any study or development of a philosophical work. Through the study of scientific evidence, rather than reasoning, speculation, and conjecture alone, I would add. The study of evolutionary biology, TV and Radio appearance, and book writing, three of his main traits. As an evolutionary biologist Dawkins looked into man, inside of man, into our set of genes, their composition and replication mechanisms, as agents of our human origin, composition, and behavior. In this book I have also chosen that path in order to attempt to learn more about our behavior towards religious infrastructures, reasons behind that behavior which sometimes is constructive and other times destructive. Would the irony be that the answers to our questions regarding our human origin, behavior, relation to all the other species, and ultimate end has always been inside of us, inside our genes?

- Indeed, a look at the agents and activities of *New Atheism* presents some paradoxical and interesting considerations. Should Atheistic thinking be mostly silent and un-organized, while aggressive religious movements promote indoctrination of children, religious wars, uncontrolled world population, misery and poverty among the masses? On the other hand, leading figures in the New Atheism movement use scientific evidence to gain understanding about our human nature and behavior while they are being criticized for their "aggressive" methods, TV and Radio appearances, as well as for their alleged campaign against Islam. *Where is the line to be set, if there is one, between progressive Atheism and aggressive Atheism?* Again, this is a topic that I pretend to address in this book, particularly in the chapters ahead.

Chapter
17

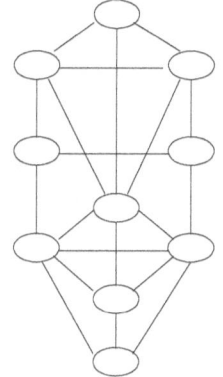

*"Oñati (<u>Basque</u>: Oñati, <u>Spanish</u>: Oñate, <u>French</u>: Ognate) is a town located in the province of <u>Gipuzkoa</u>, Basque Country, population of 10,500, 40 kilometers (25 miles) south of the **Bay of Biscay**. The name is Basque and translates roughly as "place of many hills", reflecting the landscape of the area. The town is surrounded on three sides by green mountains on the southern side by the Aloña limestone formation.*[2]

*"**Laguardia** (<u>Basque</u>: Guardia) is a town and municipality located in the southern province of Alava, Basque Country; it belongs to the region of Rioja Alavesa, a population of 1500. The place lies over a hill and it is surrounded by a wall that the **King Sancho "the Strong"** ordered to build. There are still preserved five different entries to access the walled city. Regarding the economy, its main strength is the **wine industry**. Indeed, the wine is elaborated and processed in numerous wineries."*[1]

Basque Country or Tucson, Arizona?

The analysis of the *"**Vatican leaks**"* documents continues at the research center headed by Dr. Finley at the University of Arizona, in Tucson, Arizona, USA. Finally, Kathy and Xabier have a few days to be together and try to make plans for their future. Both have just finished having dinner at Kathy's house on the foot of the **Santa Catalina Mountains**, just a couple of miles north of Tucson.

-This has been a fabulous dinner, Kathy. I am impressed by both the cuisine here in Tucson, your choice of wine, and by the views of the city from your balcony. A great evening, really.

-Well, I'm happy to hear that you feel this way, also. Now you know that we love to barbeque beef ribs using wood from the mesquite bushes which are all over the countryside. It gives them a special flavour...It's the mesquite wood, not so much my ability in the kitchen, then. Do you also like to cook?

-Yes, I do. I love to cook fish and meats, but I am not so good with desserts, though. Next time it would be pleasure to prepare something for the two of us, or for more people, of course.

The skies were beginning to fill with stars, and the city lights were giving shape and beauty to the city of Tucson in the near distance. Kathy thought the opportunity presented itself to ask Xabier a few questions. Questions about the weather? Questions about the next Rodeo in town? By now both were watching the city lights from her balcony.

-So, what are your plans, Xabier, are you going back to the Seminary of Arantzazu in Oñati, Basque Country, to become a priest one day? She said so looking at the city lights, trying to make it sound like a casual question.

-I have thought about it many times, Kathy, but many things and events have gone by since we first met that afternoon at the library of the University of Arizona. Can you see the university from here, can you see the football stadium lighted tonight?

-Yes, I can remember. I can remember how we both tried to grab the same book, you from one side of the book shelf, and myself from the other side, and then you...

-*I love you, Kathy*. I have loved you since that first day, from the moment you began to speak. –Said Xabier, who by now was behind Kathy, gently placing his hands around Kathy's waist, and whispering those words in her ears.

-*I love you too, Xabier*. I have been trying to say these words for months, wanting to know your response, wanting to know about your plans, our plans for the future.

256

At this point both Kathy and Xabier were standing next to each other at the balcony, with the city lights in the background, embracing each other. One kiss on her mouth led to another, and another. Both smiled and stood still, just looking at each other, not saying any word for a few seconds.

-Ohh, Xabier, I have a bit of news! Last night Dr. Finley said to me that he wants to offer you a job at the Council for World Peace (CWP), as a researcher and regular worker in his staff! Do you know what I'm saying?

-Yes! He also told me so two days ago, right after we all finished our work at the laboratory, translating and organizing some of the documents, and...

-So what did you say, I mean what was your answer to Dr. Finley? – Interrupted Kathy, wanting to get to the answer quickly.

-I said yes! I said I would be delighted to be part of the team on a regular basis, especially now that the *CWP* is organizing that *international meeting in Brussels*, Europe, in the year 2020. I said yes!

-I cannot believe all this is happening! So what does it mean, Xabier, what do we want to do now, I mean, you and I?

-Well, it means that we both are committed to the idea of working with the CWP, to travel to other countries to try and identify societies under stressful conditions, to identify "hot spots" in the globe and to alert member countries in the CWP of those "ready-to-explode" conditions so that resources can be gathered and contributed, of course. This report, for example, being prepared for the coming up international meeting in Brussels is going to inform on the health of the planet on those areas: *overpopulation, food resources at their limits, religious wars, climatic change, etc*. Nations and societies in the world need to face the reality of it, a planet Earth reaching its limits in those areas, those dimensions, and that we must address those problems and needs if we pretend to last as a human species beyond the next 500 years. –Suggested Xabier.

-Yes, but what about... Began to say Kathy.

-Of course, other organizations like **Greenpeace** will most likely join in, will contribute to the effort. Societies will also need to take a serious look at their respective religions and the social and political roles played by their hierarchies of power and control. We are killing each other in the name of this God and the other Gods, as thousands of women, men, and children die in the bombing of cities and towns all over the world, even today, at this very moment. We have to be realistic as a human species and consider the resources available in the planet, negative health conditions due to over industrialization and over production in some countries, the dangerous generation of CO_2 all over the planet, and make the changes and adjustments needed. That is what we need to do, as you and I know well.

-Yes, but what about... Continued insisting Kathy.

-I will also call the good folks at the Arantazu Seminary in Oñati to let them know that I no longer wish to become a priest, to let them know that the world is reaching a state of major crisis, that the planet's resources are reaching their limits, and that the CWP needs me and many other people to work with the CWP and other international organizations in order to achieve those goals, those changes needed to save our human species from auto-destruction and annihilation, for sure.

-Yes, I understand, but what about...

-Also, the time has arrived to gather people in Tucson to look into the idea of creating a Basque Center, the so called "**Eusko Etxea**", so that we do our part in protecting the Basque culture in Tucson, in the planet, we need all cultures, we need diversity of ideas, cultures, societies and people in our planet, no question about it.

-Yes, Xabier, but what about you and me? Asked Kathy, this time placing her hands in Xabier's shoulders.

-Furthermore... **Would you marry me, my dear Kathy?** Said Xabier with a smile from ear to ear, knowing that he had been teasing Kathy a bit with his lengthy statements.

-Yes, I would, I mean I do! And will we live in Tucson, Arizona, or Oñati, Basque Country? What would be your choice?

-In both places! Why not? If OK with you we will live and work in Tucson all year around, but for vacation we would go to the Basque Country to spend a few weeks with our relatives and friends. What do you say?

-*Wonderful! I love you, baby*! –Said Kathy, as they both embraced and kissed each other passionately.

NOTES

A note to the reader: Textual and graphical contents in this NOTES section are intended as an aid and service to the reader by expanding on topics and themes presented earlier in chapters throughout the book. Original sources, either books, articles, reports, or their *Uniform Resource Locator* (URLs; Web site address) in the Internet are cited. This author cannot vouch for the accuracy and/or validity of those materials in this "Internet age." It would not make sense either to ignore and not make use of the bountiful collections available on the Internet, gathered by thousands of individuals, from amateur writers, to published authors, and disciplined historians, just because these sources may not be "100% accurate, 100% of the time." Instead, it is proposed here, it is the reader's responsibility to determine if these materials are useful, accurate, valid, and sufficient for his/her personal use, and to decide if additional materials ought to be researched and gathered as well.

Chaps: 1, 2, 3, 4, 5, 6, 7, 8, 9, 10, 11, 12, 13, 14, 15, 16, 17
Bibliography

Part I: Kathy and Xabier, together again

Chapter 1: Kathy and Xabier, together again

[1] Quotes, courtesy of: http://www.notable-quotes.com

Chapter 2: A List of Crimes Resolved, Maybe

[1] Quotes, courtesy of: http://www.notable-quotes.com/c/crime_quotes.html

Chapter 3: The Vatican Secret Archives

[1] David Goldenberg, writer, in: http://theweek.com/articles/466772/10-secrets-vatican-exposed

[68] *Opening of the Vatican Secret Archives:* Benedict XVI has announced new research towards beatification of Pope Pio XII

("Hitler's Pope").
http://www.spiegel.de/international/world/0,1518,583205,00.ht
ml

Chapter 4: Creation of the Council for World Peace (CWP)

[1] *Menachem Begin* (1913-1992), 6th Prime Minister of Israel shared Nobel Peace Prize with Egyptian President Anwar Sadat, 1978 Nobel Peace Prize Winner, courtesy of:
http://www.doonething.org/heroes/begin.htm

[2] *Mikhail Gorbachev* (1931-), Russian Politician, Environmentalist, Social Activist, 1990 Nobel Peace Prize Winner, courtesy of:
http://www.doonething.org/heroes/gorbachev.htm

Part II: Planet Earth at its Limits

Chapter 5. World Population at its Limits

[3] *"Pakistan, populations pressures"*, 1 April 2013, **World Population Awareness (WPA)**, in:
www.overpopulation.org/Asia

[5] *"Family Planning Pilot Project in Philippines is a Success Story* 3 March 2013, by Bonnie Tillery, in:
www.overpopulation.org/Asia

[6] *"Fertility Rates Fall, but Global Population Explosion Goes on* "

[7] *Dan Brown*, writer, courtesy of:
http://www.goodreads.com/author/show/630.Dan_Brown

Chapter 6. Land and Sea Food Resources

[1] *Allan Savory*, writer, courtesy of:
http://www.brainyquote.com/quotes/quotes/a/allansavor603601.
html
[2] *Eric Ripert*, chef, writer, courtesy of:
http://www.brainyquote.com/quotes/quotes/e/ericripert509529.html

[4] *"Bangladesh: Land Scarcity and Rising Population",*

262

10 March 2013, Financial Express Bangladesh, in:
www.overpopulation.org/Asia

[7] "Food Security Overview", 10 Oct 2014, World Bank Organization, in:
http://www.worldbank.org/en/topic/foodsecurity/overview#1

[8] *Inside the Looming Food Crisis*", extreme weather, booming populations make building the food supply a challenge, by Dennis Dimick, 22 May 2014, **National Geographic**, in:
http://news.nationalgeographic.com/news/2014/05/140522-food-crisis-vulnerable-weather-climate-future/

[9] *"Chinese firms and Gulf sheiks are snatching up farmland worldwide. Why?"*, by Brad Plumer, 26 January 2013, **National Geographic**, in:
http://news.nationalgeographic.com/news/2014/05/140522-food-crisis-vulnerable-weather-climate-future/

[10] *"Seafood Crisis"*, **National Geographic**, October 2010, in
http://ngm.nationalgeographic.com/2010/10/seafood-crisis/greenberg-text/1

Chapter 7. Women Trafficking, Global Network

[1] *Human Trafficking*, in:
https://en.wikipedia/wiki/Human_trafficking

[2] *Sarah Elizabeth Mendelson (2005). Barracks and Brothels: Peacekeepers and Human Trafficking in the Balkans. CSIS. p. 2.ISBN 978-0-89206-464-9.*

[3] *"United Nations Convention Against Transnational Organized Crime And The Protocols Thereto" (PDF). Retrieved 2012-01-21.*

[4] Measures to prevent human trafficking, February 2009, in UNODC document, see http://www.unodc.org/unodc/en/human-trafficking/prevention.html?ref=menuside

[5] *GLOBAL REPORT* on Trafficking in Persons 2014, from United Nations on Drugs and Crime (UNODC), in https://www.unodc.org/documents/data-and-analysis/glotip/GLOTIP_2014_full_report.pdf

[6] *Polaris Project*, National Human Resource Center, see http://polarisproject.org/human-trafficking

[7] Human Traffickers, "Caught on Hidden Internet", A new set of search tools called **Memex,** developed by **DARPA**, peers into the "deep Web" to reveal illegal activity, see http://www.darpa.mil/Our_Work/I2O/Programs/Memex.aspx

[8] *Council of Europe*, chart of signatures of Treaty 197; see http://www.coe.int/ro/web/conventions/full-list/-/conventions/treaty/197/signatures?p_auth=Gn9RcCwG

[9] *India's web portal*, Anti Human Trafficking Portal, launched on 20 February 2014, see http://pib.nic.in/newsite/PrintRelease.aspx?relid=104002

[10] **The** growing exploitation of migrant women from central and eastern Europe, *Geneva, International Organization for Migration,* 1995.

[11] *Trafficking for Organ Trade*, UN.GIFT.HUB, see http://www.ungift.org/knowledgehub/en/about/trafficking-for-organ-trade.html

[12] *Smith, Heather M.* "Sex trafficking: trends, challenges, and the limitations of international law." **Human rights review** 12.3 (2011): 271-286.

[13] *"U.S. cites Russia, China among worst in human trafficking: report"*, 19 June 2013, In http://www.reuters.com/article/us-usa-humantrafficking-, idUSBRE95I1LC20130619

[14] *"Between Victim and Agent: A Third-Way Feminist Account of Trafficking for Sex Work"*, by **Shelly Cavalieri**, University of Toledo College of Law, see: http://ilj.law.indiana.edu/articles/86/86_4_cavalieri.pdf

[15] *Lori Foster*, writer, courtesy of: http://www.brainyquote.com/quotes/quotes/l/lorifoster697574.html

[16] *Win Calendar*, courtesy of: http://www.wincalendar.com/Human-Trafficking-Awareness

Chapter 8: Religious Wars (Islamic State)

[1] *Charles de Secondat*, 17th century French philosopher, courtesy of:
http://www.brainyquote.com/quotes/quotes/c/charlesdes355518.html

[2] *Benjamin Carson*, medical doctor, writer, courtesy of:
http://m.likesuccess.com/quotes/13/603866.png

[11] "Peak Oil" in: www.oildecline.com

[12] The Crusades, courtesy of www.wikipedia.org/wiki/Crusades

Chapter 9. Climatic Change

[1] Climatic Change, *"Report: Climatic change Crisis Catastrophic"*, by Hilary Whiteman, London (CNN), in www.cnn.com/2009/world/europe/05/29/annan.climate.change.human

[2] International Agreements, *National Geographic*, pg. 26, November 2015, courtesy of www.nationalgeographic.com.es

[3] Germany's energy model, by Robert Kunzig and Luca Locatelli, *National Geographic*, pg. 34, November 2015, courtesy of:
http://environment.nationalgeographic.com/environment/global-warming/

[4] "Will Global Warming Heat Us Beyond Our Physical Limits?", by Cheryl Katz, *National Geographic,* 15 December 2015; Courtesy of:
http://news.nationalgeographic.com/2015/12/151215-global-warming-heat-wave-stress-death-climate/

[5] *Steven Pinker*, writer, courtesy of:
http://www.brainyquote.com/quotes/quotes/s/stevenpink599094.html

[6] *Chellie Pingree*, politician, courtesy of:
http://www.brainyquote.com/quotes/quotes/c/chelliepin622564.html

[13] Climatic Change, "Report: Climatic change Crisis Catastrophic", by Hilary Whiteman, London (CNN), in

www.cnn.com/2009/world/europe/05/29/annan.climate.change.human

PART III: The Council for World Peace (CWP)

Chapter 10: Dr. Finley and Kathy travel to Africa

[1] *Kinshasa*, capital of the Democratic Republic of Congo (DRC), courtesy of: https://en.wikipedia.org/wiki/Kinshasa

[2] Land grabbing in Ethiopia, BBC News, 17 January 2012, see: http://www.bbc.com/news/world-africa-16590416

Chapter 11: Oñati and Laguardia, enchanted Towns

[1] Seminary in the Arantzazu complex, town of Oñati, Gipuzkoa, Basque Country, courtesy of: https://es.wikipedia.org/wiki/O%C3%B1ate#/media/File:O%C3%B1ate_-_Ayuntamiento.jpg

[2] Oñati, town in the province of Gipuzkoa, Basque Country; see: https://es.wikipedia.org/wiki/onati

[3] Laguardia, town in the province of Alava, Basque Country; see: http://www.laguardia-alava.com/index.php/es/

[4] *F. Scott Fitzgerald,* on his wife, *Zelda,* courtesy of: http://stylecaster.com/love-quotes/

[5] *Robert M. Parker, Jr.,* writer, courtesy of: http://www.brainyquote.com/quotes/quotes/r/robertmpa674168.html

Chapter 12: Planning the entry into the Secret Archives

[10] *The Vatican Secret Archives Conspiracy*, courtesy of: http://coolinterestingstuff.com/the-vatican-secret-archives-conspiracy

[11] *10 Secrets of the Vatican exposed*, courtesy of: http://theweek.com/articles/466772/10-secrets-vatican-exposed

266

Part IV:
A Solution to Sustainable Life in the Planet

Chapter 13: Human Evolution, reaching its end?

[1] *Carbon-14*, ^{14}C, or *radiocarbono-14*, is a radioactive isotope of carbon with a nucleus containing 6 protons and 8 neutrons. Its presence in organic materials is the basis of the radiocarbon dating method pioneered by Willard Libby and colleagues (1949), to date archaeological, geological, and hydrogeological samples. Carbon-14 was discovered on 27 February 1940, by *Martin Kamen* and Sam Ruben at the University of California Radiation Laboratory in Berkeley, although its existence had been suggested by Franz Kurie in 1934.

[2] *Avram Noam Chomsky* (1928-) is an American linguist, philosopher, cognitive scientist, logician, historian, political critic, and activist. He is an Institute Professor and Professor (Emeritus) in the Department of Linguistics & Philosophy at MIT, where he has worked for over 50 year. In addition to his work in linguistics, he has written on war, politics, and mass media, and is the author of over 100 books.[13] According to the Arts and Humanities Citation Index in 1992, Chomsky was cited as a source more often than any other living scholar from 1980 to 1992, and was the eighth most cited source overall. He has been described as a prominent cultural figure, and he was voted the "world's top public intellectual" in a 2005 poll. Chomsky has been described as the "*father of modern linguistics*" and a major figure of analytic philosophy. His work has influenced fields such as computer science, mathematics, and psychology. He is credited as the creator or co-creator of the Chomsky hierarchy, the universal grammar theory, and the Chomsky–Schützenberger theorem. After the publication of his first books on linguistics, Chomsky became a prominent critic of the Vietnam War, and since then has continued to publish books of political criticism. He has become well known for his critiques of U.S. foreign policy, state capitalism and the mainstream news media.

[5] "The ancestors of today's primates were small and ate insects", **Figure 1**, Chapter 2, courtesy of **Boyd y Silk (2003)** and its publisher.

[6] The genetic variety of modern hominids, in Boyd and Silk (2003), pgs. 422-446.

[7] The human throat, Boyd and Silk (2003), pg. 450.

[8] Silvio's open space, Boyd and Silk (2003), pg. 461.

[9] . **William B. ("Will") Provine** (born c. 1942)

Provine is a historian of science specializing in population biology and the Modern Synthesis in evolutionary theory. He has published the definitive study of the distinguished geneticist, Sewall Wright. A Tennessee native educated at the University of Chicago, he is Distinguished University Professor at Cornell University, where he holds appointments in the Department of Ecology and *Evolutionary Biology*, the Department of History, and the Department of Science and Technology Studies. Provine, who is a hard determinist as well as an atheist, rejects all forms of teleology in biology and claims that "evolution is the greatest engine of atheism ever invented."

The Origins of Theoretical Population Genetics and *Sewall Wright and Evolutionary Biology; articles:* Progress in evolution and meaning in life", 1989, In: M. Nitecki, ed., *Evolutionary Progress*, ISBN 0-226-58692-8

[10] On Richard Leakey, courtesy of:
http://www.britannica.com/EBchecked/topic/333898/Richard-Leakey

[11] *Donald Johanson,* scientist, writer, courtesy of:
http://www.brainyquote.com/quotes/quotes/d/donaldjoha355706.html

Chapter 14: Inside the Secret Archives

[1] *10 Secrets of the Vatican exposed*, courtesy of:
http://theweek.com/articles/466772/10-secrets-vatican-exposed

Chapter 15: The Findings, Please

[1] *"Religion, Rome and The Reich: The Vatican's other dirty secret"*, 21 May 2006, in:
http://www.independent.co.uk/news/world/europe/religion-rome-and-the-reich-the-vaticans-other-dirty-secret-479043.html

Chapter 16: Network of Atheist Organizations

[1] Quote by Emmet Fields, author of "Is the Bibble the word of God?", in:
http://www.goodreads.com/author/show/6979279.Emmett_F_Fields

[2] Most contents in Chapter 12 are extracts from "History of Atheism", in: http://en.wikipedia.org/wiki/History_of_atheism

[3] Text from Samkhya Karika, in:
http://www.ivantic.net/Moje_knjige/karika.pdf

[4] Basics of Jainism, in: http://en.wikipedia.org/wiki/Jainism

[5] Namokara Mantra in Jainism, in:
http://en.wikipedia.org/wiki/Namokar_Mantra

[6] Sophism, courtesy of: http://en.wikipedia.org/wiki/Sophism

[7] Epicurus, courtesy of: http://en.wikipedia.org/wiki/Epicurus

[8] Baruch Spinoza, courtesy of:
http://en.wikipedia.org/wiki/Baruch_Spinoza

[9] Thomas Hobbes, courtesy of:
http://en.wikipedia.org/wiki/Thomas_Hobbes

[10] Kazimierz Lyszczynski, courtesy of:
http://en.wikipedia.org/wiki/Kazimierz_ Lyszczynski

[11] Jean Meslier, courtesy of:
http://en.wikipedia.org/wiki/Jean_Meslier

[12] Baron d'Holbach, courtesy of:

[13] David Hume, courtesy of:

[14] Charles Bradlaugh, courtesy of:
www.en.wikipedia.org/wiki/Charles_Bradlaugh

[15 Karl Marx, courtesy of: www.en.wikipedia.org/wiki/Karl_Marx

[16] Friedrich Nietzsche, courtesy of:
www.wikipedia.org/wiki/Friedrich_Nietzsche

[17] Ernestine Rose, courtesy of:
http://en.wikipedia.org/wiki/Ernestine_Rose

[18] Elyzabeth Cady, courtesy of:
http://en.wikipedia.org/wiki/Elizabeth_Cady_Stanton

[19] Matilda Gage, courtesy of:
http://en.wikipedia.org/wiki/Matilda_Joslyn_Gage

[20] Passage from *The Women's Bible*, The Book of Genesis, 26, 27, 28, by Matilda Gage and her committee, see in www.amazon.com

[21] Anne Nicol Gaylor, courtesy of:
www.en.wikipedia.org/wiki/Anne_Nicol_Gaylor

[22] Ayaan Hirsi Ali, courtesy of:
www.en.wikipedia.org/wiki/Ayaan_Hirsi_Ali

[23] Ophelia Benson, courtesy of:
www.en.wikipedia.org/wiki/Ophelia_Benson

[24] An interview with Ophelia Benson by The Freethinker, in: www.freethinker.co.uk/2008/05/16/, "Not much of a believer, a world exclusive interview with Ophelia Benson."

[25] Vladimir Lenin, courtesy of:
www.en.wikipedia/wiki/Vladimir_Lenin

[26] Mao Zedong, courtesy of:
www.en.wikipedia/wiki/Mao_Zedong

[27] Enver Hoxha, courtesy of:
http://en.wikipedia.org/wiki/Enver_Hoxha

[28] Madalyn Murray O'Hair, courtesy of:
www.en.wikipedia.org/wiki/Madalyn_Murray_O'hair

[29] Christopher Hitches, courtesy of:

[30] Richard Dawkins, courtesy of:
www.en.wikipedia.org/wiki/Christopher_Hitchens

[31] New Atheist Movement, courtesy of:
www.en.wikipedia.org/wiki/New_Atheism

[32] Demography and Statistics of Atheism, courtesy of:
www.en.wikipedia.org/wiki/Demographics_of_Atheism

Chapter 17: Basque Country or Tucson, Arizona?

[1] Town of Oñati, Basque Country, courtesy of:
https://en.wikipedia.org/wiki/Oñati

[2] Town of Laguardia, Basque Country, courtesy of:
https://en.wikipedia.org/wiki/Laguardia,_Alava

Bibliography

Acharya S. (real name is D.M. Murduck), *The Christ Conspiracy: The Greatest Story ever Sold*, Kempton, Illinois, 1999; see also Adventures Unlimited Press, ISBN 0-932813-74-7.

Backman, Ronet, and Linda E. Saltzman, *Violence against women: Estimates from the redesigned survey,* Bureau of Justice Statistics (PDFNCJ 154348), August 1995. Also in: www.ojp.usdo.jgov/bjs/pdf/femvied.pdf

Benimeli, Jose A. Ferrer, *The Vatican Secret Archives (Los Archivos Secretos Vaticanos y los Masoneria: Mitos Politicos y una Condena Pontifica),* Universidad Catolica Andress Bello, Caracas, Venezuela, 1976.

Goikoetxea, Ambrose, *Euskal Herria Nation-State in the 21st. Century: A New Socio-Political Architecture*, 537 pages, Euskal Herria 21st. Century Press, Arrasate, Gipuzkoa, Basque Country, 1977; distributed by amazon.com (www.amazon.com).

Gollin, James, *Worldly Goods, The wealth and power of the American Catholic Church, the Vatican, and the men who control the money (Riquezas de este Mundo, la Riqueza y Poder de la Iglesia Católica de los Estados Unidos, el Vaticano, y los Hombres que controlan el Dinero),* 531 paginas, New York, first edition, 1971.

Gruber, E.R, and H. Kersten, *The Original Jesus: The Buddhist Sources of Christianity*, 288 pages, ISBN-13: 978-1852308353, Element Books Ltd, May 1996.

Iriondo, I., R. Sola, y A. Otegi, *Mañana, Euskal Herria, Entrevista con Arnaldo Otegi*, Baigorri Argitaletxea editorial, Bilbao, Euskadi, gara@gara.net, 2005.

Ingersoll, Robert Green, *Some Mistakes by Moses*, originally published in 1879, copyright 2009 by Cosimo Inc.

Jeffers, H. Paul, *Dark Misteries of the Vatican (Misterios Oscuros del Vaticano)*, 205 pages, Citadel Press, ISBN 13-978-0-8065-3132-8, New York, 2010.

Kasmir, Sharryn, *The Mondragon Myth (El Mito de Mondragon: Cooperativas, Politica, y la Clase Trabajadora en un Pueblo Vasco)*, Albany, NY, State University of New York Press, 1996.

Kelly, J.N.D., *The Oxford Dictionary of Popes*, Oxford University Press, Oxford 1986.

Kechris, Alexander S., *Classical Descriptive Set Theory*, Springer-Verlag, New York, 1995.

Kloppenborg, John S., *The Earliest Gospel (El Evangelio más Antiguo)*, 187 pages, Westminster John Knox Press, Louisville, Kentuky, EE.UU., 2008.

Kurlansky, Mark, *The Basque History of the World (La Historia Vasca del Mundo)*, 387 pages, Walker and Company, New York, ISBN 0-8027-1349-1, 1999.

Laboa Gallego, J.M., *History of the Popes*, La Esfera de los Libros Publishers, 2005, Avenida de Alfonso XIII, 1 bajos, Madrid 28002, tel 91296 02 00, www.esferalibros.com

Lertxundi, Jabier, *The Technocrats in MCC, the Opus Dei, and the PNV (La Tecnocracia en MCC, El Opus Dei, y el PNV)*, 207 pages, ISBN 84-931693-66, Basandere Press, Donostia, Euskal Herria (Basque Country), 2002.

Lindtner, Christian, *"The Pope in the Footsteps of the Buddha"*, http://jesusisbuddha.com/pope.htmlScott, Kenneth, *A History of Christianity*, Harper and Row publishers, 1975.

Livingstone, Elizabeth, *The Concise Oxford Dictionary of the Christian Church*, Oxford University Press, Oxford 1977.

Lost Gospel of Judah, National Geographic, DVD video format, 2006 NGHT, Inc.

Martin, Malachi, *The Jesuits (Los Jesuitas)*, 525 pages, Simon & Schuster, New York, ISBN 978 0 671 54505 5, 1987.

Martin, Malachi, *Rich Church, Poor Church (La Iglesia Rica, la Iglesia Pobre)*, 253 pags.; Putnam Pub Group, ISBN-10: 0399129065; 1984

Manhattan, Avro, *Murder in the Vatican*, Ozark Books, Springfield, Mo., 1958.

Manhattan, Avro, *Vatican Holocaust*, Ozark Books, Springfield, Mo., 1988.

Manhattan, Avro, *The Vatican in World Politics*, Copyright 1949 by Gaer Associations, Inc., 1949; see also: http://www.cephas-library.com/catholic/catholic_vatican_in_world_politics_introduction.html

Manhattan, Avro., *The Vatican Billions*, 1983, see: http://www.cephasministry.com/catholic_vaticans_billions_1.html

Montero, Daniel, *The Spanish Political Caste (La Casta, el Increíble Chollo de ser Politico en España)*, 285 pages, La Esfera de los Libros, ISBN 978-84-9734-885-0, Madrid, 2010.

Melnyk, George, University of Calgary, *Comentario* sobre el libro de George Chaney (2002), en www.historycooperative.org/cgi-bin

Moreno Bayona, Victor, *El Soborno del Cielo*, ISBN 84 7681 444 5, 190 pages, Ona Industria Grafica Press, Poligono Agustinos/Soltxate, Calle F, nave B6, 31013 Iruña-Pamplona, Navarre, Euskal Herria, 2005.

Molares do Val, Manuel, *Cronicas Barbaras,* "Mondragon", 2008 (http://cronicasbarbaras.blogs.com/crnicas_brbaras/2008/04/mondragn.html).

Moral, Jose A. del, "Saratxaga propone una alternativa al Grupo Mondragon", *Cybereuskadi*, 29 Marzo 2009, en http://cybereuskadi.com/saratxaga-promueve-una-alternativa-al-grupo-mondragon

Passelecq, George, y Bernard Suchecky, *The Hidden Encyclical of Pius XI (La Enciclica Escondida de Pio XI)*, Harcourt Brace, New York, 1977.

Phayer, Michael, *Pius XII, The Holocaust, and the Cold War.* Indianapolis: Indiana University Press, 2008, ISBN 978-0-253-34930-9.

Pagels, Elaine, *The Gnostic Gospels*, Random House, NY, 1981.

Pritchard, James B., *The Times Bible´s Atlas*, 2nd edition, Plaza and Janes Editors, 1992.

Puzo, Mario, *The Borgias, the First Great Family of Crime (Los Borgias, la Primera Gran Familia del Crimen),* Planeta Internacional, ISBN 84-08-04067-7 397 pages, 2001.

Reese, Tomas J., *Inside the Vatican*, 317 pages, Harvard University Press, ISBN 9-780674-932616, London, 2003.

Renzetti, Claire M., Jeffrey L. Edleson, and Raquel Kennedy Bergsen, *Sourcebook on Violence against Women*, 391 pages, Sage Publishers (order@sagepub.com), Washington DC, 2nd. Edition, 2011.

Riddle, J.E. (1804-1859), *The History of the Papacy, to the Period of Reformation*, Richard Bentley Publishers, London, 1854. Also, see digital contents of book: http://www.archive.org/stream/historyofpapacyt01ridd#page/142/mode/2up

Rodriguez, Pepe, *Lies of the Catholic Church (Mentiras Fundamentales de la Iglesia Católica)*, Ediciones B, Bailen 84, Barcelona 08009, Spain, 2004, www.edicionesB.com

Sastre, Alfonso, *Lope de Aguirre que Estás en los Infiernos*, 120 pages, Editorial Hiru, ISBN 978-84-96584-36-5, Hondarribia 2010.

Secret Vatican Archives, 64 pages, Archivio Segreto Vaticano, Citta del Vaticano, 2006.

Secret Vatican Archives, 64 pages, Archivio Segreto Vaticano, Citta del Vaticano, 2006

Schwartz, Judith, *Mondragon: Reclaiming Regional Production Capacity*, New Economics Institute, 3 Decemer 2009, in http://neweconomicsinstitute.org

Steinem, Gloria, *Revolution from Within (La Revolucion Interna)*, 422 pages, ISBN 0-316-81240-4, USA, 1991

Sorauren, Mikel, *History of Navarre, The Basque State* (*Historia de Navarra, El Estado Vasco*), ISBN 84-7681-299-X, Erel editorial, Paulino Caballero 38, 31003 Pamplona-Iruña, 1998

Tamayo Acosta, Juan Jose, "*John Paul II and the Opus Dei*" (http://www.voltairenet.org/article125522.html#article125522).

The Lost Gospel of Judah, National Geographic, DVD video format, 2006 NGHT, Inc.

The Times Bible´s Atlas, 2nd edition, by James B. Pritchard, Plaza and Janes Editors, 1992.

Uriona, A., "Gernika pide la paz como valor supremo", El País, Bilbao, 27 de Abril 2007.

Watkins, Gloria Jean, *Ain't I a Woman? (No soy una Mujer?)*, 223 pages, South End Press, Boston, MA, USA, 1981.

Williams, Paul L., *Murder, Money, and the Mafia: The Vatican Exposed*, Prometheus Books, 2003, also see: www.prometheusbooks.com

Wurtzel, Elizabeth, *Bitch: In Praise of Difficult Women*, 438 pages, Anchor Books, ISBN 0-385-48401-1, New York, 1999.

Zachman, J., "A framework for information systems architecture", *IBM Systems Journal*, Vol. 26, No. 3, 1987.

Recommended Websites

"The Buddha, Life and Teachings of the Lord Buddha," http://www.angelfire.com/realm/bodhisattva/buddha.html

"Buddha on Christianity", http://christianity.nibbanam.com/

"Buddhism and Christianity," http://en.wikipedia.org/wiki/Buddhism_and_Christianity

Ambrose Goikoetxea, Ph.D.

Double-Tradition content in New Testament Bible: See .
http://www.textexcavation.com/doubletraditioninventory.html

✳✳✳

Acknowledgements

I would like to express my gratitude to a number of people who have contributed to the making of this novel-trilogy, initially with their own questions, personal stories, experiences, suggestions of themes and issues to explore, and later with their own comments, likes and dislikes, and encouragement to have this work published.

Very specially, my thanks and appreciation to **Aloña Altuna**, my wife, my companion at work and in life, for listening to ideas and theories that would take shape in my mind as I ventured into each chapter. Her own questions motivated my searching deeper into events, issues, and into those very same ideas and theories. Her sister **Eli Altuna**, for taking the time to read several chapters, and for her own interest in wanting to know more about "regular women and men in the USA society", thus encouraging additional descriptions of American women and men in this book, "**The Planet Earth at its Limits**", Book 3 of this novel-trilogy.

As the drafts of the various chapters would take shape I would send them to **Lucien Duckstein**, my old and dear doctoral dissertation teacher at the University of Arizona, my life-long friend, although he has passed away before seeing this third volume published. "*Ambrose, this section fits best in chapter 6...*", or "*This point you are making does not come across well... needs better explanation*", or "*Do away with this text and space and just cite the references...*" He would say. If my writing and organization of issues could survive his critique, I would then manage to convey its contents to the readers, I felt. My deepest appreciation for sharing his talents, constructive criticism, and life-long friendship.

During the last twenty years I have visited the town of Zugarramurdi, northern **Navarre**, Basque Country, on several occasions to visit its famous "witch caves" and other places where the "Akelarre" meetings of "witches" took place, but mostly to visit with its loving town people. Dear people like **Koro Irazoki** and **Gonzalo Garmendia** and other women members of the Akelarre Association, gave generously of their time in my efforts to learn about the their lives, work, and cultural activities today to remember the women and men from their town that were taken away by the

Spanish Inquisition in 1610. When I suggested that I might be able to arrange for a meeting with City Hall officials in Logroño, they did not support the idea at first: "*Ambrose, they will not listen to you or anyone... 400 years have gone by and neither the Logroño City Hall nor the Spanish State have done anything to remember those victims.*" After several visits with Logroño's City Hall officials, I was able to secure their promise to "do something", however, and eventually City Hall representatives Zugarramurdi and Logroño met in the Spring of 2010 "to gather in peace and democracy", a significant first step. My desire to hear Logroño City Hall officials express any words of "moral responsibility", or any type of responsibility, for the deaths and damages caused by Logroño's City Hall officials in 1610 met with deaf ears, on the other hand. Still, Koro, Gonzalo, Aloña, and I tried to make history, together, and hopefully our lives are a bit richer today for trying.

My vote of thanks to **Ainhoa Aguirre**, director of the Museum of Zugarramurdi, and her dedicated support staff of young women for providing the full list of 103 women and men of Zugarramurdi and nearby towns that were processed by the Spanish Inquisition in 1610. Also my thanks to Ainhoa for allowing me to participate as an invited speaker at the Museum on 29 June 2010 to remember those women and men. Along the same vein, my thanks to **the people of Zugarramurdi's "Ayuntamiento"** (City Hall) for providing me with a full list of the town's 283 inhabitants today, with family names, in order to carry out one comparative analysis, an analysis that produced interesting results and possibly a "first time look" at the full horror and devastation perpetrated on the people of Zugarramurdi by the Auto-de-Fe carried out in Logroño in 1610.

Another vote of thanks to **Estitxu** and **Victoria Beistegui** and the people of **Sociedad Amigos de Laguardia**, in Laguardia-Biasteri, for making possible the participation of **Dancers of Laguardia** led by "**Raul**" in the town of Zugarramurdi in the summer of 2010 to help remember the men and women of 1610.

Walking into Logroño's City Hall in the summer of 2008, I met with **Concha Arribas Llorente**, chief and coordinator of the Equality Office, and her administrator **Maite Seoane Sanchez** who listened to my suggestion and plea to meet with Koro, Gonzalo and other people in the town of Zugarramurdi. My thanks to both for communicating that suggestion to their fellow officers in Logroño's City Hall. As women and dedicated public officials I thought they would respond, and they did.

This list of acknowledgements would not be complete without my thanks to *Mari Karmen*, *Nerea Arostegi*, and the women of Arrasate-Mondragon, my dear and adopted town, and "base of operations" in the making of this novel-trilogy. They represent in many ways the town's "folk people", with their daily lives and work, their concern for the representation of women's history and views in the town's schools and cultural life. Their review of several chapters and their comments were influential in my choice of themes and the depth of my research on the same.

To *Emilia Doyaga*, a distinguished member of *New York's Eusko Etxea*, who generously gave of her time and energy to distribute a questionnaire that I had prepared among *three generations of women* in the Basque Community of that State. Findings gathered in that survey served later as a basis for the contents of two chapters in this book. It was not clear in my mind that women in the Basque Diaspora stayed in touch with women's issues back in the "old" country, and vice versa. I am indebted to Emilia and each one of the participating women, on both sides of the Atlantic, for sharing with us all their concerns, anxieties, and aspirations.

To *Sam Zengotitabengoa*, editor of the *Journal of the Society of Basque Studies in America* (SBSA, www.societyofbasquestudiesinamerica.com), and his dedicated support staff in Brooklyn, New York for publishing three articles of mine with my findings and observations on the social, cultural, and political life in the "old country", Euskal Herria today. Following my comeback to Euskal Herria in 2004, after having spent most of my adult and professional life in the USA --also my very dear own country-- I found that I could not publish my writings with a "Basque-American" perspective, a perspective deemed "politically incorrect" by many publishing houses in the Basque Country, publishing houses that were receiving "subsidies and financial support" from offices in the Madrid Government and the PNV-led Basque Government itself. My findings revealed a collection of circumstances, events, and public strategies that were not in the best interest of Basque Society, Basque communities and Eusko Etxeak in the long run, and neither in the interest of future generations, in my opinion, findings that were not in line with the image of Basque society today that those publishing houses wanted to project to the general public. Sam and his editorial staff, however, gave generously of their talents, energy, and space so that this Basque-American could air his views and, for that gesture towards diversity of thought, I am immensely grateful.

Fortunate I am, as well, for having access to documents housed in *Kultur-ate*, Arrasate's own public library, a rich source of the history of the peoples, women and men, in this unique piece of land in the Basque Country. Its wonderfully helpful staff, all women, played a key role in my being able to be close to the people and the land while writing this trilogy.

As luck would have it once in a while, I am also very fortunate to have met *Juan Manuel Tudanca*, an architect and archaeologist for the city of Logroño in the summer of 2008, as my wife Aloña and I walked through the narrow streets in the old part of the city looking for any signs giving testimony to the Auto-de-Fe carried out by the Spanish Inquisition in that city in 1610, where eight women and five men died in the city's jails, and five women and one man were burned alive at the stake. His findings played a major role in the events of the following two years, as reflected in the story and dialogue of main characters in this novel.

My thanks also to *Mireille Molette*, my friend, neighbor, and French teacher in Fairfax, Virginia, USA, for her insightful comments. Her curiosity about Basque culture in general, and women's rights in particular, also played a role in the selection of topics developed in this trilogy.

Special mention and vote of thanks to *Valentin Goikoetxea* and *Asun Beistegi*, relatives of mine in Laguardia, for their desire to know more about "the women of the Second Republic", and how their new women roles in government are helping change our society today in the USA, Spain, and Basque Country.

This author is also thankful to **Juanjo Hidalgo**, editor-in-chief of AUNIA (www.aunia.org) for giving this author the opportunity to publish his interactions and dialogue with some of the women and men in Logroño's City Hall, as well as for presenting "a theory of the meteorite" to audiences in Spain and Basque Country that sheds new light, hopefully, into the full impact and devastation that the Spanish Inquisition perpetrated on the people and town of Zugarramurdi in 1610. Along these lines, my thanks also go to **Marta Brancas**, a historian and newspaper reporter who had published earlier on women's lives in that same magazine and urged me to contact Juanjo. To both my thanks for their trust and generosity.

As most historic novels would demand, this one also required a considerable research effort over a five year period. I am in debt to the many authors reflected and mentioned in this trilogy, and very specially to **Mark Kurlansky** for this historical narrative *The Basque History of the World (1999)*. In that book Kurlansky presents key figures and events in the culture, history, and political life of the Basque peoples in the last five hundred years in a fact-rich, revealing, and easy-to-read manner. It was at the Eusko Etxea of New York in 2003 that I had the opportunity of meeting Mr. Kurlansky and joining many people in a ceremony held to admit him into our Hall of Fame at that Eusko Etxea. His writings speak clearly, purposely, and in an entertaining flow of words about the history of the Basque peoples, with their strengths and weaknesses, their music and dance, their basic rights and aspirations for a free and independent homeland, their pluralistic society open to women and men of all thoughts, creeds, and concepts of well being.

Last, but not least, my thanks and appreciation to **Dr. Eugene Stakhiv**, my boss and chief at the US Army Corps of Engineers, in Alexandria, Virginia, USA, for giving me the opportunity to work with him and a number of professionals well connected to a large array of engineering, social, and cultural challenges at home and in the global community. My concern for the well-being of our global community was reinforced and enriched by working with him and his team.

✳︎✳︎✳︎

Other Books by this Author

For the purchase of the following books, please contact the distributor (www.amazon.com) or the author directly at agoikoetxea1@telefonica.net; also, please visit the page www.euskalherriasiglo21.org to download articles by this author free of charge:

(1) Euskal Herria Estado-Nación en el Siglo 21: Una Nueva Arquitectura Socio-Política (in Spanish), 535 pages, *Editorial Euskal Herria Siglo 21*, Arrasate 2007 (Distributed por ELKAR, www.elkar.com)

(2) Enterprise Architectures and Digital Administration: Planning, Design, and Assessment (*Arquitecturas Empresariales y Administración Digital: Planificación, Diseño, y Evaluación (en Inglés)*, 526 pages (In English), *World Scientific Press*, New York, 2007 (Distributed by World Scientific, http://www.worldscibooks.com/business/6239.html)

(3) When the Parallel Worlds Co-Existed, Book 1 of this novel-trilogy, "Women, the New Architects of Society", already written, and available to readers at Amazon.com (www.amazon.com), English and Spanish versions, and at ELKAR distributors (www.elkar.com), in its Spanish version:

> *Synopsis:* The story of Kathy Thompson, a young Jewish American woman in search of her own identity in a society still dominated by men, and of Xabier Elurmendi, a young Ertzaina (Basque police). Both meet in the USA, and through them we are witnesses to today's "social and political conflict" in the Basque Country. Together they face situations and experiences of intrigue, ritualistic murders, paedophile princes of the Church, corrupt politicians, and a plot to assassinate the Pope Benedict XVI in distant places like Arrasate-Mondragon (Basque Country), Madrid, Rome, Istanbul, Tel-Aviv, Lhasa (Tibet), and other places along the "old silk road." A novel politically and religiously incorrect, but revealing and entertaining."

(4) **The Pope's Red Shoes**, <u>Book 2</u> of this series, "Women, the New Architects of Society", already written and published.

> *Synopsis:* In this book the planning, logistics, and the break in are carried out by Kathy and Nerea with the help of the "Circle of Wise Women", obtaining the code of Gethsemane, a code that reveals the true origin of Christianity before it became a state religion. Only a small piece of the code is missing, and Kathy and Xabier must travel to Beijing, Tibet, New Delhi, Tel-Aviv, and Jerusalem along the old "Silk Road" to find that missing piece, each time risking their lives at the hands of local power lords, including members of "Mount Harmon", an ultra secret religious sect bent on recuperating the code of Gethsemane by any means. Kathy and Xabier arrive at an unexpected and mutually agreed upon decision towards the end of this trilogy.

(5) **"Findings of a Basque-American in Euskal Herria Today: Betrayal, Reality, and the Winds of Change"** *("Conclusiones de un Vasco-Americano en el País Vasco Hoy Día: Engaño, Realidad, y Cambio")*, article, pages 27-42, *Journal of the Society of Basque Studies of America*, Vol. XXVIII, New York, 2008. Can be downloaded free of charge in <u>www.euskalherriasiglo21.org</u>; more details in <u>www.societyofbasquestudiesinamerica.com</u>.

(7) **"400-Year Anniversary of the Burning of Basque Women and Men by the Spanish Inquisition in the Auto-de-Fe of 1610 -- Part I"**, article published in the *Journal of the Society of Basque Studies of America*, Vol. XXIX, New York, 2011. Can be downloaded free of charge in <u>www.euskalherriasiglo21.org</u>; more details in <u>www.societyofbasquestudiesinamerica.com</u>.

(8) **Love Poems: Paintings and Portraits with Words,** a book collection of 45 poems in English, Catalan, Euskera, and Spanish, 275 pages, Euskal Herria 21st Century Press, Laguardia-Biasteri, Basque country, 2012.

Author's Biographical Note

Dr. Ambrose Goikoetxea, Ph.D.
Director, Euskal Herria 21st Century Foundation
with offices in Laguardia, Alava
Arrasate, Gipuzkoa, Basque Country, and
Boston, Massachusetts, USA
e-mail: agoikoetxea1@telefonica.net

This Basque-American author was born (1952-) in the town of *Biasteri-Laguardia*, province of Alaba, Euskal Herria (Basque Country) from a family of carpenters on his father's side (the *Goikoetxeas*), farmers, monks and nuns on his mother's side (the *Martinez*), all "liberals" on both sides of the family for generations. At the age of six, and right after the Spanish Civil War, the family first migrated to Mexico City where it  lived during five years, returned to Basque Country for another five years, and finally migrated to the USA where he lived and worked during the next forty five years. *B.S.* (Bachelor of Science) in Aeronautical Engineering, California Polytechnic Institute (Cal-Poly), Pomona, California, 1969; *M.S.* (Master of Sciences), Mechanical Engineering, University of California at Los Angeles, 1970; and *Ph.D.* (Doctor of Philosophy) in Systems Engineering and Economics, University of Arizona, Tucson, 1977, USA.

He went on to work as a professor at several universities, and as an engineer at several corporations in the USA, for during years until 2004 when he returned from his experience in the "*Basque Diaspora*" to Basque Country to continue his work, this time applying his skills and experience gained in American society to social needs in Basque society. A brother of his is today a medical doctor in San Diego, California, a sister is an English teacher and social worker at Simi Valley, California, a son is an AIDS clinical investigator at a major hospital and research center in San Diego, California, and a second son is a software engineer and computer systems architect in Boston, Massachusetts, USA.

Dr. Ambrose Goikoetxea is the author of over 35 papers published in refereed national and international journals, 5 technical books taught in engineering, information systems, mathematics, economics, and business universities in over 30 universities in the USA, Latin America, China (ROC), and Europe. Additionally, since 2004, he has written and published 12 books on social and political issues, including the novel-trilogy "*Women, the New Architects of Society.*"

Founder and Director (part-time) of the *Euskal Herria 21st Century Foundation*, based in Arrasate-Mondragon since February 2007, an organization that works with citizens to re-build the social and political fiber in Euskal Herria (Basque Country); bilateral projects with *Eusko Etxeak* and other *Basque centers* in the USA and Latin America (see web site: www.euskalherriasiglo21.org). From 2004 to 2007 he worked in the Department of Information Sciences at the *University of Mondragon* (MU) where he taught graduate and undergraduate courses in software engineering, design of software processes with UML (Unified Modelling Language) tools, enterprise computer architectures, and digital government administration. There, as Director of the *e-Democracy Project*, his team lent technical support to members of the Basque Parliament in an assessment of the use of the new information technologies (e.g., e-mail, digital TV, electronic signature, etc.) in 74 Parliaments and regions with legislative capacity in the European Union (EU).

Earlier, 1999-2004, he was a Sr. Information Systems Engineer at the Center for Excellence in Software Engineering (W908) of the *MITRE Corporation*, Virginia, EE.UU. In that capacity he supported business systems architecture development in the IRS Modernization Enterprise Architecture, applications test planning and business rules integration in the Customer Account Data Engine (CADE), and performance assessment of messaging middleware (MQSeries). At MITRE he also completed an architecture design to support intra-site and inter-site data backup, failover, and recovery for the Army's Defense Message System (DMS). Prior to joining MITRE he was the Performance and Capacity lead engineer for the Global Transportation Network (GTN) at **Lockheed Martin Corporation**, in Manassas, Virginia (1997-1999) where he created the system performance and capacity planning (**PCP**) group, designed and instituted PCP processes, responsible for setting up a suite of modeling and measurement tools.

A member of several engineering professional organizations, and a lecturer in the Department of Engineering Management, Department of Operations Research, and the Department of Management Science of **George Washington University,** 1990-2004. Associate Professor in the Systems Engineering Department, **George Mason University**, 1985-1999. President and Technical Director of Integrated Technologies and Research, Inc., from 1995 to 1997, where he designed and developed decision support systems for the **U.S. Army Corps of Engineers**. In 1985 and 1986 he was **NASA-ASEE Research Fellow** at the Goddard Space Flight Center, in Greenbelt, Maryland, designing decision support systems for NASA managers to assist with systems engineering and configuration functions of space projects; also, a member of the Man-Machine Interface Design Group. 1979, NASA-ASEE Research Fellow, **Jet Propulsion Laboratory** of the California Institute of Technology (Cal-Tech); evaluation and selection of projects in the areas of solar-thermo power plants, underground nuclear plant location analysis, and urban public transportation systems.

Organizer and **General Chair** of the *IX-th International Conference on Multiple Criteria Decision Making (MCDM)*, Fairfax, Virginia, August 5-8, 1990, attended by 185 participants and speakers from over 25 countries. Dr. Goikoetxea is a recognized speaker at international conferences on system performance modeling, decision analysis, distributed database design, and risk analysis. More recently, as **Program Chair** of the *Association for Development of the Information Society* (IADIS), Dr. Goikoetxea brought together Mondragon University and Universidade Alberta of Portugal to celebrate an international conference on Applied Computing and Web-Based Communities (see www.iadis.org/ac2006, www.aidis.org/wbc2006) in San Sebastian, Basque Country, 25-28

February 2006 with the participation of 250-275 persons from 25 countries.

Currently, as a retired person, he teaches English courses to corporate people in the industrial complex of the Basque Country, a a part-time activity, and continues to do weight-lifting at the local gym three times a week. *"**Keep mind and body busy**"*, he says.

For additional detail, please contact this author at agoikoetxea1@telefonica.net

Thank you,
Merci beaucoup,
Gracias,
Eskerrik asko!

www.ingramcontent.com/pod-product-compliance
Lightning Source LLC
Chambersburg PA
CBHW030422290526
45786CB00001B/91